TAVERN

on the

GREEN

JENNIFER OZ LEROY
AND KAY LEROY

ARTISAN

First published by Artisan in January 2009
A Division of Workman Publishing Company, Inc.
225 Varick Street
New York, NY 10014-4381
www.artisanbooks.com

Library of Congress Cataloging-in-Publication Data

LeRoy, Jennifer Oz.
Tavern on the Green / Jennifer Oz LeRoy and Kay LeRoy.
p. cm.
Includes index.
ISBN 978-1-57965-357-6
1. Cookery. 2. Tavern on the Green. I. LeRoy, Kay. II. Title.

TX714.L4675 2009
641—dc22
2008009860

Design by Stephanie Huntwork
Studio food styling by Jamie Kimm and Anna Elisa de Castro
Studio props styling by Roy Finnamore

Printed in China
First printing, November 2008

2 4 6 8 10 9 7 5 3 1

CONTENTS

INTRODUCTION

*O*ne of the most important gifts my parents ever gave me was education. We were raised in the greatest city in the world and enrolled in the best schools. Dalton, the only choice for a LeRoy, was a breeding ground for the future executives of the world.

"What does your father do?" was a common question there. The most frequent answer was lawyer or doctor.

But mine was "My father owns Tavern on the Green and Maxwell's Plum."

I often got responses like "My parents got married there!" Beginning in 1986 some of my friends' mothers would ask me, "How could your father close Maxwell's Plum? My husband and I met there!" As a child, I shrugged my shoulders and wondered why they were apparently upset with *me*. It was only later that I began to understand the impact my parents and their restaurants had on New York and the rest of the world.

I say "my parents" because, although my father is recognized as the founder and impresario of Tavern on the Green, my mother, Kay, was a very large part of its creation. She may not have been raised in Hollywood (like my father was), but where she came from you either "produced" your own destiny or didn't survive. Born in Ireland, she moved to England as a child. She had to start supporting herself in her teens, caring and cooking for an extravagant, highly demanding family at an age when most of us are still learning about life. As challenging a time as it was for her, when, at twenty-two, she met my father, she was a great cook and had as much class as any princess. My mother has always exhibited a natural sense of style and sophistication that no one could have taught her. I thank her for teaching me that using tact and approaching life with aplomb at all times are better indicators of class than money or family heritage.

To this day, I meet people from all over the world who tell me stories about a wonderful time they had at Tavern on the Green or Maxwell's Plum, or even at a dinner party my parents hosted (at our home, neither a twenty-one-course meal nor a Mongolian hot pot for 200 close friends was farfetched). My mother did most of the cooking herself. I have fond memories of my mother's cooking, especially the pancakes she'd often make on school mornings. They were my favorite, partly because she'd fashion them in special shapes, such as teddy bears and flowers.

. . .

As people begin to tell me a story about their experience with the LeRoys or a LeRoy venue, I always give them my full attention and try to slow time down, so I can share their memories. These storytellers have a glow as they recall their experiences.

When I was young, our holidays were invariably over the top. For Thanksgiving, Tavern would send over several turkeys accompanied by piles of mouthwatering side dishes. Of course, there'd also be a wide selection of desserts, along with something special the pastry chef would create just for us. Years later, once I'd begun working at Tavern, I was usually scheduled for a shift or two on holidays. But, on Thanksgiving, I would try to take a break, run home in my kitchen whites, and give everyone a holiday hug. I will never forget how proud my father was as he told our guests about my dedication to the Tavern kitchen.

My brother, Max, sisters Bridget and Carolyn, and I were lucky enough to grow up in the Dakota, the legendary New York apartment building that's just a few blocks from Tavern. On many occasions my friends and I would Rollerblade right over to the restaurant's big wooden doors, where we were greeted by a friendly doorman, who in my eyes seemed ten feet tall.

"Good afternoon, Jennifer."

"Hello, John," I'd reply, giving him a big hug.

In the lobby, the host or hostess would also welcome us warmly. "Hello, Jennifer! Would you and your friends like to sit in the garden today or the Crystal Room?"

"The Crystal Room, please."

We'd be escorted down the winding, mirrored, and chandeliered hallway (we'd be carrying our Rollerblades, but we swore that one day we'd leave them on and race from one room to another) into one of the most desirable dining rooms in New York.

As we explored the restaurant, those friends who were first-timers would often notice how some of the chandeliers seemed familiar. There was a reason for that. When I was eleven, my father took me shopping for a chandelier for my bedroom; he liked my choice so much he bought twelve more for a Tavern hallway. (To this day, when I wander down that hall of mirrors, I remember how my father held my hand as we looked for my very own first chandelier.)

When I turned thirteen, I started getting invited to lots of bar and bat mitzvahs. And what better place to throw such an important celebration than Tavern on the Green? I remember going to many fantasy parties that year, such as the casino-themed one or the party that turned the entire restaurant into a jungle. At each, the food seemed to go on for miles. The rooms were filled with beautiful *frutti di mare* towers, carving stations and the make-your-own-sundae stations, always my favorite stop: all different kinds of ice cream, crushed cookies and sprinkles, and sauces of every flavor imaginable.

In sum, for a child like me, Tavern on the Green was like a combination of Willy Wonka's chocolate factory and Versailles.

.   .   .

I have so many memories at Tavern on the Green that these days, when I walk through the front doors, it's like walking into the house I grew up in. I remember my father telling us stories over breakfast about people he'd met at work the night before. One day, when I was about twelve, my father asked me to accompany him to the restaurant that evening. He had a twinkle in his eye, and I got a feeling I should get dressed up and be on time.

When our car pulled up to Tavern, a giant red carpet was laid outside the entrance and there were cameras flashing everywhere. Once we got inside, I shook the hands of movie stars left and right. Still, I wasn't completely convinced celebrities were anything special. (At the time, I was so horse crazy that unless you had four legs and a tail, I wasn't going to be impressed.)

That all changed about an hour later, when my father spotted Christian Slater and asked if I wanted to meet him. *Heathers* had come out the year before, making him a teen heartthrob, and I was so excited I nearly fainted. This was the moment when I began to appreciate my dad and Tavern more than ever—I realized not every girl got to meet a major teen idol at her father's place of business!

As the years passed, I would meet many influential people at the restaurant, such as director Martin Scorsese and writer Elie Wiesel. But I think of another of my earlier brushes with celebrity with particular fondness. When I was fourteen, I was the captain of my school's basketball team and, along with the entire LeRoy family, a huge fan of the New York Knicks. So it was exciting to hear that there was going to be a charity event at Tavern hosted by the Knicks players and other professionals, including L.A. Laker Magic Johnson. Part of the festivities that night involved games in which you could interact with the athletes, including a round-robin shoot-out with Magic Johnson and twenty kids. I was fortunate enough to be the one girl chosen to participate, alongside nineteen very competitive boys.

All the team practices at school really paid off that night. After each round, Magic would ask, "Did you make the basket, dear?" and I would smile back at him and politely say yes. Before I knew it, I was in the final round and, when it was all over, it was just Magic and me standing on the base line! Being the winner and getting a signed basketball from Magic as a prize was the greatest moment of my basketball career.

Special memories like these mean so much. Having spent so many of my formative and early adult years at Tavern, I now hope to spend the next thirty providing the setting where great memories are created for many others, both New Yorkers and the innumerable visitors who put a meal with us at the top of their list. Most of all, I wish to share life's joys with my family and, as you'll see (and taste!) in the pages that follow, our family's most illustrious member is Tavern on the Green itself!

—JENNIFER OZ LEROY

1

From

QUAINT SHEEPFOLD

to

SHIMMERING CITY ICON

THE HISTORY OF
TAVERN ON THE GREEN

On the western edge of New York City's Central Park, where the bustle of West Sixty-seventh Street yields to 843 tranquil acres of open space, perches a majestic building unlike any other. It is a destination, a showplace, a visual treasure. To approach this gathering place in the early evening is to be swept into a twinkling wonderland of towering trees, wrapped from the tips of their branches to the base of their trunks in more than ten miles of tiny white lights. To amble through its glittering, mirrored hallways, and to be seated in one of its six elaborate dining rooms for an unforgettable meal, is a down-the-rabbit-hole experience, one that attracts luminaries and wide-eyed tourists alike.

Indeed, no other restaurant in the world is host to such a cross-section of rap stars and writers, politicians and professional athletes, moguls and mob bosses, stage and screen actors, ingenues and iconoclasts, as well as first-time visitors to the city. If the walls of Tavern on the Green could talk, the voices of such diverse personalities as Frank Sinatra, Barbra Streisand, Billy Crystal, Donald Trump, Kelly Ripa, Woody Allen, Star Jones, Jerry Seinfeld, Rudy Giuliani, and Richard Burton would fill its dazzling rooms. Speaking of well-known voices, for several years, Howard Stern's birthday broadcast emanated from our rooms. What's more, the résumés of many a successful chef, restaurateur, or hospitality professional includes a stint at Tavern—Michael Lomanaco, Drew Nieporent, Marc Poidevin, Patrick O'Sullivan, David Rosengarten, and Bill Yosses among them. Even hardened New Yorkers, who are notoriously tough to impress, admit that there is a romance here that doesn't exist anywhere else. Without this unabashedly unself-conscious presence in the park, which novelist Fannie Hurst called "the heartbeat of the asphalt city," New York would be significantly diminished. Tavern's spectacular setting and radiant charm has made it *the* place for New York's most prestigious charity and political functions, Broadway openings, and film premieres. But the building that houses Tavern on the Green has a storied past, one as colorful and unparalleled as dozens of multitiered crystal chandeliers, expansive pastoral murals, and wall-to-wall cabbage-rose carpeting that now define its fantastical interior.

.   .   .

Believe it or not, it began as a sheepfold: a shelter for scores of sheep that spent the day grazing in the nearby Sheep Meadow. The full-time shepherd attending this flock, as well as his family, were also housed in the building. From the moment construction began in 1870, the brick-and-stone structure was the subject of intense public interest, not least because it was being built by order of William "Boss" Tweed, the city's commissioner of public works. Tweed, who as the head of New York City's infamous Tammany Hall was also the Democratic Party leader and a state senator,

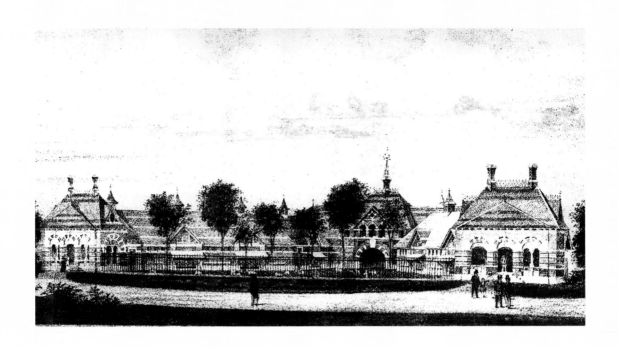

TOP: *Architect Jacob Wrey Mould's rendering of the sheepfold.*
ABOVE: *Once the building was completed, 200 sheep were housed there and taken over to the Sheep Meadow each day for grazing.*

had just pushed through a new city charter that gave him and his associates more control over the municipal treasury. The Tweed ring insisted that contractors should bill far in excess of what the jobs actually cost, so Tweed and his cronies could line their own pockets with the difference. Reformers eventually targeted them, and Boss Tweed was convicted of larceny and forgery in 1873, dying in prison five years later. Out of the scandal came some good—for instance, Tweed secured the plot for the Metropolitan Museum of Art—but not before Tweed and his ring plundered sums estimated between thirty million and two hundred million dollars.

Another rare bright spot from Tweed's reign as public works commissioner was the sheepfold, considered to be one of the finest examples of Ruskinian Gothic architecture in the city (the American Museum of Natural History, farther north on Central Park West, is another). The 23,000-square-foot, U-shaped animal quarters, which cost the city seventy thousand dollars to build, was designed by Jacob Wrey Mould, an English-born architect and sculptor who worked under Calvert Vaux, one half of the landscape architecture team Olmsted and Vaux, whose design proposal for Central Park won them the commission for the greensward. Mould contributed greatly to the aesthetic beauty of this audacious scheme to create a pastoral oasis in the center of Manhattan, pushing the city's northward growth to either edge of the narrow island. Mould's whimsical, intricate sandstone carvings of birds and seasonal plants ornament the banisters around Bethesda Terrace in the heart of the park. Belvedere Castle, the park's most enchanting folly, is also a Mould design. Whatever the commission, be it a grand stairway or a home for a shepherd and his sheep, the architect was celebrated for his precise technical drawing. Despite the sheepfold's appeal on paper, Mould's collaborator, Frederick Law Olmsted, objected to its location from the outset, since gaining access to it required walking across a bridle path. Furthermore, he ridiculed the Tweed plan to draw visitors to the sheepfold's pavilions by hanging portraits of sheep and specimens of wool on the walls. Tammany Hall proved too powerful, however, and the building was erected on the edge of the bridle path.

For more than half a century, it housed two hundred South Down sheep, the shepherd, and his family. Twice a day the crook-carrying shepherd and his pack of sheepdogs would hold up carriage traffic (and later, automobiles) as he drove the gray-faced flock to and from the Sheep Meadow. As ill-conceived as the sheepfold's siting may have been, the presence of sheep in the adjacent meadow perfectly suited the bucolic philosophy underlying the park's design.

By the turn of the twentieth century, however, the lawns and meadows of Central Park had turned into stretches of bare earth pockmarked with patches of weeds. Save for a road built in 1905 for equestrians and carriage drivers just behind the sheepfold at Sixty-sixth Street, Mould's building and its surroundings underwent few changes as the city regarded its parkland with benign neglect.

All that changed in 1934, when Robert Moses, the chair of the State Council on

Parks Commissioner Robert Moses (second from left) and Mayor Fiorello La Guardia
(second from right) preside over the opening of Tavern on the Green on October 20, 1936.

Parks, also became the city's parks commissioner. Throughout his long reign (he held both jobs simultaneously until the early 1960s), Moses, one of the most powerful and polarizing figures in the city's history, promoted a vision of urban planning in which towers, boroughs, and parks were linked by a series of highways. This approach endowed the city with cultural assets (such as Lincoln Center), but also fell into disfavor with those who saw their landscape transformed by urban sprawl and smog. But there were no such complaints when, just months into his municipal job, Moses announced his scheme for the rehabilitation of Central Park, a plan that layered ball fields, playgrounds, and other recreational facilities over Olmsted and Vaux's vision of a pastoral landscape. The plan did not include the renovation of the Central Park Casino on the park's east side, where former mayor Jimmy Walker danced with chorus girls on the black glass dance floor. In a move aimed to usurp the former nightclub's prominence, Moses announced that the picturesque sheepfold across the park would be converted into a moderately priced restaurant, a "Tavern on the Green." Claiming that the sheep that had grazed in the meadow for more than sixty years were producing malformed progeny due to inbreeding, he banished them to Brooklyn's Prospect Park and reassigned the shepherd to duties at the lion house in the Central Park Zoo, also slated for renovation. Moses ultimately sued to oust the management of "Jimmy Walker's Versailles," as the pricey casino came to be known, and eventually had the building torn down.

Tavern's main dining room in the late 1930s.

When Moses made public his plans for the sheepfold in February 1934, a fleet of government-paid relief workers under the New Deal's Civil Works Administration (CWA) had already begun its conversion—a typical Moses move—in hopes of meeting the commissioner's projected Memorial Day deadline. Although Moses was known for his ability to get things done, budget shortfalls and shortages of materials pushed the opening well past Labor Day. More than a thousand relief workers rotated in three shifts on a twenty-four-hour-a-day schedule in the months leading up to Tavern's opening. They laid two terrazzo dance floors, one in the courtyard and one inside the building; hauled in kitchen equipment; scraped the paint off old beams in the spaces designated as dining rooms; laid the mastic floors; and landscaped the grounds. Tavern's tables were set up in both arms of the U-shaped space while the dance floor was positioned at its base with the kitchen just behind it. The courtyard between the two wings was paved with flagstones, outfitted with nineteen hitching posts, and lined with London plane trees.

On Saturday, October 20, 1936, Tavern on the Green finally opened its doors, just in time for the annual inspection of Parks Department personnel and equipment. Employees of the park gathered in their olive-green uniforms once a year on Central Park's Great Lawn for review by the mayor, parks commissioner, and general superintendent. On that fall day, more than two thousand park workers from Manhattan, Brooklyn, Queens, Staten Island, and the Bronx marched in double lines by borough from the West Sixty-fifth Street entrance onto the lawn for review by Mayor Fiorello La Guardia. As the park band played, La Guardia, Moses, and Superintendent W. Earle Andrews reviewed the starch-suited troops and the latest equipment acquired by the department for the care and maintenance of the park.

Afterward, the three men, along with the parks commissioner's wife and daughter and a slew of photographers and reporters, strolled over to the former sheepfold. They were greeted at the door by a coachman dressed in his finest riding regalia: a cherry-red fitted boxcoat, white breeches, black boots, and a black top hat. The mayor was handed a brass key to the building, which he ceremoniously inserted into the keyhole, opening for the first time the doors to the restaurant that would eventually become synonymous with the city, and play host to millions of guests from all over the world. Following a tour of the dining rooms and kitchen, during which he chatted with the chef and helped himself to a breakfast sausage, La Guardia pronounced his satisfaction with Central Park's newest attraction.

The Central Park Catering Corporation had been awarded the concession contract for Tavern on the Green, one of just two restaurants in the park at the time—the other one was the cafeteria at the zoo. From the beginning, Tavern's prominent location brought it the same level of scrutiny New Yorkers give such municipal icons as the Yankees, the Statue of Liberty, and the Chrysler Building. Indeed, when the restaurant was rumored to be planning a dress rehearsal dinner (what's known these days as a

The Opening Day Menu at
Tavern on the Green

*T*he Tavern has never strayed too far from its tradition-bound fare; indeed, several of the dishes served up from the very beginning remain on the menu today, albeit with embellished names. Slow-Poached Jumbo Shrimp Cocktail, Slow Roast Dry-Rubbed Prime Rib au Jus, and Mashed Potatoes are favorites to this day.

CANAPÉ OF ANCHOVIES
HONEYDEW MELON SUPREME OF FRUIT
BLUE POINT COCKTAIL
SHRIMP COCKTAIL

CELERY, OLIVES, GHERKINS

CONSOMMÉ JULIENNE
CREAM OF TOMATO AUX CROÛTONS
MANHATTAN CLAM CHOWDER

BROILED HALIBUT STEAK
FRIED LONG ISLAND SCALLOPS
BONED SQUAB
VEAL STEAK
ROAST PRIME RIB OF BEEF AU JUS
BAKED HAM, SOUTHERN STYLE
BROILED CALF'S LIVER
TENDERLOIN OF BEEF RAGOUT

BROCCOLI HOLLANDAISE
FRENCH STRING BEANS
CREAMED SPINACH
BAKED IDAHO, CANDIED SWEET, OR MASHED POTATOES

ALLIGATOR PEAR SALAD

COCONUT CUSTARD PIE
ASSORTED PASTRIES
PETITS FOURS
FRENCH ICE CREAM
PINEAPPLE CHEESE CAKE

COFFEE OR TEA

BAR: COCKTAILS PRICED FROM 35¢ TO 75¢

"soft" opening), with tickets priced at $25, Superintendent Andrews ordered the invitations recalled. He reminded the Catering Corporation that this was a breach of the price rules he had set for the resaurant: Diners were to be charged no more than $1.50. Andrews insisted that Tavern be "a place where the average citizen can sit down and eat a decent meal amid pleasant surroundings." The controversy continued as a series of articles in *The New York Times* revealed that management was raising prices for dinner service, which wound up costing a patron about $3.30 for a "balanced meal" from the à la carte menu. This discovery led to gripes from competitors, who complained that they had to pay taxes while Tavern sat on tax-exempt city property (this was part of the deal Moses had cut with officials). Franc Boland, spokesman for the Hotel Association of New York City, didn't want Tavern stealing customers who typically patronized "the better class of restaurants" just outside the park. (Boland conceded that the cafeterias and concessions incidental to the zoo and other recreational facilities filled a legitimate place in the park because "otherwise the people who went there might die, famished.") Ultimately, the price of a full breakfast was set at fifty, sixty-five, and seventy-five cents and à la carte. Lunch was eighty-five cents and dinner was offered for $1.50. And in a tradition that continues to this day, supper dancing was offered from ten o'clock to closing.

Embraced by New Yorkers as a gathering place, Tavern on the Green quickly became an integral part of the city's social life. One could stop by for a sandwich and a cold glass of beer or tuck into a full-course dinner. In summer, Tavern recalled the open-air restaurants of Paris's Bois de Boulogne by offering dining on the big terrace facing the West Drive. The restaurant also began serving a canter breakfast for the riders in the park, and offered an afternoon tea.

. . .

Just as it hit its stride in the late 1930s, Tavern was taken over by the Civilian Patrol Corps as its headquarters until 1943, when new management assumed the lease and renovated the space as a year-round restaurant. By the mid-1950s, Tavern on the Green was showing its age. Renowned modernist Raymond Loewy, one of the founding fathers of industrial design, was engaged to give the space a face-lift—a process that resulted in the addition of the Elm Room. (It was named after the tree it wrapped around, and much of its footprint is now the Park Room.) He introduced a populist machine-age look, with coffered ceilings camouflaging recessed lighting, linoleum floors laid out in a large gridded pattern to mimic the pattern overhead, bentwood chairs, and aluminum-rimmed enamel-topped tables. Tavern's menu, too, kept up with the times. The new owners proudly served the "fancy" food of the era: lobster Newburg, ham with pineapple, and chicken in cream sauce.

While Loewy was tinkering with the interior, the building's grounds fell under attack—by fifty angry Upper West Side mothers, children in tow. Apparently,

TOP: *The entrance of Tavern, circa 1950.*
ABOVE: *Warner LeRoy's renovation of Tavern required gutting the interiors completely.*

while the renovations were under way on the inside, a bulldozer was plowing up a plot adjacent to the restaurant to turn it into an additional parking lot. The mothers-and-children brigade surrounded the bulldozer and effectively stopped work for the day. Several days later, the bulldozer was back, the protesters returned, and work was stopped again, this time with the press watching. The dispute ended in a victory for the concerned neighborhood families, who won their children a new playground in the park, across the driveway from Tavern, one that continues to welcome hundreds of city kids each day.

In 1962, Restaurant Associates took over the lease. Over the years, Tavern on the Green, although moderately successful, became badly outdated and virtually forgotten by most New Yorkers. By the early 1970s, the tradition-bound Tavern was quite out of sync with the psychedelic times. In 1974, Restaurant Associates shuttered the "rustic little money-losing pub," as *New York Times* food writer Eric Asimov later described it.

Rather than signaling the end of an era, however, the closing led Tavern into its most prominent and glamorous phase ever. Warner LeRoy, basking in the glory of his wildly successful first Manhattan restaurant, Maxwell's Plum, acquired the lease and embarked upon an extravagant ten-million-dollar renovation of the recently landmarked building. Although the sum was unheard of, it came as little surprise to anyone who knew him. Architecture and *New York Times* critic Paul Goldberger described him as "New York's mad genius."

Of Maxwell's, a former East Side coffee shop turned into an SRO (standing room only) restaurant and *the* swinging singles hangout of the era, Peter Benchley of *The New York Times Magazine* wrote, "It is one of the true paradoxes of the city's night life. By being consciously—almost self-consciously—democratic, by avoiding all pretense to exclusivity, it has become one of the most smashingly successful places in the city, attracting everyone from movie stars to restaurateurs to—yes, even the fabled Brooklyn secretary. And contrary to the social imperative, they all seem to coexist in relative bliss." Indeed, the toast of New York—Bill Blass, Warren Beatty, Julie Christie, Emilio Pucci, and Cary Grant among them—were regulars. In Maxwell's, Warner brought to life his credo that "a restaurant is a fantasy, a kind of living theater in which diners are the most important members of the cast." With the restaurant's hallmark collection of Tiffany glass, its Lalique crystal fountain, its antique chandeliers from the Vanderbilt Hotel, and potted fresh flowers, one could say Warner was just doing what comes naturally.

The son of Hollywood royalty, Warner grew up around movies and movie sets, which later influenced his idea of what a restaurant should be. His father, Mervyn LeRoy, who is best known as the producer and uncredited director of *The Wizard of Oz*, and was also behind such classics as *Mister Roberts* and *Gypsy*, and his mother, Doris Warner, the daughter of the founder of Warner Brothers Studios, installed a popcorn machine and cotton candy maker in their lavish home for their son's enjoyment. It wasn't unusual for the young Warner to join the likes of Frank Sinatra and Judy Garland for a movie in the family's fifty-seat screening room, in which the projector hid behind a Picasso.

Tavern was a perfect fit for the showman in Warner, who seemed to know it was in his future before he had even considered bidding on the lease (see "Emerald Mirage," page 16). When he walked into the courtyard of the run-down building, he imagined something wholly original and incredible: He would build a room in that space that would look like the *inside* of a wedding cake. Using lavish amounts of brass, stained glass, etched mirror, original paintings, and antique prints, and dozens of chandeliers dripping with crystals, Tavern was reincarnated. Hand-hewn rafters reemerged, and the soaring vaulted ceilings above them reappeared after being hidden for decades by pedestrian plaster. The Elm, Rafters, and Chestnut rooms were paneled in exceedingly rare wormy chestnut. He even added a room that recalls an ornate tiered cake and called it the Crystal Room, after the more than twelve Baccarat, Waterford, and Osler crystal chandeliers that glisten overhead. The Terrace Room, in which rustic baroque gives way to flights of rococo fancy, was also a creation of his. No matter how successful he was in resuscitating the restaurant, Warner's Tavern wasn't immune from public scrutiny. The construction of both additions, now so inextricably linked to the erstwhile sheepfold, was a violation of the building's landmark status and resulted in a one-hundred-thousand-dollar fine.

. . .

Tavern on the Green took New York by storm from the moment it reopened on August 31, 1976. It dazzled the city with its decorative whimsy, its eclectic menu, and its playfulness. Tavern, once so "out" that it had to close, was now very "in" indeed. Of the results of the two-year renovation, Goldberger wrote, "It is all, on one level, absurd; and yet it is all, on another level, quite wonderful. Mr. LeRoy's creation, as a piece of design, goes beyond the conventional limits of taste to create a new and altogether convincing world of its own." Celebrities flocked to the restaurant to see and be seen. On any given night, there could be a party for a movie premiere in one room, a group of NFL players in a second, and a celebrity wedding reception in yet another. Often described as an innovator, Warner was lovingly referred to by his longtime employees as the P. T. Barnum of restaurants because "nothing was ever big enough." He always began with the biggest idea and expected his staff to join him in his outsize fantasies for the restaurant. He did nothing subtly—and that included his mode of transportation and dress. Squired about town in a peach-colored limousine, he invariably emerged in one of his signature velvet or brocade suits.

One of the most outrageous events Warner ever held at Tavern was a 1995 Blue Moon Ball benefit for the Central Park Conservancy. He donned an iridescent blue-sequined tuxedo accessorized with blue cowboy boots and blue-tinted sunglasses for

The Crystal Garden decorated for the 1995 Blue Moon Ball.

this jaw-dropping bash. Warner insisted on swapping out overnight the three thousand white lightbulbs in the restaurant for blue ones, deploying three teams of three people with ladders at midnight to get the job done; they worked right up until guests began streaming in the next evening. Huge arrangements of all-blue flowers—delphiniums were flown in from France—filled the rooms. Metallic blue tablecloths printed with silver metallic stars were specially made for the event, and statuesque silver candelabras, one of Warner's favorite accoutrements, graced each table. He loved live theater and managed to infuse the party with a bit of it by bringing in the world-renowned Mummers to greet guests at the door. On entering the cocktail reception tent that covered the restaurant's parking lot, guests chatted among models clad in blue leotards and Cartier jewelry to add even more bling to the affair. The pièce de résistance, however, was the tableau Warner created in the gardens. In anticipation of the ball, during the seasonal changeover from lanterns punctuating the trees in Tavern's gardens to the famous blaze of lights, he had blue bulbs installed rather than the traditional white. Instead of turning them on as each tree was completed (the usual practice), he had them kept dark until the night of the event. Just after all the evening's nearly eight hundred guests had been led into the building by the Mummers, Warner gave the signal to the employees standing by at each of fifteen light switches and the night was instantly illuminated in dazzling twinkling blue. That blue was made more ethereal by fog emanating from dry ice packed around the trunks of the trees and by a giant moon slowly rising and setting over the restaurant (it hung from a crane hidden from view). A loud collective "oh!" rose from the crowd who, if they had had any doubts, now knew they were in for a most memorable night, one that raised over $1 million!

· · ·

Warner stopped at nothing to achieve his vision. "Working for Warner was thrilling. You never knew what directive would drop in your lap each day," says one longtime employee. Once, on seeing an old photograph of the Tivoli Gardens in Copenhagen, he enlisted one staff designer to figure out how to make and hang the cloth lanterns that now illuminate the terrace on summer evenings. The day after watching Tim Burton's 1990 fantasy film *Edward Scissorhands*, Warner insisted his designers track down the topiaries that filled the eccentric Scissorhands's mansion garden—in those pre-Google days, doing so required more than fifty phone calls (see "Tavern's Topiaries," page 135)—and still came up short.

When he couldn't find the right color paint for the Crystal Room, Warner had it flown in from Europe, paid Customs overtime to clear it, and then sent a special truck to retrieve it for transport to the warehouse. He was known to check the noise levels in the restaurant by walking around with a sound meter and, though Tavern was situated among trees on the edge of the park, insisted there be no leaves on the ground outside the restaurant, a quirk that kept his maintenance crew on their toes.

As opulent a backdrop as it was for celebrations, Tavern was always a fantastic work in progress. In 1988, it underwent yet another renovation to expand its popular store, relocate the bar, and create the lovely Park Room and Garden. Subsequently, the Crystal Garden, which faces the Sheep Meadow, was outfitted with state-of-the-art sound and light systems to encourage dancing during the summer months.

For all his showmanship, Warner was a serious, brilliant businessman. He was the first restaurateur to bring all of the talent needed to run such a big operation in-house. Tavern boasts its own horticulturist, florist, electrician, carpenter (and wood shop), printer, upholsterer, and interior design team. So intent was Warner on remaining open continually that when the electricity in the restaurant needed to be updated, he rented freezer and refrigerator trucks to temporarily store the food, and the show went on. Even during union strikes, Warner got loyal employees to cross the picket line. He simply refused to let the place close.

Since Warner's death in 2001—the one day, aside from that of the untimely passing of beloved chef Patrick Clark, that the restaurant has ever closed for business under our family's reign—Tavern on the Green has continued to thrive under Jennifer's direction. Although then only twenty-two, Jennifer had grown up at Tavern. At nineteen, she began working there, starting with menial kitchen jobs—cutting lemons and slicing countless pats of butter—because she wanted to learn every aspect of the business. After a stint in the pastry kitchen, she became the expeditor—the most intense role in any kitchen, but even more so here, where the job involves directing the assembly of up to four thousand meals daily. Jennifer proved that she could work as hard as anyone, and when Warner opened the grandly renovated Russian Tea Room in 1999, he put her in a management position. Eventually she worked her way up to operations manager and ultimately became Warner's logical successor.

Since then, Tavern's snuggery of a bar has been redecorated, its massive (13,000 square feet) kitchen has received a comprehensive refurbishment, and an employee cafeteria has been installed. Warner would swoon over the newly commissioned hand-painted murals and antique treasures that continue to dazzle the eye of the next generation of Tavern diners, just as the gently tweaked new menus dazzle their palates.

· · ·

Today, Tavern on the Green remains the premier celebration restaurant in New York City. It serves as the fairy-tale backdrop for all the milestone occasions—engagements, weddings, birthday parties, bar and bat mitzvahs, graduations, charity benefits—and, for thousands of tourists, as a once-in-a-lifetime dining experience. More than 700,000 guests fill its breathtaking rooms each year, with more than 10,000 of those visitors coming through the doors from Thanksgiving to Christmas Day. Nevertheless, as Bryan Miller of *The New York Times* once observed, "Every day is a holiday in this cheerful, leafy setting." Indeed, Tavern sparkles inside and out, 365 days a year, beguiling patrons and passersby with its otherworldly aura, bringing to life that oft-repeated sentiment "Only in New York."

Emerald Mirage

As we drove home, it seemed to me a shimmering emerald waterfall was gushing forth on Fifty-seventh Street, just a few doors east of Hammacher Schlemmer. We had been to a dinner party at Warner's mother's house at 25 Sutton Place—one of those dinner parties with finger bowls and lots of wine. So at first I thought it was the wine causing the mirage of the emerald waterfall, but, looking back, I saw that it was the most beautiful chandelier I'd ever seen, hanging in the window of Nesle.

"Warner, stop. There's a fantastic . . ." I said, but he'd seen it too. And he didn't just stop—he slammed on the brakes and backed up. We gazed up at it, in all its glittering glory. It was perfect. We were in love. We had to have it.

The next morning we were waiting outside the store before Mr. Nesle unlocked the door. "It's an Osler," he said, "made in Austria for the Maharaja of Udaipur . . ." We weren't really listening. We just knew we wanted it.

Back home at the Dakota, the question arose: Where to put it? Hmm, the place was already quite crammed—with several chandeliers and a lot of other things, too. Oh, well, we decided we had to have it anyway. We'd find a place for it.

A few days later, the bids were opened for Tavern on the Green. We never went there (did anyone?), but since it was just a few blocks from our apartment, we decided to walk over and take a look around. To me it was the Blanche Dubois of Central Park. It was dusty, dingy, grimy. Even the rats poking around the edges of the courtyard seemed dispirited. And the gray February afternoon, already darkening, didn't make it look any better. I turned to Warner. His face had that ecstatic smile—the smile he always wore when he saw what he wanted. He marched across the cracked paving stones of the courtyard and spread out his arms. "This will be the Crystal Room," he said. "It will feel like dining inside a wedding cake. We'll have chandeliers and hydrangeas all around, and here"—he pointed upward—"is where we'll hang the emerald chandelier."

—Kay LeRoy

2

COCKTAILS

SANGRIA D'ESPAÑA

*T*his wine punch, served from a pitcher, instantly sets a celebratory tone; it's a casual, communal drink typically placed on the table for guests to serve one another. Serve it with a wooden spoon for holding back the fruit while pouring the liquid into ice-filled glasses. If you don't have a really large pitcher, divide the mixture between two glass pitchers, to be sure you have room for the soda, which is added just before serving. For a truly Spanish drink, add sliced peaches or plums to this colorful mix. • SERVES 4 • *photograph on page 18*

---

4 ounces brandy

4 ounces Cointreau or Triple Sec

1½ cups fruity red wine, such as Zinfandel or Spanish Garnacha

1 cup Sweet-and-Sour Mix (recipe follows)

1 lime, cut into small wedges

1 orange, cut into small wedges or slices

1 small bottle (10 ounces) club soda, well chilled

Sprigs of mint, for serving

In a large, heavy glass pitcher, combine the brandy, Cointreau, red wine, and sweet-and-sour mix. Reserve 4 lime and 4 orange wedges for serving, and add the remaining citrus fruit to the pitcher. Stir together well and refrigerate for at least 1, and up to 4 hours before serving time.

When ready to serve, stir the club soda into the pitcher. Half-fill each of 4 wine or highball glasses with ice cubes and garnish the edge of each with one of the reserved lime and orange wedges. Pour some sangria into each glass and serve at once.

SWEET-AND-SOUR MIX

---

3 cups sugar

4 cups water

2 cinnamon sticks

1½ cups fresh lime juice

In a large saucepan, combine the sugar, water, and cinnamon sticks; stir until the sugar has dissolved. Bring the mixture to a boil over medium-high heat. Reduce the heat so the mixture just simmers, and add the lime juice. Cook gently for 4 to 5 minutes more, then remove from the heat and let cool. When cool, remove the cinnamon sticks (these can be rinsed, dried, and reused) and pour the mixture into a storage container. Refrigerate for up to 1 week. • MAKES 4 CUPS

STILETTO

*T*he wine and liquor director at Tavern is busy year-round, developing special drink menus for the holidays, sourcing new wines and liquors, and revamping the standard cocktail menu. This fruity concoction, served at Tavern in a hurricane glass, is offered on the Valentine's Day menu. • SERVES 6

12 ounces pineapple vodka

3 ounces peach syrup or liqueur

3 ounces Chambord

3 ounces bottled pomegranate juice

3 ounces pineapple juice

6 ounces bottled peach juice

Thin circles of fresh orange, lime, and lemon, for garnish

In a pitcher half-filled with ice, combine all the ingredients except the citrus circles and stir to mix well. Half-fill six goblets with ice and divide the mixture among them. Cut halfway through each citrus circle and perch an orange, lime, and lemon pinwheel on the rim of each glass. Serve at once.

EVERYONE LIKES A GOOD DRINK

We have some of the best bartenders in the business who can serve (or invent!) pretty much any cocktail you can imagine. Everyone likes a good drink, even Martha Stewart, who loves to order Tavern's "Very Berry" Cosmo (page 26). Jack Nicholson, however, is in another league. When he comes in, he doesn't order a drink—he orders a bottle of bourbon with a lot of ice.

THE MIDTOWN MANHATTAN

*L*egend has it that the Manhattan was created at New York's Manhattan Club in 1874, at a party given by Lady Randolph Churchill (mother of Winston) to honor the newly elected New York governor, Samuel Tilden. As with many classic cocktails, the recipe can cause contentious discussion among aficionados, particularly on the subject of whether rye or bourbon whiskey is correct. Bitters, of course, are de rigueur. • MAKES 1 COCKTAIL

3 ounces premium or super-premium
    bourbon whiskey, such as Wild Turkey or
    Knob Creek

1 ounce sweet vermouth

1 drop Angostura bitters

1 dash Bénédictine

1 maraschino cherry

Chill a large martini glass. In a cocktail shaker half-filled with ice, combine the bourbon, vermouth, bitters, and Bénédictine. Shake energetically 40 times, then strain into the chilled glass. Garnish with the cherry and serve at once.

NOTE · **Use a clean, chilled glass for each cocktail, no matter how late it gets.**

MADISON AVENUE MOJITO

*M*uddled cocktails are somewhat labor-intensive because they are best made one at a time. For a party, assemble all the ingredients and equipment on a sideboard; print the recipe on a small card placed next to the bar area. Guests can make their own cocktails using the recipe as a guide. • SERVES 1; REPEAT AS NECESSARY

1 thin lemon wedge

2 thin lime wedges

6 sprigs of mint

Crushed ice, as needed

1½ ounces white rum

¾ ounce Cointreau

Club soda, as needed

In a double old-fashioned or a highball glass, combine the lemon wedge, 1 lime wedge, and 5 of the mint sprigs. Muddle using a wooden "muddler" for 5 to 10 seconds to release their flavor by pushing and turning the muddler, smashing the ingredients. Add a scoop of crushed ice, then pour the rum and Cointreau over the top. Stir with a cocktail spoon and top up with a splash or two of club soda. Make a short slash in the flesh side of the remaining lime wedge and perch on the edge of the glass. Top with the remaining sprig of mint and serve at once.

MAXWELL'S PLUM

When Maxwell's Plum opened in 1965, with a sprawling, exquisite bar as the centerpiece of the exuberant space, it represented the pinnacle of the singles scene. Indeed, at its most popular, the restaurant served more than 1,200 customers a day. This pretty, plum-colored cocktail, developed at Tavern as an ode to Warner LeRoy's first foray into the restaurant business, is especially popular in the fall. • SERVES 2

---

4 ounces plum vodka

1 ounce Triple Sec

1 ounce fresh orange juice

4 ounces bottled cherry juice

2 slices ripe plum (optional)

Chill 2 large martini glasses. In a cocktail shaker half-filled with ice, combine all the ingredients except the lime zest. Shake energetically for 10 to 20 seconds, then strain into the chilled glasses. Cut a slit in each slice of plum, and slide over the rim of each glass, if desired; serve at once.

A STEP BACK IN TIME

The Maxwell's Plum cocktail . . . vichyssoise . . . sole meunière . . . beef Stroganoff—all are timeless offerings. And yet they do evoke a time and a place: Manhattan in the 1970s, before the culinary revolution brought us shizu leaves, pork belly, and tartare made with something other than chopped beef. Dinners were candlelit and elegant, classic Continental dishes were revered, and Tavern opened its doors to a discriminating and approving audience.

In that spirit, most chapters in this book feature a Tavern recipe for these beloved classics. Take "A Step Back in Time" and create—and enjoy—these dishes once again.

TAVERN'S "VERY BERRY" COSMO

*I*n typical Tavern-on-the-Green fashion, this signature cocktail is a colorfully embellished version of the late twentieth-century classic, the Cosmopolitan, which fueled the craze for all manner of flavored vodka martinis. The rich red of this version is a nod to the ruby-red slippers from *The Wizard of Oz*, the classic film produced by Warner's father, Mervyn. The family's association with the film didn't end when production wrapped, however. When filming was completed, young Warner was given Toto, Dorothy's beloved dog, as a gift. The film lives on in Warner's daughter Jennifer; at her birth, Mervyn declared her "our Oz," thus her middle name. Jennifer subsequently proudly bestowed the name on her horse farm in upstate New York.

✦ SERVES 2 ✦ *photograph on page 25*

2½ ounces berry-infused vodka, such as Stolichnaya or Skyy	Dash of fresh lime juice
½ ounce Triple Sec	4 raspberries
1 ounce cranberry juice	2 blackberries, plus extra for garnish (optional)

Chill 2 large martini or cocktail glasses. In a cocktail shaker half-filled with ice, combine the vodka, Triple Sec, cranberry juice, and lime juice. Shake energetically for 10 to 20 seconds, then strain into the chilled glasses. Gently drop 2 raspberries and a blackberry into each glass and serve at once, or skewer 2 raspberries and 2 blackberries on a toothpick and place across the top of the glass before serving.

FLIRTINI

*W*hen sparks begin to fly, this sparkling fruit-infused cocktail is just the drink for sipping. ✦ SERVES 4 ✦ *photograph on page 25*

2 ounces peach syrup or liqueur	4 ounces orange vodka
8 ounces bottled mango juice	8 ounces chilled prosecco
2 ounces Triple Sec	4 star anise pods, or pieces, for garnish

Chill 4 large martini glasses. In a cocktail shaker half-filled with ice, combine the peach syrup, mango juice, Triple Sec, and vodka. Shake energetically for 10 to 20 seconds, then strain into the chilled glasses. Top each glass with about 2 ounces of prosecco. Float a star anise pod on the surface of each drink and serve at once.

OH! WHAT A PEAR!

*M*ore than three hundred marriage proposals take place at Tavern every year. When word gets back to the bartender that she said yes, he promptly sends out this celebratory cocktail to toast the happy couple. ✦ SERVES 2 ✦ *photograph on page 25*

5 ounces pear vodka

1 ounce pear liqueur

2 ounces bottled pear juice

½ ounce fresh lime juice

2 slices of ripe pear, for garnish

Chill 2 large martini glasses. In a cocktail shaker half-filled with ice, combine all the ingredients except the pear slices. Shake energetically for 10 to 20 seconds, then strain into the chilled glasses. Cut a small slit halfway through each pear slice, crosswise, and perch a slice on the rim of each glass. Serve at once.

MIMOSA

*B*runch is one of the most difficult reservations to secure at Tavern on the Green. It's not uncommon each Saturday and Sunday to find guests leisurely sipping one of these in the snuggery while their tables are being readied. Chilling the juice and Cointreau is an essential step if you want to experience a Mimosa, Tavern-style. ✦ SERVES 6 ✦ *photograph on page 28*

12 ounces fresh orange or tangerine juice

2 tablespoons Cointreau

1 bottle chilled Champagne

In a glass pitcher, combine the orange juice and Cointreau. Chill for at least 1 hour before serving time. Chill 6 flute glasses. Stir the juice well and divide it among the chilled glasses. Top each glass with the Champagne, pouring slowly to avoid bubble-up and overflow, and serve at once.

CLASSIC BLOODY MARY

The Bloody Mary may run a close second to the Mimosa as the most popular brunch cocktail at Tavern, but its Gotham origins make the horseradish-spiked eye-opener the favorite of most New Yorkers. The first Bloody Mary is usually traced to the 1930s and George Jessel, a multitalented show business icon, who found the combination of vodka and tomato juice a rejuvenating pick-me-up. His creation was subsequently elaborated upon by a French bartender at the legendary King Cole Bar in New York's St. Regis Hotel, who added black and cayenne peppers, Tabasco sauce, Worcestershire sauce, and lemon juice. Dill and horseradish were later additions. At one time, Maxwell's Plum sold more Bloody Marys than any other establishment in the country!

If fresh horseradish is not readily available, you can substitute ⅛ cup of prepared (bottled) sauce. • SERVES 8

---

1 quart (4 cups) tomato juice

6 ounces Worcestershire sauce

1 ounce fresh lemon juice

2 tablespoons Tabasco sauce

1 tablespoon red pepper flakes

1 tablespoon crushed black pepper

1 teaspoon dried dill

¼ cup freshly grated horseradish

16 ounces (2 cups) premium vodka

8 leafy green stalks from a celery heart, for garnish (optional)

8 lemon wedges, for garnish (optional)

In a large punch bowl, combine the tomato juice, Worcestershire, lemon juice, Tabasco, red pepper flakes, black pepper, dill, and horseradish and mix well. Assemble 8 tall glasses and half-fill them with ice. Add 2 ounces (¼ cup) of vodka and about 1 cup of the tomato juice mix to each glass and stir once. Add a celery stalk and a lemon wedge to each glass, if desired, and serve at once.

A Tour of Tavern on the Green

*I*n its more than six decades as a restaurant, Tavern's footprint has grown from the original U-shaped building that accommodated two dining rooms and a kitchen to a dynamic, ever-changing cluster of six breathtaking rooms, each exuding a particular vibe. When Warner leased the place in 1974, he added the iconic Crystal Room onto the inside base of the U and padded one side of its uprights with the Terrace Room. Once in his hands, Tavern's interiors became a constant work in progress. Although each room always appeared to be decorated to the hilt, Warner was constantly tinkering, adding seemingly out-of-sync touches that somehow perfectly suited the interior. He treated the space like a stage set and viewed himself as its set designer. The building's handsome brick exterior does nothing to announce the fantasyland that visitors encounter from the moment they walk through the doors. The hallways alone recall a mini Versailles, the walls paved as they are with tiles of beveled mirrors. Such a glamorous entry is signature Warner LeRoy; his gift for showmanship is evident in every corner of this wonderland.

CRYSTAL ROOM

Tavern's iconic dining room, the choice of film directors and newlyweds alike, is the crown jewel of the restaurant's flamboyant spaces, a vision in shimmering Baccarat, Osler, and Waterford crystal chandeliers and floor-to-ceiling windows. During its construction in 1974, reviewers described it as a glass castle in what was then known as a dangerous and run-down park. Today, the Crystal Room looks out on the true glories of Central Park, making it the most popular place to eat in the restaurant. The twelve enormous chandeliers plus a dozen pairs of crystal sconces mounted on ornate columns illuminate the rococo ceiling, a vision in plaster mastery, with an ornate pattern that looks as if it were squeezed from a pastry bag. Warner spared no expense in creating this dazzling utopia. As if the view of the park on three sides wasn't enough, he commissioned two of Tavern's four famous murals, here a fantasy garden in keeping with the room's fairy-tale aura, along the back wall, one mural spanning the top three feet of it and the other beneath the chair rail. His goal was to make the space look like the inside of a wedding cake. Indeed, it is a confection in which several hundred people enjoy a Tavern meal each day.

MAXIMILIAN'S PAVILION ROOM

Once simply called the Pavilion Room, for its gazebo motif of white lattice ceiling elements and colonnaded balustrade, this oval-shaped room was recently renamed to honor Maximilian LeRoy (Kay's son and Jennifer's brother, who passed away in 2005). This dedication to Max's memory followed a complete renovation of the space, making what had arguably been the least desirable room in the restaurant—it's the only one without windows—more beautiful and coveted.

Kay in particular had grown tired of the somewhat garish colors of the fantasy garden mural adorning the walls. Inspired by John Vanderlyn's *Panorama of the Gardens of Versailles*, which occupies 167 linear feet of an elliptical room in the Metropolitan Museum of Art, she commissioned Ron Genereux to do a new mural (see "Those Fabulous Murals," page 258). The breathtaking panorama of Central Park that resulted celebrates the park's beauty; it's an extraordinarily realistic series of scenes of one of the world's most famous urban landscapes on a perfect spring day.

Now, in Maximilian's Pavilion, you feel like you are in the middle of Central Park, rather than in a windowless room (albeit one that can open up to the Crystal or Rafters rooms, its new romantic soft palettes blending seamlessly with the adjacent areas). Maximilian's Pavilion enchants all who cross its threshold, but for us, its most captivating feature is the only three people depicted in the mural—Max, of course, Warner, and the late Jeffrey Higginbottom, who was our longtime design director. They're sitting in the Crystal Room seemingly toasting Central Park!

CHESTNUT ROOM

A favorite of guests in the winter months, the Chestnut Room conjures an eccentric collector's idea of a ski lodge. The walls are clad in rare wormy chestnut in which nail and spike holes and some original saw marks evoke farmhouse rusticity. But combined with the expansive etched and frosted mirrors and bullet glass, this is no mere warming hut. Four eight-foot-high, five-tiered copper and brass William and Mary chandeliers hang from the beamed ceiling while the mirrors reflect several copper stags, Tavern's mascot, and weathervanes hung on the walls around the room. Each mirror depicts a scene from the 1949 version of *Little Women*, with June Allyson, Margaret O'Brien, Elizabeth Taylor, and Janet Leigh as the March sisters, another Mervyn LeRoy film.

Guests who dine in this room inevitably pause to contemplate the brilliant mix of brass, glass, mirror, copper, and porcelain. The enormous turkey platter mounted on one wall especially catches the eye. Warner "borrowed" it from our kitchen at home, having fallen in love with it. The next thing we knew, the huge plate had become a piece of wall art in the Chestnut Room!

RAFTERS ROOM

Named for the eight two-foot-thick, hand-hewn girders that span the width of this steep-pitched ceiling, the Rafters Room follows the original footprint of the erstwhile sheepfold. A long, narrow space, studded along the wormy chestnut walls with crystal and mirrored sconces and on the ceiling with four tiered, colored-crystal chandeliers, it recalls a great baronial hall. Warner designed the stained-glass panels that decorate the walls. The room, a favorite for banquets, boasts a captivating view of the Rafters Garden.

TERRACE ROOM

A miniature version of the Crystal Room, this dazzling glass pavilion sparkles under the light of two Waterford crystal chandeliers and a magnificent hand-carved plaster ceiling. It, too, offers an enchanting view of the park and boasts a private garden that is often tented in the cold months to accommodate larger parties. Though Warner decreed there be candles in all the dining rooms, he was especially insistent that every table in the Terrace Room have a towering candelabra for private events. He maintained that the double-paned windows reflected candlelight in triplicate, turning the room into a magical space, not least because they were also reflected in the fabulous antique Venetian mirror hanging there. Warner wanted the space to be a showpiece and often forced clients to use candelabra no matter their desires—he offered to throw in the flowers for free just to fulfill his own fantasy!

PARK ROOM

The most intimate of Tavern's dining rooms, the Park Room is illuminated by a pair of stunning Baccarat chandeliers by night and by a windowed wall overlooking the Park Garden and period fountain by day. On the opposite wall, a fifty-two-foot mural of turn-of-the-century Central Park spans the length of the room. It's a sentimental favorite because Warner had the muralist, Joyce Kubalak, paint his four children—Bridget, Carolyn, Max, and Jennifer—among the New Yorkers frolicking in period dress. The pretty space has been the setting for countless celebrations—we've had many a family fete here ourselves—from bat and bar mitzvahs and birthdays to graduations and anniversaries.

3

PASSED

and

NIBBLED

CRAB CAKES
WITH AVOCADO TARTAR SAUCE

*T*hese little cakes are a miniature version of the beloved crab cake entrée on Tavern's dinner menu. Of course, you can make them larger and serve them as a main course for four. Don't skip the step of chilling the mixture before forming and sautéing the crab cakes: When chunky crabmeat is the main ingredient (rather than bread crumbs), the cakes need time to firm. If desired, toast the baguette slices until pale golden brown. • MAKES 12 COCKTAIL-SIZE CRAB CAKES; MAY BE DOUBLED
· *photograph on page 36*

---

1 tablespoon butter

2 ribs of celery, finely chopped

2 tablespoons finely chopped yellow onion

½ cup heavy cream

1½ tablespoons Dijon mustard

1½ tablespoons finely chopped, well-drained pimiento

1¼ cups plus 3 tablespoons fine, dry bread crumbs

1 teaspoon zest from a scrubbed lemon (see Note, page 41)

Salt and freshly ground white pepper

1 large egg, lightly beaten

1 pound lump or backfin crabmeat, gently squeezed to remove excess moisture

TO FINISH

2 tablespoons vegetable oil

2 tablespoons butter

12 slices baguette (about ⅓ inch thick)

Avocado Tartar Sauce (recipe follows)

In a small sauté pan, heat the butter over low heat. Add the celery and onion, cover, and sweat gently until tender, about 10 minutes. If the vegetables begin to brown, add a tablespoon of water to keep them moist. Add the cream and increase the heat to medium. Simmer uncovered for 5 minutes, stirring frequently to prevent a boil-over, until reduced and quite thick. Remove from the heat and let cool.

In a large mixing bowl, whisk together the cream mixture, mustard, pimiento, the 3 tablespoons bread crumbs, lemon zest, ½ teaspoon salt, and ¼ teaspoon white pepper. Whisk in the egg, and then add the crabmeat, breaking it up a little but leaving some lumps intact. Toss the mixture together gently until evenly mixed. Mark and divide the mixture in the bowl into 4 equal portions, to make portion control easier.

Spread the remaining 1¼ cups bread crumbs in an even layer on a dinner plate. Scoop up about one third of each marked quarter of the crab mixture and gently squeeze out any excess liquid (you are aiming for 12-dollar-coin-size cakes). Form with your hands into a small patty. The mixture will be quite wet and loose. Place the crab cake on the plate of crumbs, then use a metal spatula to scoop bread crumbs over the top of the cake. Slide the spatula gently underneath and carefully turn the cake over into your palm to let the excess bread crumbs on the bottom fall back onto the plate, then place the cake back onto the spatula. Slide gently onto a platter or tray and repeat to make the remaining crab cakes, shaking the plate of crumbs each time to make an even layer. Cover the plate of crab cakes and refrigerate for at least 1 hour, preferably 2, and up to 3 hours.

In a 12-inch skillet, combine the oil and butter and place over medium-low heat. When the butter has melted and the foam subsides, gently slide the crab cakes into the pan. Cook for 5 to 6 minutes, until golden brown. Carefully turn the cakes over and brown the other side (it will take slightly less time). Place the baguette slices on a platter, and top each with a crab cake, then top each cake with about ½ teaspoon of the tartar sauce. Place on a buffet or pass at once.

AVOCADO TARTAR SAUCE

2 tablespoons capers, rinsed and drained

4 small cornichons, sliced

1 tablespoon flat-leaf parsley

1 tablespoon chives

1 teaspoon thyme leaves

1 cup Mayo/Aioli (page 42, made with 1 clove garlic), or store-bought mayonnaise (mixed with 1 pressed clove garlic)

1 small, ripe Hass avocado, peeled and finely diced

1 tablepoon fresh lemon juice

Salt and freshly ground black pepper

In a mini-prep or standard food processor, combine the capers, cornichons, parsley, chives, and thyme. Pulse quickly on and off, scraping the sides, to dice but not puree the ingredients. Add the mayo and pulse just until evenly combined. Scoop out into a bowl and gently fold in the avocado, lemon juice, ½ teaspoon salt, and ¼ teaspoon pepper. Taste for seasoning and refrigerate, covered, for up to 1 hour before serving. • MAKES 1½ CUPS

WINE·STEAMED
SHRIMP COCKTAIL
WITH LEMON REMOULADE

*I*n this slightly New Orleans take on the classic shrimp cocktail, steaming the shrimp over wine, rather than water, adds a complex flavor that marries beautifully with the bright yet satisfying rémoulade. Rémoulade sauce is a classic building block of the French Creole cuisine celebrated in the Big Easy. Prepare for rave reviews!

◆ SERVES 6; MAY BE DOUBLED

1 cup dry white wine or vermouth

1½ pounds large shrimp (13- to 15-count), peeled and deveined but with tails left intact

Lemon Rémoulade (recipe follows)

Finely grated zest of 1 scrubbed lemon, for garnish (optional; see Note)

Small, whole sprigs of flat-leaf parsley, for garnish (optional)

In the base of a large steamer pot, bring the wine to a simmer. Fill a large bowl with water and ice and place near the stove. Place the shrimp in the steamer basket, cover, and steam for 3 minutes. Immediately plunge the shrimp into the ice water. Simmer the wine until reduced by about three quarters, to about 1 tablespoon.

Retrieve the shrimp with a slotted spoon and spread on a clean kitchen towel while you prepare the rémoulade.

Stir the reduced wine into the rémoulade sauce. Divide the rémoulade among 6 large martini glasses and divide the shrimp among the glasses, hooking the tails over the edge. If desired, garnish each glass with a little lemon zest and a few sprigs of parsley. Place on a buffet or pass on platters (if passing on platters, use stemless martini glasses to avoid tipping).

continued

A NOTE ON CITRUS ZEST

Just a touch of orange, lime, or lemon zest imparts far more tang and brightness than even triple the quantity of the fruit's juice, but how you remove the zest is important. Most citrus fruits are waxed before shipping, so always scrub the fruit under hot water and then dry it before removing the zest.

If the zest will be used to flavor a liquid and will be strained out, you can remove large strips with a vegetable peeler, taking care not to remove too much of the bitter white pith that lies inconveniently just beneath the colorful zest.

For sauces, desserts, and braises—in fact, any time the zest will remain in the dish at serving time—use a zester. For many years, we used a tool with five tiny eyes at the top, which removed the zest in tiny curls, and this can be useful for garnishing. But when you want the flavor only, with no chance of discovering tough bits of zest lurking in a dish, a Microplane citrus grater is the best choice. Similar to a wood rasp, the Microplane yields ethereal drifts of superfine zest that add their bright essence—but no texture—to the finished dish.

When removing the zest of a citrus fruit, try to leave as much of the bitter white pith behind as possible. If there is a great deal of pith still attached to your citrus strips, remove it by sawing back and forth gently with a small sharp knife, held almost parallel to the strip.

LEMON RÉMOULADE

2 large or 3 small gherkins, sliced

1½ tablespoons capers, rinsed and drained

1 shallot, sliced

½ cup loosely packed flat-leaf parsley

2 teaspoons grated lemon zest

Salt and freshly ground black pepper

Tabasco sauce

⅔ cup Mayo/Aioli (made with 2 cloves garlic), or store-bought mayonnaise (with 2 pressed garlic cloves)

In a mini-prep or standard food processor, combine the gherkins, capers, shallot, parsley, lemon zest, and ¼ teaspoon each of salt, pepper, and Tabasco (add more Tabasco, to taste, if desired). Pulse on and off quickly, scraping the sides, to dice but not puree the ingredients. Add the Mayo/Aioli and pulse just until evenly combined.

◆ MAKES ABOUT ¾ CUP

MAYO/AIOLI

1 to 3 large, firm garlic cloves (depending on the recipe; see each recipe for guidelines)

1 large egg plus 1 large yolk, at room temperature (see Note, page 231)

Salt

2 teaspoons white wine vinegar

1 teaspoon Dijon mustard

1 cup extra-virgin olive oil

½ cup canola oil

1 tablespoon boiling water

2 tablespoons fresh lemon juice

Freshly ground white pepper

Push the garlic through a press and scrape into a food processor; add the whole egg, egg yolk, ½ teaspoon salt, vinegar, and mustard. Process until evenly blended. With the motor running, drizzle in the olive and canola oils very slowly at first, adding at a slightly faster rate after the first ⅓ cup or so has been emulsified. Add the boiling water, lemon juice, and ¼ teaspoon white pepper, and pulse two or three times.

The mayo/aioli will improve and mellow if allowed to rest for 24 hours; cover and refrigerate, then return to cool room temperature before serving. It will keep for up to 5 days in the refrigerator. ◆ MAKES ABOUT 2 CUPS

BLINI
WITH DOMESTIC CAVIAR

*I*nstead of the golden caviar called for below, you can use a mixture of several different kinds and colors for a sophisticated presentation similar to that at Tavern on the Green. Slivered smoked salmon is a delicious substitute for the caviar.

If you don't need this many blini for your party, use half the batter and freeze the remaining batter for up to 1 month. Before using, give the frozen batter a generous 3 or 4 hours at room temperature to thaw. If you try to rush the thawing process, the yeast will exhaust its rising power before it hits the pan. • MAKES ABOUT 50 BLINI

2½ teaspoons (1 package) quick-rise active
 dry yeast

1¼ cups whole milk, heated to 110°F

1½ cups flour

2 large eggs, separated

About 4 tablespoons (½ stick) unsalted
 butter

½ cup crème fraîche or sour cream

12 ounces domestic golden caviar or
 salmon roe

In a bowl, combine the yeast, warm milk, flour, and egg yolks. Stir together to blend and then whisk until smooth. Cover the bowl with a towel and let the batter rise in a warm place until doubled in bulk, about 1½ hours.

In a large, clean bowl, beat the egg whites with an electric mixer or whisk until stiff peaks form. Fold into the batter gently but thoroughly. The batter should be very fluffy.

Preheat the oven to 175°F.

In a large nonstick frying pan over medium-low heat, melt about 2 teaspoons of the butter. (Alternatively, use a nonstick griddle, brushing it lightly with melted butter.) Ladle 1 rounded tablespoon of batter into the pan for each blini, being careful not to crowd the pan. Cook until the bottoms are lightly browned and bubbles have formed on the top, about 3 minutes. Flip the blini over and cook until browned on the second side, about 2 minutes. Transfer to a warmed platter, cover with aluminum foil, and place in the oven.

Cook the remaining blini in the same way, adding butter to the pan as needed. The blini can remain in the warm oven for up to 30 minutes before being topped and served.

To serve, spread a dollop of crème fraîche over the top of each blini. Top each with a generous half teaspoon of caviar or salmon roe. Place the platter on a buffet, or pass at once.

TUNA TARTARE
ON RUFFLED CHIPS

*P*ieces of diced ahi sparkle like jewels in this glamorous appetizer, a good choice for a dressy cocktail party.

Japanese hot mustard is sold in small tubes; look for it in Asian markets and well-stocked food stores. For the ruffled potato chips, use the tube-packed commercial variety, which are typically very good and remain whole while others often arrive mostly broken.

Do not assemble these pretty appetizers too far in advance, or the chips will get soggy. ◆ SERVES 10; MAY BE DOUBLED

GINGER SOY DRESSING

1 small egg yolk (or use about ⅔ of a large yolk)

½ teaspoon peeled and grated fresh ginger

½ small garlic clove, finely chopped

1 teaspoon Japanese prepared hot mustard

2 teaspoons mirin (Asian sweet wine)

2 teaspoons low-sodium soy sauce

3 tablespoons rice vinegar

¼ cup peanut oil

1½ tablespoons Asian sesame oil

12 ounces sushi-grade ahi tuna fillet, cut into ⅛-inch dice

2 shallots, finely chopped

2 tablespoons snipped chives, plus a handful of longer pieces

Salt and freshly ground black pepper

30 ruffled or plain potato chips

In a mini-prep or standard food processor, combine the egg yolk, ginger, garlic, mustard, mirin, soy sauce, and rice vinegar and process until smooth. With the motor running, very slowly drizzle in the peanut and sesame oils and process just until emulsified. Transfer this dressing to a bowl, cover, and refrigerate up to 2 days.

In a bowl, toss together the tuna, shallots, snipped chives, ½ teaspoon salt, and ¼ teaspoon pepper. Add just enough of the dressing to moisten the mixture thoroughly and toss again (do not add so much that the mixture is soupy; reserve any remaining dressing for a green salad). The tuna is best served immediately, but it can be covered and refrigerated for up to 30 minutes.

Arrange the potato chips on a large platter and scoop a generous dollop of tuna tartare onto each chip. Scatter with the remaining chive pieces and place on a buffet or pass at once.

HOME·CURED SALMON "PASTRAMI" HAND ROLLS

For special occasions, it's fun to turn a big salmon caught in the wild into a "pastrami." But plan ahead, because you need to start fixing it at least three days in advance of your event. This unique dish is also fun to serve—it's interactive, and it's great to eat.

The salmon "pastrami" will keep for about a week, loosely wrapped, in the refrigerator. If you choose to use only half the pastrami, the rest may be frozen for several months and thawed gently to make more hand rolls, or even to use as a topping for blini or a filling for indulgent sandwiches with cream cheese and capers. (In this case, you would halve the serving ingredients below for its debut serving.)

If wild-caught salmon is unavailable, farm-raised may be substituted. • SERVES 36 FOR A LARGE BUFFET OR OPEN HOUSE

CURING MIXTURE

1 large white onion, coarsely chopped

1 cup coarsely chopped carrot

1 cup coarsely chopped dill

1 cup coarsely chopped flat-leaf parsley

1 small bunch of chives, cut into 2-inch lengths

1 tablespoon dry mustard powder

1 teaspoon coriander seeds, crushed

1 teaspoon crushed red pepper flakes

1 teaspoon chili powder

Kosher salt

1½ tablespoons sugar

Juice of 2 limes

1 large side of wild-caught salmon, about 3 pounds, picked over for leftover bones

PASTRAMI MIXTURE

½ cup molasses

2 teaspoons cayenne pepper

5 bay leaves, crumbled

1¼ tablespoons freshly ground black pepper

1¼ tablespoons hot paprika

1¼ tablespoons ground coriander

TO SERVE

Six 16- to 18-inch soft lavash rounds or squares

2 large red onions, finely diced

1½ cups capers, rinsed and drained

3 cups crème fraîche

⅔ cup finely snipped chives

THREE TO FIVE DAYS BEFORE THE EVENT

In a food processor, combine the onion, carrot, dill, parsley, and chives and pulse on and off quickly until the ingredients form a rough paste. Transfer to a mixing bowl and add the spices, 2 tablespoons kosher salt, the sugar, and lime juice. Mix together well.

On a large work surface, lay a 4-foot-long piece of plastic wrap and spread half of the curing paste down the center in a flat, wide strip, keeping it at least 2 inches away from all the edges. Lay the salmon, skin side down, over the paste and spread the remaining paste over the flesh side of the salmon. Fold in the edges of the plastic wrap and then lay another 4-foot piece of plastic wrap over the top, tucking the edges of the top piece underneath to make an airtight seal. Place the wrapped salmon on a large rimmed baking sheet, to catch any leaking juices, and refrigerate for at least 48 hours, turning over every 8 hours (the salmon will keep this way for up to 5 days, and the flavor will only improve).

Check occasionally while curing: If the juices from the pan threaten to overflow, drain them.

THE NIGHT BEFORE THE EVENT

Unwrap the salmon and scrape off the curing paste. Rinse briefly to get rid of any excess paste. Pat the salmon dry thoroughly with a clean kitchen towel, and place on a rack inside a roasting pan that will fit in your refrigerator.

In a small saucepan, combine the molasses, cayenne pepper, and bay leaves and bring to a boil. Strain the mixture into a heat-proof jug and allow it to cool for 10 minutes. In a small bowl, combine the black pepper, paprika, and coriander and toss together.

Brush the flesh side of the salmon with the molasses mixture and allow it to dry for 10 minutes. Sprinkle about 1½ tablespoons of the dry spice mixture over the surface of the salmon and rub it in with your fingertips.

Brush another layer of the molasses mixture over the salmon and again allow it to dry for 10 minutes, then sprinkle with more of the spice mixture.

Repeat the process once more, then drape a clean tea towel over the roasting pan and refrigerate it overnight (do not cover with plastic wrap or the outside texture of the pastrami will be too soft).

THE DAY OF THE EVENT

Several hours before serving, brush the salmon with the remaining molasses and rub in the remaining spice mixture. When ready to serve, slice it very thin down to, but not through the skin, on the diagonal, into long strips.

To finish, assemble on the buffet table the slivered "pastrami," a platter of lavash, and bowls of chopped red onion, capers, crème fraîche, and chives. Guests assemble their own "hand rolls" by placing some slivers of salmon inside a piece of lavash, then topping with the condiments as desired. Finally, the lavash is rolled into a firm cylinder and eaten by hand.

GONE TO THE DOGS

Pets are not allowed inside Tavern 364 days a year. However, there is one night every February when the city's dognoscenti descend on our restaurant with their bulldogs, shih tzus, and poodles in tow. It's the annual bash in honor of the Westminster Kennel Club Dog Show, a great party given by Iris Love, with the help of her friends Ann Radice and columnist Liz Smith. Love is a dog lover, Guggenheim heiress, and lifelong New Yorker who is famed for her prized dachshunds. Since the early 1980s, she and her pals have been bringing together more than five hundred fellow dog folks from around the world at Tavern to shine the spotlight on their beloved breeds. One regular who is now sorely missed at these gatherings was the philanthropist Brooke Astor, for many decades the queen of New York Society. (When Mrs. Astor died in 2007, at age 105, Iris Love took in her two cherished dogs, Girlsie and Boysie.)

The invitations to the yearly soiree, featuring a picture of Love and a few of her canines dressed like famous historic figures or Egyptian deities, have become collectors' items. Guests are always treated to an elaborate buffet that showcases Love's passion for her pooches. One year she asked the banquet staff to make fire-hydrant-shaped ice sculptures. For another extravaganza, Love requested that the pâté be molded to resemble a pair of her beloved dachshunds.

SMOKED OR CURED SALMON
AND CHIVE ROULADES

*P*resliced salmon pieces tend to be too small to work well for this stunning and tasty appetizer, necessitating much more patching than the trimming technique described below, so we call for a whole piece of (unsliced) salmon. Alternatively, ask your fishmonger for help in obtaining the largest possible slices of salmon for this dish.

When you are laying the fish out on the plastic wrap, think of it as a puzzle where a little overlapping or the odd bare patch won't make a bit of difference to the finished product.

This is the supreme make-ahead dish: The rolls can be frozen for up to 1 month before serving (if you do this, allow twice as much time for thawing the rolls before slicing). It may also—and very successfully—be made with the cured salmon "pastrami" on page 47. • SERVES 12 TO 14

---

1 pound smoked salmon

2 teaspoons butter, at room temperature

¼ cup fish or chicken stock (low-sodium canned is fine)

1½ teaspoons powdered gelatin

2 drops Tabasco sauce

1 drop Worcestershire sauce

½ cup heavy whipping cream, very cold

2 tablespoons finely snipped chives

3 tablespoons domestic caviar, such as wasabi tobiko, or salmon roe

---

With a long, thin, and very sharp knife, slice the salmon into large pieces on a steep diagonal, as thin as possible, or have your fishmonger do it. If the resulting slices are thicker than ¼ inch, place between two sheets of plastic wrap and pound gently with a rolling pin or meat mallet to an even thickness of ¼ inch. Trim the pieces into rectangles about 6½ by 3½ inches. (The trimming is not an exact science: In a perfect world, you would have six rectangles exactly the same size, but in fact you will need to patch and trim the very forgiving slices of fish to achieve the approximate size called for. The rolls will still look gorgeous.) As you trim, reserve a few good-size pieces of fish for possible patching, and keep about ¼ cup of trimmings for the salmon mousse.

In a food processor, combine the ¼ cup salmon trimmings and the butter and process until only just blended, stopping to scrape down the sides of the bowl as needed. Chill a large bowl in the refrigerator.

In a small saucepan, combine the fish stock and gelatin and let stand for 5 minutes. Place the pan over low heat and stir just until the gelatin dissolves. Remove from the heat and stir in the Tabasco and Worcestershire sauces. Pour into the food processor with the salmon mixture and pulse quickly 3 or 4 times, just to blend. Transfer to a second large bowl.

In the chilled bowl, use an electric mixer or whisk to whip the cream to stiff peaks. Add about one third of the whipped cream to the salmon mixture and fold together gently but thoroughly to lighten it. Gently fold in the remaining whipped cream and the chives, just until no white streaks remain. Cover and refrigerate the mousse for 10 minutes to allow the gelatin to begin setting.

Place on a work surface a piece of plastic wrap slightly larger than a salmon rectangle, and place a salmon rectangle on top, positioning it so that a long side is facing you. Patch with trimmings, if necessary, to make a 6½ by 3½-inch rectangle. Spoon about 3 tablespoons of the salmon mousse lengthwise across the center of the salmon. Using the plastic wrap, pull the edge of the salmon nearest you up and over the mousse and down in the back to meet the other edge, without overlapping. (Don't worry if there are a few gaps; these may be concealed with the caviar garnish during final assembly.) Twist the ends of the plastic to seal and pat into an even log. Repeat with the remaining ingredients to make 5 more rolls. Place all the rolls in the freezer for at least 2 hours.

Remove from the freezer and let stand for 10 minutes. Remove the plastic and trim off the untidy ends. Slice each salmon roll into 8 rounds about ¾ inch thick, and place on a platter. Let stand for 5 to 10 minutes longer to complete the thawing. Place about ¼ teaspoon of the caviar near the edge of each round and place the platter on a buffet, or pass at once.

OYSTERS ON THE HALF-SHELL
WITH GRATED CARROTS AND WARM CHAMPAGNE JUS

*A*bracing mignonette always makes a nice accompaniment to just-shucked oysters, and this creamy sauce is no exception.

Fanny Bay oysters are small and lean; if you can't find them, use any other small to medium oyster.

Be sure to use a double-folded kitchen towel or an old oven glove when opening oysters, to protect the hand that is holding the oyster while you are wielding the knife.

✦ SERVES 10 TO 12; MAY BE DOUBLED

---

2 carrots, peeled and coarsely grated	Salt
24 small oysters, preferably Fanny Bay	Tabasco sauce
¾ cup Champagne or white wine	⅛ to ¼ teaspoon fresh lemon juice
1 small shallot, very finely chopped	Kosher or rock salt, for serving
1½ tablespoons vermouth	Fresh seaweed, for garnish (optional)
¾ cup heavy cream	

In a steamer basket set over simmering water, steam the grated carrot until completely tender, about 5 minutes. Spread out in a single layer on a paper towel and set aside.

Scrub the oysters with a stiff brush under running water. Working over a bowl to catch the escaping juices, insert an oyster knife into the hinge of each one and gently pry open. Remove the oysters from their shells (freeing the connective muscle underneath), place them in a small bowl, and rub them all over with your fingers to catch any grit. Reserve the rounded bottom shells for serving. Strain the oyster juices through a fine-mesh sieve into a small saucepan (this gets rid of any stray bits of grit, which are very unpleasant if not removed!). Cover and refrigerate the oysters while you finish the sauce.

Heat the pan of oyster juice over high heat and add the Champagne, shallot, and vermouth. Bring to a boil and reduce by two thirds, to about ¼ cup (this will take about 10 minutes). Add the cream and stir constantly over medium heat for 5 minutes more. Stir in ⅛ teaspoon salt, a drop of Tabasco, and a few drops of lemon juice, to taste. Remove from the heat.

On a large, rimmed serving platter, make a ¾-inch layer of kosher or rock salt to hold the oyster shells level. Place an oyster on each half-shell, and top each one with a small mound of carrots and a spoonful of the sauce. Garnish with fresh seaweed, if desired. Place on a buffet or pass at once.

GRATINÉED OYSTERS
WITH LEEK CREAM

A more refined way to serve oysters than Oysters Rockefeller, this version is all monochromatic elegance; there's no chunky spinach here. A platter of these gems is perfect on a New Year's Eve buffet accompanied, of course, by flutes of Champagne. • SERVES 8 TO 10

1 pound leeks, white and light green parts only	3 tablespoons heavy cream
	2 teaspoons Dijon mustard
24 oysters	4 ounces (about 2 cups) grated Gruyère cheese
6 tablespoons (¾ stick) butter	
1½ tablespoons Pernod	Salt and freshly ground white pepper
1½ tablespoons flour	Kosher or rock salt, for serving

Cut the leeks halfway through lengthwise, to make sure you can rinse out any grit. Run them under cold water, spreading the layers apart. Squeeze back together tightly to get rid of excess water; slice thin and then chop fine.

Scrub the oysters with a stiff brush under running water. Insert an oyster knife into the hinge of each one and gently pry open. Remove the oysters from their shells (freeing the connective muscle underneath), place them in a small bowl, and rub them all over with your fingers to catch any grit. Reserve the rounded bottom shells for serving. Cover and refrigerate the oysters while you prepare the leek cream.

In a saucepan, melt the butter over medium-low heat. Add the leeks and stir occasionally for 5 to 8 minutes, until completely softened. Add the Pernod and simmer until it has completely evaporated. Sprinkle the flour over the top and stir to combine. Cook, stirring, for 1 to 2 minutes, then stir in the cream, increase the heat to medium, and simmer until thickened, about 7 minutes. Lower the heat again and stir in the mustard, half of the cheese, a scant ½ teaspoon salt, and ¼ teaspoon white pepper. Remove from the heat and stir occasionally until the cheese has melted and the mixture is smooth. Let stand for 30 minutes at room temperature, or up to an hour, covered and refrigerated, before finishing the oysters.

About 15 minutes before serving time, preheat the oven to 350°F.

Make a bed of kosher or rock salt in a large oven-to-table baking dish. Nestle the reserved bottom shells into the salt and place an oyster in each. Top with a generous tablespoon of the leek cream and sprinkle each with a pinch of the remaining cheese. Bake for about 4 minutes, until the edges of the oysters have just begun to curl and the cheese is melted. Do not overcook, or the oysters will get tough. Place the baking dish on a heat-proof trivet on a buffet table, with a glassful of small cocktail forks placed to one side. Provide another glass for the used forks.

ICED RADISHES
WITH SWEET DILL BUTTER

*S*ome marvelous varieties of radishes—white, black, French Breakfast, and Misato Rose, to name a few—are now showing up in farmers' markets. When you can, choose a mix of colors and varieties for this simple, appealing dish.

We make a delicious dill butter for these appetizers, but if you like, serve the radishes with plain unsalted butter, as the French do. Whatever way you decide to serve them, use the best butter you can afford, such as French butter or cultured butter from Vermont.

The radishes may be refrigerated, uncovered, for up to 2 hours before serving. They should be served cold; place on a bed of crushed ice if they will be on a buffet for more than 30 minutes. • SERVES 8 TO 10; MAY BE DOUBLED

---

8 tablespoons (1 stick) best-quality unsalted butter, at room temperature

Sea salt

2 tablespoons minced dill, plus extra sprigs for garnish

16 radishes, washed and chilled, stem and root ends trimmed flat, and halved crosswise

In a small bowl, stir together the butter, a scant ½ teaspoon sea salt, and dill until evenly combined. Spoon the dill butter into a pastry bag fitted with a small star tip, forcing the butter down as far as possible toward the tip end of the bag before twisting the top closed. Chill for at least 30 minutes and up to overnight. Return to room temperature for 20 minutes before piping, so the butter will flow.

Arrange the halved radishes on a platter with the larger cut side up. Pipe a small rosette of the butter in the center of each half. Decorate the platter with dill sprigs and pass at once or place on a buffet.

BRUSCHETTA OF HEIRLOOM TOMATOES
WITH BURRATA CHEESE

*B*ruschetta has been the darling of cocktail parties for almost a decade now, and it never seems to go out of style. When tomatoes are at their peak, there's no better way to eat them, short of biting into them as you might an apple!

Note that burrata cheese can be so soft that in some cases you may be almost spreading it rather than slicing.

If desired, you could cover and refrigerate the tomato mixture for up to one hour before serving, but be sure to return it to room temperature for ten to fifteen minutes so the flavors can develop. • SERVES 10; MAY BE DOUBLED

1½ pounds ripe heirloom tomatoes

⅓ cup finely chopped flat-leaf parsley

3 large garlic cloves, very finely chopped or pushed through a press

Salt and freshly ground black pepper

2 tablespoons best-quality extra-virgin olive oil

1 tablespoon best-quality balsamic vinegar

Ten ½-inch-thick slices of large-diameter baguette or similar-size rustic Italian bread

Olive oil spray

10 ounces burrata cheese, or best-quality fresh mozzarella, sliced into pieces slightly smaller than the slices of bread

Wash and core the tomatoes and halve them crosswise. Scoop out and discard the seeds and cut the flesh into ¼-inch dice. In a bowl, combine the diced tomatoes, parsley, garlic, ¾ teaspoon salt, ¼ teaspoon pepper, olive oil, and vinegar. Toss together gently. Set aside.

Preheat the oven to 375°F.

Place the bread slices on a baking sheet and spray (or brush) both sides lightly with olive oil. Bake for 10 minutes, then turn over and bake for about 5 minutes more, until only just barely golden. Season with salt and pepper and place on a large serving platter.

Top each bruschetta with a slice (or smear) of the burrata, then place a spoonful of the tomato mixture on each slice; transfer the platter to a buffet, or pass at once.

CROUSTADES
WITH THREE FILLINGS

*T*hese easy croustades make a nice textural change from pastry shells or plain baguette slices, and their depth makes them better suited to richer and moister fillings than to a standard canapé.

Choose one filling from the three offered below—each filling recipe fills 48 croustades—or double the croustade recipe and make two of the fillings. If you're serving a crowd, you can triple the number of croustades here and make all three fillings!

Don't use sprouted wheat or any other heavy loaves such as "seven-grain" for these—they'll be too stiff to bend easily. But pumpernickel bread makes a nice change for salmon-based fillings.

Mini-muffin pans vary in cup size: If the cups measure 1¾ inches, use a 2- to 2¼-inch cookie cutter. For 2-inch cups—which hold up better than the smaller cups—use a 2½-inch cutter. • MAKES ABOUT 48 TOAST CUPS; MAY BE DOUBLED OR TRIPLED

---

6 tablespoons (¾ stick) unsalted butter

½ teaspoon paprika

½ teaspoon Worcestershire sauce

Nonstick vegetable oil spray

One 1-pound loaf presliced whole wheat sandwich-style bread

In a very small saucepan, melt the butter over low heat. Remove from the heat and stir in the paprika and the Worcestershire. Spray two mini-muffin pans with nonstick spray. (If your muffin pans are nonstick, this is not necessary.)

Preheat the oven to 325°F.

Roll the bread slices firmly with a rolling pin to flatten them to about ⅛ inch. Use a 2- or 2½-inch cookie cutter to cut as many rounds as possible (see Tip). Brush both sides of each bread round with some of the melted butter and ease into the muffin pans to form little cups. Place in the oven and toast for 10 to 15 minutes, until just barely golden and firm.

To finish, follow the instructions in each subrecipe below.

You can also make the croustades well in advance. To store, carefully place in a large airtight container, separating the layers with parchment or wax paper. They will keep for up to 1 week in the refrigerator or for up to 3 months in the freezer. To use, return to the muffin pans and warm in a low oven for 5 to 10 minutes, to recrisp.

TIP · **After cutting out the rounds, whiz the trimmings and crusts in a food processor and store in the freezer; use whenever a recipe calls for fresh bread crumbs.**

continued

GARLIC·SHRIMP FILLING

1½ pounds small, peeled shrimp

3 tablespoons butter

3 tablespoons extra-virgin olive oil

5 shallots, very finely chopped

5 garlic cloves, very finely chopped or pushed through a press

¼ cup dry white wine

¼ cup fresh lemon juice

Salt and freshly ground black pepper

½ cup coarse, chopped flat-leaf parsley

⅓ cup seasoned dry bread crumbs, for topping

Coarsely chop the shrimp and set aside.

In a large sauté pan, heat the butter and oil over medium-low heat. Add the shallots and garlic and sauté until softened, being careful not to let the garlic brown. Add the wine and lemon juice and deglaze the pan; add the shrimp and simmer for 1 to 2 minutes, until pink and firm. Remove from the heat and stir in ½ teaspoon salt, ¼ teaspoon pepper, and the parsley.

Preheat the oven to 350°F.

Put the croustades on a baking sheet. Spoon about 1 tablespoon of the shrimp mixture into each croustade and top with about ¼ teaspoon of the bread crumbs. Drizzle a tiny bit of any juice remaining in the pan over each croustade and warm in the oven for 5 minutes. Serve at once. ◆ MAKES ENOUGH FILLING FOR 48 CROUSTADES; MAY BE HALVED

CURRIED CHICKEN FILLING

3 ounces cream cheese, softened

Scant 1 teaspoon curry powder, plus additional for serving

5 ounces diced cooked chicken (¼-inch dice), about ¾ cup

⅓ cup slivered blanched almonds, coarsely chopped

1½ tablespoons heavy cream

1 tablespoon chutney, coarsely chopped

Salt

In a bowl, combine the cream cheese and curry powder and beat with a wooden spoon until fluffy. Fold in the chicken, almonds, cream, chutney, and ¼ teaspoon salt.

Place the croustades on a platter and spoon about 1 tablespoon of the filling into each one. Top with a tiny sprinkle of curry powder and serve. ◆ MAKES ENOUGH FILLING FOR 48 CROUSTADES; MAY BE HALVED

CREAMY CRAB FILLING

16 ounces picked crabmeat
(see Note), well-drained

½ cup (4 ounces) cream
cheese, softened

¼ cup crème fraîche

Freshly ground white pepper

1 tablespoon tomato paste

2 teaspoons dried dill

Domestic caviar (black,
salmon, wasabi tobiko,
or golden whitefish), for
garnish

Chop the crab fine (there should still be a bit of texture).

In a bowl, fold together the crab, cream cheese, crème fraîche, ¼ teaspoon white pepper, tomato paste, and dill until evenly blended. Transfer the mixture to a piping bag fitted with a star tip and refrigerate the bag inside a resealable plastic bag until just before serving time (up to 3 hours).

Place the croustades on a platter and pipe about 1 tablespoon of the crab mixture into each one. Top with about ⅛ teaspoon caviar and serve at once. • MAKES ENOUGH FILLING FOR 48 CROUSTADES; MAY BE HALVED

NOTE · **Because the mixture is chopped, there is no need to use the more expensive lump or backfin crabmeat.**

FOOD AND DRINK TIDBIT

Tavern's bartender goes through more than 4,000 cases of house wine every year.

TOP ROW: *Jon Bon Jovi and Richie Sambora; Julia Child.* MIDDLE: *Demi Moore and Bruce Willis at
the* Pulp Fiction *party; Ron Silver, Madonna, and Joe Mantegna at the* Speed-the-Plow *party.*
BOTTOM: *Peter Jennings and his wife; Michael Douglas.*

Fabulous Bashes

About half of Tavern's astounding business is in banquets, specially planned private events that span the city's financial, media, arts, and cultural circles. Milestone celebrations, too, are a part of the mix. And it's not surprising. Parties have been part of the restaurant's DNA since Warner reopened it in 1976. He rarely needed a reason to throw a bash, and his love of staging events drew luminaries from all over the world into Tavern's dining rooms.

Michael Jackson celebrated his thirtieth-anniversary concert here with with more than a thousand guests, who were greeted by the "munchkins" from *The Wizard of Oz* singing their signature anthem and then were escorted to the gardens for a carnival complete with live animals.

Hillary Clinton, Usher, Barbara Walters, and Whitney Houston have all celebrated birthdays here. Tavern's pastry kitchen staff spent days baking Walters a six-foot cake out of which jumped an enormous purple gorilla.

One of India's most prominent families rented out the entire restaurant to host the marriage of their daughter, who paraded alongside her husband up to Tavern's doors on a pair of elephants. Liza Minnelli performed at the reception.

Broadway legend Bob Fosse so loved Tavern's flamboyance that he provided money in his will for a party in his honor on his passing. He requested a dance floor be installed in the Crystal Room for the enjoyment of several hundred of his closest friends, including his girlfriend, Ann Reinking, *and* his wife, Gwen Verdon.

Not all of Tavern's clients are of celebrity stature, but they throw no less over-the-top fetes. For a little girl's princess-themed fourth birthday party, custom hot-pink tables and chairs were built, each child received a princess outfit, and a balloon artist, face painter, Cinderella, and a court jester were on hand to entertain.

GOAT CHEESE–RADICCHIO QUESADILLAS

*M*aking quesadillas is a fun spectator sport if you don't mind guests in the kitchen. The grilled radicchio may be set aside for up to two hours at room temperature before you make the quesadillas. The final cooking, however, should be done just before serving, so reserve this dish for a casual gathering. • SERVES 8 TO 10; MAY BE DOUBLED

---

2 tablespoons extra-virgin olive oil

1 tablespoon balsamic vinegar

1 small garlic clove, pushed through a press

1 teaspoon minced rosemary leaves

Salt and freshly ground black pepper

1 small head of radicchio

2 tablespoons butter, melted

6 large flour tortillas

2½ tablespoons store-bought tapenade

11 ounces fresh goat cheese, crumbled (about 2⅓ cups)

Preheat the broiler.

In a small bowl, whisk together the oil, vinegar, garlic, rosemary, ⅛ teaspoon salt, and a good pinch of pepper.

Quarter the radicchio lengthwise into wedges. Swirl them in a bowl of water and spin dry in a salad spinner. Lightly baste all sides of each radicchio wedge with the oil mixture, then set the wedges on a broiler pan and place in the broiler about 6 inches from the heat source. Broil, watching closely, until slightly charred, 3½ to 5 minutes. Baste the tops of the wedges, then turn over and baste the other side. Continue to broil until deep brown and crisp on the surface but completely tender inside, 2 to 4 minutes. Turn off the broiler and preheat the oven to 175°F.

Cut the radicchio crosswise into thin slivers. Have the melted butter, tortillas, tapenade, and goat cheese ready near the stove.

Place a dry griddle or large cast-iron skillet over medium-high heat and brush the pan with some of the melted butter. Thinly spread one side of a tortilla with about one third of the tapenade. Place in the pan, tapenade side up, and immediately scatter with one third of the crumbled cheese, leaving a ¼-inch border uncovered around the edge. Top with one third of the slivered radicchio and place a tortilla on top; brush with a little more butter. Press down with a spatula and cook until the cheese begins to liquefy and the underside is mottled brown, 3 to 5 minutes. Turn over with a wide spatula and cook until the other side is golden, about 2 minutes. Transfer to a large baking sheet and keep warm in the oven while you make the remaining 2 quesadillas in the same way.

Transfer the quesadillas to a cutting board and, using a large, sharp knife, cut each one into 6 equal wedges. Fan the wedges on a warmed platter and serve at once.

MUSHROOMS STUFFED
WITH BACON AND BLUE CHEESE

ere, steaming the mushrooms helps get rid of some of their substantial water content, making for a more concentrated mushroom flavor. (Don't be surprised at how much they shrink; just be sure to start with large mushrooms!) Plan on a few extra mushrooms per person, as they tend to be very popular.

If desired, the steamed mushrooms and stuffing may be separately covered and refrigerated for up to twenty-four hours before assembling, baking, and serving.

◆ SERVES 10 TO 12; MAY BE HALVED OR DOUBLED

---

4 ounces lean smoked or unsmoked bacon (about 5 slices)

42 large white button mushrooms (each 2½ to 3 inches in diameter, about 1 pound total weight), brushed clean

2 tablespoons fresh bread crumbs

2 tablespoons chopped flat-leaf parsley

1 teaspoon minced sage

3 ounces blue cheese, crumbled

Salt and freshly ground black pepper

2 tablespoons dry white wine or vermouth

In a heavy skillet, cook the bacon over medium-high heat until crisp, turning occasionally. Drain the bacon on a double layer of paper towels; when cool, crumble into a large bowl.

Preheat the oven to 400°F.

Lightly oil a baking dish large enough to hold all the mushrooms snugly in a single layer, or use 2 smaller dishes.

Trim off the rough bottom ends of the mushroom stems, then remove the stems and chop them fine. Add to the bowl with the bacon, then add the bread crumbs, parsley, sage, blue cheese, ½ teaspoon salt, and ¼ teaspoon pepper. Mix thoroughly. The mixture should hold together slightly. If it seems dry, moisten with a few drops of water or wine.

Put the mushroom caps, rounded side down, in a steamer basket set over simmering water. Cover and steam until tender and glossy, about 5 minutes. Lift out the basket, allowing any moisture to drain away.

Spoon a generous teaspoon of the stuffing mixture into the stem cavity of each mushroom cap and smooth it into an even, rounded mound (add additional filling to the largest caps as needed). Place the mushrooms, stuffing side up, in the prepared baking dish. Drizzle the wine around the edges of the dish.

Bake, uncovered, until golden, about 30 minutes. Let cool for 5 minutes and transfer to a platter. Place the platter on a buffet (the mushrooms will still be very good at room temperature), or pass at once.

CHRISTMAS DEVILED EGGS
WITH CAPER MAYONNAISE AND
RED AND GREEN CAVIAR

No matter the season, year, or decade, deviled eggs are always in style. They appeal to young and old alike, and theirs is often the first platter to be emptied at a cocktail party. Here, they are dressed for the holidays with indulgent dollops of salmon and wasabi caviars.

Allowing the eggs to stand in the water for at least an hour after cracking the shell makes for faster and easier peeling. • MAKES 24 DEVILED EGGS; MAY BE DOUBLED

---

12 extra-large or jumbo eggs
  (see Note, page 231)

¼ cup distilled white vinegar or apple cider
  vinegar

⅓ cup mayonnaise

1 teaspoon whole-grain mustard

1½ teaspoons white wine vinegar

3 tablespoons capers, rinsed and well drained

1 tablespoon finely chopped flat-leaf parsley

Salt and cayenne pepper

1 ounce (2 tablespoons) salmon caviar

1 ounce wasabi tobiko caviar

Carefully place the eggs in a wide, deep saucepan and add water to cover. Place over medium heat and bring to a boil. As soon as the water begins to boil, remove the pan from the heat, cover, and let stand for 11 minutes.

Transfer the eggs to a bowl of ice water, add the white vinegar, and let stand for 6 minutes. Strike each egg against the side of the bowl to crack the shell slightly; roll back and forth to gently crackle all over. If you have time, let stand in the water for at least 1 hour.

Peel the eggs and cut them in half lengthwise. Scoop out the yolks and place in the bowl of a food processor. Reserve the whites, cut sides down, in a single layer to prevent splitting. (The whites can be refrigerated, loosely covered with a towel, for up to 2 hours before filling.)

Add the mayonnaise, mustard, white wine vinegar, capers, parsley, ¼ teaspoon salt, and ⅛ teaspoon cayenne to the food processor. Pulse to combine, scraping down the sides of the bowl as necessary. Taste and adjust the seasoning, then scoop the mixture into a pastry bag fitted with a small star tip. The filled pastry bag can be refrigerated for up to 2 hours before piping (allow to soften for 10 minutes before piping, so the mixture will flow easily).

About 10 minutes before serving, arrange the egg white halves cut sides up on a platter and pipe some of the filling into the center, keeping it relatively flat to provide a surface for the caviar. Top each egg with ¼ teaspoon each of salmon caviar and wasabi caviar. Place the platter on a buffet, or pass at once.

LAMB CHOPS
WITH ITALIAN SALSA VERDE FOR DIPPING

*I*talian "salsa verde" (green sauce) is quite different from the Mexican version of the same name, which is made with tomatillos. Baby lamb chops are ideal for eating standing up; when they're "frenched," or trimmed, the clean bone is perfect for holding on to. Although they are a little on the pricey side, they're just right for a clubby party or one with a high ratio of meat-eaters. Note that lamb chops from New Zealand are more affordable than domestic chops and are very tasty indeed! • SERVES 6; MAY BE DOUBLED

SALSA VERDE

3 mild, white Spanish anchovies or
   2 oil-packed anchovies

2 garlic cloves, very finely chopped or
   pushed through a press

2 cups firmly packed flat-leaf parsley

⅓ cup packed mint leaves

1½ tablespoons capers, rinsed and drained

1½ teaspoons Dijon mustard

2 teaspoons white or red wine vinegar

½ cup extra-virgin olive oil

¼ cup extra-virgin olive oil

Salt and freshly ground black pepper

2 garlic cloves, very finely chopped or
   pushed through a press

18 baby lamb rib chops, bones "frenched"

If using Spanish anchovies, soak in warm water to cover for 5 minutes, then drain and pat dry. In a small food processor, combine the anchovies, garlic, parsley and mint leaves, capers, mustard, and vinegar. Pulse until smooth, scraping down the sides. With the motor running, drizzle in the ½ cup olive oil in a steady stream and continue to process until smooth. Cover and chill for at least 1 hour and up to 3 hours to let the flavors marry (any longer and the beautiful green color of the parsley will begin to fade). Return to room temperature for 10 minutes before serving.

In a shallow baking dish, combine the ¼ cup olive oil, ¾ teaspoon salt, a generous grinding of pepper, and the garlic; and stir. Add the lamb chops and coat them well with the mixture. Cover and let marinate in the refrigerator for 2 hours, or at room temperature for 1 hour.

Preheat a broiler or cast-iron ridged griddle pan to medium-high heat. Grill the lamb chops for about 1½ minutes on each side for medium-rare, or until done to your liking, then let stand for 2 minutes. Place a ramekin in the center of a platter and fill wil the salsa verde. Arrange the chops, meaty side inward, around the ramekin and serve at once.

MINI RARE STEAK SANDWICHES
WITH HORSERADISH CREAM

*T*hese adorable little sandwiches are popular with all ages and genders. They're perfect for a cocktail party that might stretch into the dinner hour, and to temper the results of an extra cocktail. Be sure to provide plenty of these; they are always one of the first appetizers to disappear. • MAKES 48 TINY SANDWICHES

1½ pounds flank steak
2 tablespoons extra-virgin olive oil
Salt and freshly ground black pepper
⅓ cup bottled horseradish
⅓ cup sour cream

⅓ cup mayonnaise
4 French baguettes, each cut into 24 slices
    (½ inch thick)
Sprigs of parsley, for garnish (optional)

Place a rack in a roasting pan or on a broiler pan. Brush both sides of the steak with 1 tablespoon of the oil, and season generously with salt and pepper. Place on the rack and let stand at room temperature. In a small bowl, whisk together the horseradish, sour cream, and mayonnaise.

Preheat the broiler. Place an oven rack about 4 inches from the heat source.

Broil the steak on the rack in the roasting pan for 4 minutes, then turn and broil until firm but still quite pink in the center, about another 4 minutes. Let rest for 5 minutes.

Cut the steak with the grain into slices about 2 inches thick, then thinly cut the slices crosswise across the grain.

Spread one side of each baguette slice with a teaspoon of the horseradish cream. Arrange half the slices horseradish side up on the counter, and place 2 or 3 slices of steak on each one. Top with the remaining baguette slices and gently press down on each sandwich to compact it. With a bread knife, cut each sandwich in half and secure with a toothpick. Arrange on one or two platters and garnish with the parsley sprigs, if desired. Serve immediately or place on a buffet.

4

SOUPS

ELEGANT VICHYSSOISE

*B*ack around the time when stiletto heels came on the fashion radar, this soup was a signal to guests that the host or hostess was well-traveled, sophisticated, and quietly—but totally—*with it*. It is no less delicious and pleasing today. • SERVES 10 TO 12 • *photograph on page 72*

9 large leeks, white and light green parts only

6 tablespoons butter

6 large baking potatoes, peeled and cut into 1-inch chunks

9 cups chicken stock or broth (low-sodium canned is fine), or as needed

1¾ to 2⅓ cups heavy cream or crème fraîche

Salt and freshly ground white pepper

3 tablespoons finely snipped chives, for serving

Trim away the root ends of the leeks and cut lengthwise into quarters. Rinse thoroughly under cold running water to remove any grit. Squeeze to remove the excess water, then cut crosswise into ½-inch slices.

In a heavy pan or Dutch oven, melt the butter over medium heat. Add the leeks and cook, stirring frequently, for 5 to 7 minutes, until softened. Do not allow to brown.

Add the potatoes and enough chicken stock to cover by about 1½ inches. Bring the stock to a simmer, partially cover the pan, and cook gently for 15 to 20 minutes, until the potatoes are very tender.

Pass the soup through the finest disk of a food mill or puree thoroughly, in batches, in a heavy-duty blender. (Always be sure to hold the top of the blender firmly with a folded towel when blending hot liquids!) Rinse the original pan, wipe with a paper towel, and return the pureed soup to the pan. Stir in 1¾ cups of the cream and simmer gently until the soup thickens slightly, to a creamy consistency. If the soup is too thick, add a little more stock, cream, or water. If too thin, simmer for a few more minutes to evaporate some liquid and reduce slightly (the soup will thicken as it cools).

Stir in 1 tablespoon salt and ½ teaspoon white pepper; taste for seasoning (remember that cold dishes require more powerful seasoning). Cool the soup to room temperature, then place in a large glass pitcher, cover, and refrigerate for at least 2 hours and up to overnight.

Just before serving, adjust the consistency with a little more cream, if necessary, and taste and adjust the seasoning. Pour the soup into chilled cups or bowls and garnish each serving generously with snipped chives.

CUCUMBER·AVOCADO PUREE

*S*ummer weeknights at Tavern draw more neighborhood residents than any other time of year; there's really nowhere else one can sit in gardens as lush as ours *and* look out onto Central Park *and* enjoy a cooling soup, refreshing drink, or light snack. This velvety make-ahead soup is pure summer: bright green, cool, and clean. Show it off in clear juice tumblers for optimum impact. • SERVES 6 TO 12, DEPENDING ON PORTION SIZE

1½ pounds English cucumber

2 tablespoons sherry vinegar, plus additional as needed

Kosher salt

2 cups plain whole-milk yogurt

1½ cups buttermilk

3 tablespoons finely chopped dill

2 ripe, cold Hass avocados, peeled, pitted, and chopped

Freshly ground white pepper

With a peeler, peel half of the cucumbers. Halve all the cucumbers lengthwise and use a small spoon to scoop out and discard the seeds.

Coarsely chop all the cucumbers and transfer to a bowl. Add 2 tablespoons vinegar and 1 tablespoon of kosher salt. Toss together and let stand for 30 minutes.

With a slotted spoon, transfer the cucumbers to a blender or food processor, reserving the liquid in the bowl. Add the yogurt and buttermilk, 2 tablespoons of the dill, and about ½ cup of the cucumber liquid to the blender (discard the remaining liquid in the bowl), and puree until smooth. Place the blender pitcher in the refrigerator and chill for at least 1 hour and up to 12 hours.

To serve, return the blender pitcher to its base and add the avocados and a little white pepper. Blend until smooth; taste for seasoning and adjust with salt, white pepper, or a drop or two of sherry vinegar. Pour into chilled bowls, juice glasses, or Moroccan tea glasses. Sprinkle some of the remaining dill over each serving and serve at once.

LOBSTER AND FENNEL BISQUE
WITH TARRAGON CRÈME FRAÎCHE

sk any Tavern employee—from the hostesses to the staff horticulturist —to name a favorite indulgence at the restaurant, and he or she will tell you it's a toss-up between this rich, creamy soup and the crab cakes (see page 38). When the occasion calls for a soup that's a bit more formal than chowder, this is the one to choose. Whenever you serve lobster, always save the lobster heads, cooked or raw. Keep them in a big bag in the freezer and, when you have enough, make lobster bisque or stock. If you don't have a very heavy knife with which to chop up the heads, wrap them in an old, clean kitchen towel and bash with a rolling pin or a meat mallet to break them up. The smaller pieces allow more flavor to be released into the stock.

In place of the lobster heads, two fresh crabs may be substituted. • SERVES 6

½ cup canola or light olive oil

2 pounds lobster heads, cut into large pieces

2 leeks, white and green parts only, coarsely chopped and well rinsed in a colander

2 carrots, coarsely chopped

3 ribs of celery, coarsely chopped

1 head of fennel, trimmed and coarsely chopped

¾ cup tomato paste

3 cups dry white wine

4 whole heads of garlic, halved crosswise

10 sprigs of thyme

1 bay leaf

Salt and freshly ground white pepper

1½ gallons distilled water, or as needed

2 cubes best-quality fish or vegetable bouillon

1 teaspoon saffron threads

⅛ teaspoon crushed red pepper flakes

1½ tablespoons cornstarch

½ cup heavy cream

¾ cup crème fraîche

1 tablespoon finely chopped tarragon leaves

9 ounces cooked lobster meat, chopped or shredded

Place a large, heavy-bottomed stock or soup pot over medium-high heat, and add ¼ cup of the oil. When it is very hot and just beginning to smoke, add 2 handfuls of lobster-head pieces. Sear for 5 minutes, stirring occasionally. Transfer the seared lobster to a platter with a slotted spoon, let the pot heat up again until very, very hot, and sear another batch of lobster. Continue searing and removing a little at a time (this will impart the optimum flavor) and set the platter aside.

Add the remaining ¼ cup of oil to the pot and, when it is very hot, add the leeks, carrots, celery, and fennel and sauté for 5 minutes, stirring frequently. Stir in the tomato paste and sauté for 5 minutes more, or until very deep brown (but don't let it scorch). Add the wine, garlic, thyme, bay leaf, 1 teaspoon salt, ½ teaspoon white pepper, and all the seared lobster pieces. Cover with water by 2 to 3 inches (the amount will depend on the size and shape of your pot), toss in the bouillon cubes, and bring to a boil. Lower the heat so the liquid barely simmers and cook very gently, uncovered, for 1½ hours, skimming any oil or foam from the top occasionally.

Strain the soup into a large, clean saucepan through a fine-holed colander, pressing down hard on the solids with a spoon to extract all the flavor. Add the saffron and red pepper flakes, bring the stock to a boil over medium-high heat, and reduce by half, about 20 minutes. In a small bowl, whisk together the cornstarch and 2 tablespoons water, and add the mixture to the stock. Stir over medium heat for 10 minutes more, until thickened.

Stir in the heavy cream; taste again for seasoning. At this point, you may let the soup stand, covered, for up to 1 hour before serving. (If you do, reheat the soup gently before serving.)

When ready to serve, whisk together the crème fraîche and tarragon. Ladle the soup into warmed soup bowls and top with some of the cooked lobster meat, dividing it evenly. Garnish with a large dollop of tarragon crème fraîche.

MANHATTAN CLAM CHOWDER

*T*avern's opening-day table d'hôte menu in 1936 offered guests a choice of Consommé Julienne, Cream of Tomato aux Croutons, or Manhattan Clam Chowder, which has remained on the menu—with tweaks by Tavern's various chefs over the years—365 days a year. • SERVES 6

---

2 ounces salt pork or slab bacon,
   cut into ¼-inch dice

3 sprigs of flat-leaf parsley

2 sprigs of thyme

1 bay leaf

2 pints shelled fresh clams, chopped,
   with all their liquor

2 large potatoes, peeled and cut into ½-inch
   dice

1 cup water

2 leeks, white and light green parts only,
   chopped and well washed

1 green bell pepper, cored, seeded, and diced

1 large rib of celery, diced

1 large carrot, diced

6 large tomatoes (about 2½ pounds), peeled
   and coarsely chopped

1 tablespoon tomato paste

¼ cup tomato puree

Salt and freshly ground black pepper

6 Garlic Croûtes (page 206), for serving

2 tablespoons finely chopped flat-leaf parsley,
   for serving

In a small skillet set over medium heat, fry the salt pork until crisp. Using a slotted spoon, transfer the pork to a double layer of paper towels to drain. Discard the fat in the pan.

Using a small piece of kitchen string, tie the parsley sprigs, thyme sprigs, and bay leaf together. Place this bouquet garni in a large soup pot or saucepan. Add the clams, potatoes, cold water, leeks, bell pepper, celery, carrot, tomatoes, tomato paste, tomato puree, 1 teaspoon salt, and about ⅛ teaspoon pepper. Place the pot over high heat, add the reserved pork, and bring to a boil. Regulate the heat so that the soup simmers gently; cook, uncovered, for 2 hours, stirring occasionally.

Remove from the heat and discard the bouquet garni. Ladle into warm bowls, float a Garlic Croûte in the center of each bowl, scatter with a little parsley, and serve.

TRUFFLED CAULIFLOWER SOUP

*N*ever thought of cauliflower as a luxury ingredient? You haven't tried this soup. Truffle oil is pricey, but a little goes a very long way, and a two-ounce bottle should last several months. It is a natural partner for cauliflower, lending an earthy, musky touch that perfectly complements the creamy pureed cauliflower. • SERVES 6; MAY BE DOUBLED

---

2 to 2¼ pounds cauliflower
1½ cups heavy cream
1½ cups whole milk

Salt and freshly ground white pepper
1 tablespoon truffle oil (white or black)

Remove and discard the leaves and thick stalks of the cauliflower. Separate into walnut-size florets with about 1 inch of the stem attached.

In the top of a steamer set over simmering water, steam the cauliflower for 20 to 25 minutes, until completely tender.

In a blender or large food processor, combine the steamed cauliflower, cream, and milk; puree until completely smooth, scraping down the sides. Transfer to a large saucepan and stir in 1 teaspoon salt and ¼ to ½ teaspoon white pepper, to taste. Warm through on low heat. Pour into bowls or demitasse cups and drizzle a few drops of truffle oil over each portion (don't be tempted to overdo it—truffle oil goes a *long* way!), and serve at once. Alternatively, cool to room temperature, cover, and refrigerate for up to 6 hours, then warm through just before serving.

LIFE IMITATING ART

The opening night party for a revival of Noël Coward's *Private Lives* took place at Tavern in May 1983. The show, about two divorced people who meet on their honeymoons with their new spouses, headlined the recently divorced Elizabeth Taylor and Richard Burton. Each star sat at a separate oval table, Taylor with her current flame, Victor Luna, and Burton with an entourage. Within two minutes of arriving, Burton and his group of fifteen friends got up and left.

CHILLED GARDEN GAZPACHO

*I*n Spain, gazpacho traditionally contains bread, making for a thicker soup. If you prefer the authentic approach, soak about four ounces of stale, crustless French or sourdough bread in cold water for five minutes, making sure it's evenly saturated. Squeeze out most of the water, then combine in a blender or food processor with the tomato juice mixture before adding the thyme sprigs. Puree until smooth, and refrigerate as directed.

Note that the soup must be refrigerated overnight, to bring out its really wonderful flavor. ◆ SERVES 6; MAY BE DOUBLED

---

5 large garlic cloves, very finely chopped or pushed through a press

Fine sea salt and cayenne pepper

¼ cup tomato paste

1 tablespoon sherry vinegar

⅓ cup best-quality extra-virgin olive oil, preferably from Spain

1 tablespoon fresh lemon juice

3 cups tomato or tomato-vegetable juice

2 sprigs of thyme

2 large, ripe tomatoes, peeled, seeded, and finely diced (see Note)

1 large yellow bell pepper, cored, seeded, and finely diced

1¼ cups peeled, finely diced English cucumber

1¼ cups finely diced red onion (about 1 small)

2 ripe avocados, peeled, pitted, and diced

1 cup Garlic-Herb Croutons (recipe follows; optional)

In a large glass or ceramic pitcher, whisk together the garlic, 1 teaspoon salt, ¼ teaspoon cayenne (or to taste), tomato paste, vinegar, olive oil, lemon juice, and tomato juice. Add the thyme sprigs, cover with plastic wrap, and refrigerate overnight for the flavors to marry.

Just before serving, remove the thyme sprigs and whisk the tomato juice mixture well. In a large bowl, combine all the diced vegetables. Divide the diced vegetables evenly among chilled soup bowls or cups. Pass the pitcher of liquid, so guests can pour it over the vegetables. Garnish with the croutons, if desired.

NOTE · **To peel fresh tomatoes, cut a shallow cross on the bottom of each tomato and submerge in boiling water for about 10 seconds to loosen the skin. Drain immediately and stop the cooking by running under cold water. The skins will slip off easily.**

GARLIC·HERB CROUTONS

Use French, Italian, ciabatta, or sourdough bread to make these tasty croutons. Any that are unused may be frozen in an airtight container for up to about 2 months. Thawing them takes less than 30 minutes, but they do benefit from a 5-minute crisping on a baking sheet in a 350°F oven before using.

1 tablespoon canola oil

1 tablespoon extra-virgin olive oil

1 large garlic clove, sliced

2 cups slightly stale, crustless bread cubes (from about three ½-inch slices)

2 teaspoons very finely chopped flat-leaf parsley

1 teaspoon rosemary leaves

Salt and freshly ground black pepper

In a large skillet, heat the oils over medium heat; add the sliced garlic and sauté until just golden. Remove the garlic with a slotted spoon and add the bread cubes. Sauté, turning often, about 6 minutes, until golden on all sides. Transfer to a bowl and toss with the fresh herbs, ¼ teaspoon salt, and ⅛ teaspoon pepper. Drain on paper towels, if desired. · MAKES 2 CUPS

SUMMER PEA SOUP

*P*ea season is very short, so it's worth spending a little extra time on this lumi-nous soup to take advantage of it. In order to maintain the optimum, vivid green color, the peas must be cooked and blanched in batches. This is a show-stopping soup, so it should ideally be served in clear crystal juice tumblers or bone china demi-tasse cups. • SERVES 4 TO 8, DEPENDING ON PORTION SIZE

---

3 cups shelled English green peas
   (from about 3 pounds of pea pods)

¼ cup sugar

½ cup salt

⅓ to ⅔ cup vegetable stock or broth
   (low-sodium canned is fine)

⅓ cup distilled water, very cold

Kosher salt and freshly ground white pepper

2 teaspoons plain, whole-milk yogurt,
   very cold

1 teaspoon very small mint leaves, for garnish

To help the peas retain their bright color during cooking, place them in a bowl, cover the surface with ice, and toss the peas and ice together to chill.

Fill a large stockpot with water and bring to a boil. Add the sugar and the ½ cup salt. Lift about one quarter of the peas out of their bowl with a strainer, letting the ice fall back into the bowl, and transfer to the stockpot. Cook the peas until completely tender, 6 to 8 minutes.

While the peas cook, fill a large bowl with ice water and submerge a colander in it. When the first batch of peas is tender, transfer to the colander as quickly as possible. Lift the colander from the ice bath, drain the peas well, and transfer to a food processor. Repeat with the remaining peas.

Once all the peas are cooked, puree them for a good 2 minutes, scraping down the sides of the bowl. You should have about 2 cups of puree.

Transfer to a blender and add ⅓ cup vegetable stock and the distilled water. Blend the mixture until smooth. Check the consistency of the soup; if desired, add up to ⅓ cup more broth. Add a tiny pinch of kosher salt and white pepper to taste, and blend again. For a really silky-smooth soup, use a flexible spatula or a wooden spoon to work the soup through a chinois or fine-mesh strainer. If desired, store, covered, in the refrigerator for up to 2 hours; stir before serving, since the soup will separate.

Pour into chilled juice tumblers or demitasse cups, or, for larger portions, Chinese rice bowls. Dollop ¼ to ½ teaspoon of the yogurt in the center of each, then sprinkle with about ⅛ to ¼ teaspoon of the mint. Serve at once.

BLACK BEAN SOUP
WITH LIME AND MADEIRA

*B*lack beans are celebrated throughout Latin America, but their appeal has spread into Tex-Mex and classic American cooking. This deep, dark, and earthy soup gains a touch of sophistication from Madeira—one of the undisputed prides of Portugal's respected fortified wine tradition. • SERVES 10 TO 12

1 pound dried black beans

10 cups water

2 cups chicken stock or broth (low-sodium canned is fine)

1 smoked ham hock

2 ounces salt pork, rind trimmed away, cut into ½-inch dice

3 large white or yellow onions, coarsely chopped

3 ribs of celery, coarsely chopped

2 carrots, coarsely chopped

3 sprigs of thyme

3 sprigs of sage

2 bay leaves

¼ teaspoon cayenne pepper

½ cup Madeira cooking wine

1 tablespoon tomato paste

2 tablespoons red wine vinegar

1 tablespoon molasses

Kosher salt

1 lime, ends trimmed, sliced into paper-thin rounds

2 tablespoons finely chopped flat-leaf parsley

Soak the black beans in water to cover for 12 hours, or overnight. Drain well. In an 8-quart soup pot or Dutch oven, combine the drained beans, water, and the chicken stock. Place over high heat and bring to a boil. Lower the heat so the liquid simmers gently and cook, covered, for 1 hour, occasionally skimming off any foam that may rise to the surface. Add the ham hock and simmer for 10 minutes more.

While the soup is simmering, place the salt pork in a heavy skillet over low heat and sizzle gently until the fat is rendered and the pork is golden, about 15 minutes.

Increase the heat to medium-high and add the onions. Sauté for 5 minutes, stirring occasionally. Add the celery and carrots and cook, stirring frequently, for 5 minutes. Tie the herbs together with kitchen twine. Add the softened vegetables, salt pork, and herbs to the soup pot; simmer partially covered for 1 hour.

Remove the herb bundle and the ham hock from the soup. (If desired, discard the skin and bones from the hock, dice any meat that's left, and use it as garnish.)

Let the soup stand for 5 to 10 minutes to cool slightly. Puree in a blender in batches, filling the blender by only two thirds and holding the lid on securely with a folded towel. Return the puree to the original pot. Warm the soup over low heat and stir in the cayenne pepper, Madeira, tomato paste, vinegar, and molasses.

Taste for seasoning and, if necessary, add salt in ¼-teaspoon increments to taste. If too thick, add a little water. Ladle the soup into wide, shallow bowls and carefully float a slice or two of lime on the surface. Scatter a little parsley on top, and serve.

All That Jazz

*I*n the 1990s, Warner was a best friend to jazz. During that decade, jazz clubs all but disappeared in New York City, which made the idea of bringing it to Tavern all the more interesting to him. With the same flair he had used to transform Tavern nearly twenty years earlier, Warner turned the Chestnut Room into a great venue for hearing jazz.

In his inimitable style, he insisted on bringing in the best piano, one favored—and signed on the inside—by many a great jazz master. This very large, slick black Steinway D had once graced the stages of the Kennedy Center and Carnegie Hall. With the piano, revered for the ease with which one's fingers could glide along the keys, in place, jazz impresario Lenny Triola lured the legends to play there.

Many credit Warner with significantly renewing the careers of Illinois Jacquet and Little Jimmy Scott and launching those of others, including Nancy LaMott, Benny Greene, and Cyrus Chestnut. For many—including Harry Sweets Edison, Tommy Flanagan, Lionel Hampton, Etta Jones, and Al Gray—the Chestnut Room was a last glorious stop. And the performers weren't the only big personalities in the room: among those who have come to listen are Madonna, Bob Hope, Carroll O'Connor, Bill Cosby, Danny Aiello, Mel Tormé, Liza Minnelli, Bill Bradley, and none other than ol' Blue Eyes himself.

AN ELECTRIC PERFORMANCE

Lainie Kazan was one chanteuse who enjoyed sold-out appearances at Tavern, but they weren't without drama. There were no "backsatge" areas for talent at the restaurant, a stumbling block for Lainie. Warner was determined to book her, so the contract called for a trailer to be used as a dressing room. He rented a luxurious RV and stowed it in the parking lot. On opening night, just before she was to go on, the dashing diva blew the electricity by plugging her hair dryer and curling iron in at the same time. Rattled, she threatened to stay in her trailer and emerged only after intense coaxing from Tavern staff—to great acclaim from the adoring audience waiting in the Chestnut Room.

SWEET CORN CHOWDER
WITH SMOKED PAPRIKA MAYO

*S*ummer is chowder season, and this all-American soup takes its flavor straight from the golden cornfields to your bowl. Every chowder has potatoes, but not every chowder gets a smoky garnish like this luxurious—and super-simple—mayonnaise. • SERVES 6 TO 8

12 cups chicken stock or broth
(low-sodium canned is fine)

1 ham hock

2 large boiling potatoes, scrubbed

6 tablespoons (¾ stick) butter

1 large onion, chopped

2 fresh jalapeño chiles, cored, seeded,
and finely chopped

6 cups fresh corn kernels (from about 8 ears
of corn) or 6 cups frozen corn, thawed

1 cup heavy cream

¼ cup fresh lime juice

2 to 3 teaspoons sugar (use only if corn is not
very sweet)

¾ cup diced red bell pepper (¼-inch dice)

Salt and freshly ground white pepper

Smoked Paprika Mayo (recipe follows)

In a large soup pot, simmer the chicken stock and the ham hock together for about 30 minutes. Remove the ham hock and discard it, or reserve the meat for another use. Set the stock aside.

Steam the potatoes above lightly salted boiling water until tender, about 20 minutes. Remove from the steamer and cool. Peel, cut into ½-inch cubes, and set aside.

In another large soup pot over medium-low heat, melt the butter and cook the onion and chiles for 10 minutes, stirring occasionally. Add the corn and continue cooking for 10 minutes more, then add the stock.

Bring to a simmer and cook for 5 minutes. Remove from the heat and let cool briefly. Puree the soup in a blender in batches, filling the blender by only two thirds and holding the lid on securely with a folded towel. If desired, use a flexible spatula to force the soup through a medium sieve (not too fine) and return to the pan. (Straining will yield a soup with a very silky consistency; you could also pass it through the medium blade of a food mill.) Add the cream, lime juice, and sugar, if necessary. Add the bell pepper, cubed potatoes, 1½ teaspoons salt, and ½ teaspoon white pepper and bring back to a simmer. Taste for seasoning and correct with lime juice or sugar, if necessary.

Serve in large shallow soup bowls, swirling each with a tablespoon of the smoked paprika mayo.

SMOKED PAPRIKA MAYO

¾ cup Mayo/Aioli
(page 42, made with
2 garlic cloves) or store-
bought mayonnaise)
(mixed with 2 pressed
garlic cloves)

¼ teaspoon Spanish smoked
paprika *(pimentón)*

½ to 1 teaspoon fresh lemon
juice, to taste

Salt

Put the mayo and paprika in a bowl and whisk to combine. Whisk in the lemon juice and taste for seasoning; adjust with salt, paprika, and lemon juice as desired. Store, covered, in the refrigerator for up to 4 days. • MAKES ¾ CUP

WRAP IT UP

Longtime florist Paul Brummer is as well known for his flower-bedecked candelabras as for his three-layer bows. To wrap a candelabra with flowers, secure foliage such as ruscus or ivy with florist tape to the top of the base of the candelabra. Wrap the foliage around the stem and arms in barber-pole fashion, securing it to the final arm with the florist tape. Weave seasonal flowers in and out of the foliage—the more the better!

CARROT AND GINGER SOUP
WITH DILL CRÈME

*T*he ginger in this pretty soup adds an unexpected peppery snap, and the luscious dill crème makes it a refined option for lunch or as a starter for a light fall supper. • SERVES 8

1 tablespoon extra-virgin olive oil

2½ pounds ripe, dark-orange carrots, peeled and cut into 1-inch chunks

½ yellow onion, coarsely chopped

1 tablespoon peeled and finely chopped or grated fresh ginger

½ leek, white and green parts only, coarsely chopped and rinsed well in a colander

Salt

1½ quarts (6 cups) chicken or vegetable stock (low-sodium canned is fine)

¾ cup mascarpone cheese

4 to 5 tablespoons dry white wine

2 to 3 tablespoons finely chopped dill

Place a large saucepan or soup pot over low heat and add the olive oil. When it is warm, add the carrots, onion, ginger, leek, and ¾ teaspoon salt. Sauté for 10 minutes, stirring occasionally, until the vegetables are barely tender.

Add the stock and bring to a boil. Reduce the heat and simmer the soup, uncovered, for 30 to 40 minutes, until the carrots are tender all the way through. Remove the pan from the heat and let cool for 20 minutes.

Puree the soup in a blender in batches, filling the blender by only two thirds and holding the lid on securely with a folded towel. Using a flexible spatula, force the soup through a medium sieve into a large, clean saucepan, and taste for seasoning. If desired, cover the pan and let the soup stand for up to 1 hour.

In a small bowl, whisk together the mascarpone, 4 tablespoons of the white wine, the dill, and ¼ teaspoon salt. The crème should be a nice drizzling consistency; if necessary, whisk in another tablespoon of wine.

Reheat the soup, ladle into bowls, and serve each bowl with a substantial drizzle of dill crème in the center.

CURRIED APPLE SOUP

*D*uring the fall, or a holiday meal, this soup is special and delicious. There is nothing more sophisticated than a sit-down soup course, but if your celebration calls for a more casual approach, serve it in juice tumblers or Moroccan tea glasses, setting the extra soup out in a large pitcher for refills. • SERVES 6; MAY BE DOUBLED

4 tablespoons (½ stick) unsalted butter

1 large onion, very finely chopped

1½ cups unfiltered apple juice or cider

1 quart (4 cups) chicken or vegetable stock (low-sodium canned is fine), or as needed

1 pound Granny Smith apples (2 to 3 apples)

1 tablespoon curry powder

⅓ cup flour

1 cup whole milk

1 cup heavy cream

Salt

Tabasco sauce

FOR GARNISH

1 tablespoon butter

Scant ½ cup sliced almonds

In a large, heavy soup pot or saucepan, melt the 4 tablespoons butter over low heat and add the onion. Cook very gently, stirring occasionally, for about 15 minutes, until the onion is completely tender and translucent.

In a small saucepan, combine the apple juice and half the chicken stock; warm over medium heat. Meanwhile, peel the apples and then grate them on the largest holes of a box grater, grating down to the cores. Discard the cores.

Stir the apple into the pan with the onion and continue cooking until softened, about 5 minutes. Increase the heat to medium, stir in the curry powder, and cook for 1 minute. Sprinkle the flour evenly over the mixture and cook for 2 minutes more, stirring occasionally. Slowly add the warm apple juice mixture to the onion-apple mixture, whisking all the time; continue whisking and cooking until the mixture thickens.

Add the milk, cream, ½ teaspoon salt, and a dash or two of Tabasco, and bring the soup to just below a simmer. Adjust the soup to the desired consistency by adding some or all of the remaining chicken stock, and taste for seasoning. (If desired, cool the soup to room temperature and refrigerate for up to 12 hours; reheat before serving, but do not let it boil.)

To serve, melt the tablespoon of butter in a small saucepan over medium heat. Add the almonds and sizzle until golden. Ladle the soup into bowls and top each with about 1 tablespoon of almonds.

FRENCH‑STYLE
ROOT VEGETABLE SOUP
WITH SAGE

*T*his is always a winner as a prelude to Thanksgiving turkey. Adding wine to this classic fall soup—as is the style in France—lends a marvelously sophisticated flavor. • SERVES 10 TO 12

3 tablespoons unsalted butter

2 tablespoons extra-virgin olive oil

2 large onions, finely chopped

2 leeks, white part only, well washed and finely chopped

2 large sprigs of thyme

1 pound celery root, peeled and coarsely chopped

1 pound parsnips, peeled and coarsely chopped

2 cups dry white wine

1½ quarts (6 cups) chicken or vegetable stock (low-sodium canned is fine)

Salt and freshly ground white pepper

Canola or vegetable oil, for shallow-frying

About 36 large, clean, and perfectly dry sage leaves

In a large soup pot or saucepan, melt the butter over medium-low heat and add the oil. Add the onions, leeks, and thyme and cook gently without browning for about 10 minutes, until translucent. Add the celery root and parsnips and partially cover the pan. Cook for 10 minutes more, checking occasionally and adding a few tablespoons of water if the vegetables begin to brown.

Add the wine, adjust the heat so the liquid simmers briskly, and cook, uncovered, for about 20 minutes, stirring occasionally, to reduce by half.

Add the chicken stock, partially cover the pan, and simmer for about 45 minutes, until the vegetables are very tender. Remove from the heat and let the soup cool, uncovered, for 20 minutes.

Discard the thyme sprigs and puree the soup in a blender in batches, filling the blender by only two thirds and holding the lid on securely with a folded towel. Strain through a medium sieve back into a clean pan; stir in 1 teaspoon salt and a generous pinch of white pepper. Set aside.

In a large skillet, heat about 1 inch of oil over medium-high heat until the oil sizzles when you dip in the corner of a sage leaf. Add half the sage leaves to the hot oil and fry, nudging occasionally with a slotted spoon, for about 1 minute or until golden brown. Transfer to a double layer of paper towels, and repeat with the remaining sage. Salt the sage leaves to taste. (Don't wait more than 20 minutes before serving, or the sage leaves will get soggy.)

Warm the soup through and divide among the soup bowls. Scatter each serving with a few sage leaves, and serve.

5

PASTA

and

GRAINS

ARTICHOKE, PECORINO, AND PASTA TIMBALE

*T*his luxurious, delectably creamy timbale can easily be converted to a striking vegetarian main course by omitting the pancetta. One of the building blocks of fine French cuisine, it is also used in Italy, where it is called besciamella. Make the pastry and the Béchamel sauce the night before, to lessen the time and labor needed on "the Big Night."

As always when making pastry, it's best to weigh the ingredients, but dry cup measurements for the flour and sugar are fine, as long as you remember to spoon them into the cup and swipe a knife across the top to level the contents. • SERVES 8 TO 10

• *photograph on page 92*

PASTRY SHELL

15 tablespoons (7½ ounces; 1⅞ sticks) unsalted butter

3¾ cups (18¾ ounces) all-purpose flour

1½ tablespoons sugar

Rounded ½ teaspoon salt

4 large egg yolks, lightly beaten

8 to 10 tablespoons ice water

BÉCHAMEL SAUCE

3 tablespoons unsalted butter

4 tablespoons flour

1 cup dry white wine

1 cup heavy cream

1 cup whole milk

Salt and freshly ground white pepper

¼ teaspoon ground nutmeg

1¼ cups grated imported Pecorino Romano cheese

FILLING

One 9- or 10-ounce package frozen artichoke hearts

8 to 10 ounces diced pancetta

4 tablespoons (½ stick) unsalted butter

4 shallots, finely chopped

8 ounces mixed wild, cremini, or oyster mushrooms, brushed clean and sliced thick

2 cups frozen petits pois (one 9- to 10-ounce package), thawed

4 garlic cloves, very finely chopped or pushed through a press

Salt and freshly ground black pepper

Kosher salt

¾ pound dried imported rigatoni

1 pound fresh whole-milk mozzarella cheese, diced

2 fire-roasted red peppers from a jar, drained and cut into rough 1-inch pieces

1 large egg beaten with 1 tablespoon milk

MAKE THE PASTRY

Cut the butter into small chunks, place on a plate, and place in the freezer for 5 to 10 minutes.

In an 11-cup or larger food processor, combine the flour, sugar, and salt and process just to blend. Remove the cover and scatter the pieces of cold butter over the top. Pulse on and off 3 or 4 times—2 or 3 seconds for each pulse—until the butter is the size of small peas. Remove the cover and drizzle the yolks and 8 tablespoons ice water over the top. Pulse again 5 or 6 times, until the dough starts to come together and form several large, very rough clumps. If the dough does not begin to come together within 15 to 20 seconds, add 1 or 2 tablespoons ice water. Scrape down the bowl once, and avoid overprocessing or the pastry will be tough.

Turn out onto a lightly floured surface and shape quickly into a rough cylinder. Cut off about one third of the cylinder and form both pieces into round, flattened disks. Wrap each tightly with plastic wrap and refrigerate for at least 2 hours or overnight.

Let the dough stand at room temperature for 30 to 40 minutes before rolling out (otherwise, the dough will be too stiff and cold to roll).

MAKE THE BÉCHAMEL

Place a large, heavy saucepan over medium heat and add the butter. When the foam has subsided, add the flour and whisk until a smooth paste forms. Keep cooking, stirring frequently, for about 2 minutes; do not let it brown. Whisk in the wine until the sauce is smooth. Bring to a slow simmer and cook for 2 minutes, then whisk in the cream and milk, ½ teaspoon salt, ¼ teaspoon white pepper, and the nutmeg. Regulate the heat so the sauce simmers very gently and cook, uncovered, stirring occasionally, for 10 to 15 minutes, until bubbling and only just slightly thickened. Stir in the Pecorino and remove from the heat.

Cool to slightly warmer than room temperature and spray the top of the sauce lightly with vegetable oil spray to prevent a skin from forming. If desired, cover and refrigerate overnight; bring to room temperature before proceeding with the recipe.

FOR THE FILLING

Put a very large pot of water on to boil, for the pasta. Cook the artichoke hearts according to the package instructions; halve them and set aside.

In a heavy skillet, preferably cast iron, crisp the pancetta over medium-low heat until golden brown. Meanwhile, place a very large skillet or sauté pan over medium-low heat and melt the butter. When the foam has subsided, add the shallots and cook, stirring occasionally, for about 5 minutes, until tender. Increase the heat to medium-high, add the mushrooms, and cook, stirring frequently, for 5 to 6 minutes, until tender and all the moisture has evaporated. Add the peas and cook, stirring, for 2 minutes, then add the garlic and stir for 30 seconds more. Season to taste with salt and pepper and remove the pan from the heat.

Add 2 tablespoons kosher salt to the pasta water, and add the rigatoni. Cook the pasta until almost al dente. Drain the pasta in a colander, shaking well, and fold together with the pea mixture (if the mixture will not fit into the big skillet, return everything to the empty pasta-cooking pot). Thoroughly stir in about three quarters of the Béchamel sauce.

ASSEMBLE THE TIMBALE

Preheat the oven to 375°F.

On a lightly floured surface, roll out the larger disk of dough to a round about 17 inches in diameter and ⅛ inch thick. Ease the dough down into a 10-inch springform pan, gently pushing it into the corners without stretching or tearing the dough. Trim the edges of the dough with scissors, leaving a 1-inch overhang.

Spoon about one quarter of the pasta mixture into the mold and top with one third of the diced mozzarella; press down with the back of the spoon to compact gently. Spoon in another quarter of the pasta, smooth the top, then cover evenly with the artichoke hearts, the red peppers, and another third of the mozzarella. Make another layer with one quarter of the pasta and top with the remaining third of the mozzarella. Finish with the remaining pasta, smoothing the top and pressing down gently.

Drizzle the remaining Béchamel sauce over the top. Quickly roll out the smaller disk of pastry to a round about 1 inch larger than the top of the pan. Brush the top edges of the lower pastry overhang with some of the egg wash and fit the pastry top over it, matching the edges. Crimp the edges together with a fork, sealing firmly and making an attractive pattern. Trim the pastry again with scissors so that the edges are exactly even.

Slash the top of the pastry in 2 or 3 places and brush with the remaining egg wash. Bake on the center rack of the oven for about 1 hour, until the top is deep golden-brown. Transfer the pan to a rack to cool for 15 minutes before unmolding onto a platter (see Note).

Use a serrated knife to cut the timbale into wedges, then use a triangular-shaped pie server to transfer each wedge to a plate. Serve at once. (If you serve cold, much of the flavor will be lost.)

NOTE · Unmolding a timbale may appear daunting, but it's actually a piece of cake! Gently place a rimless or upside-down baking sheet over the pastry top of the timbale. Now grasp both sides and quickly invert. Gently wiggle the springform pan up and off (if you release the clip, the edge of the overhanging pastry may shatter). Place a large round serving platter gently over the revealed bottom of the timbale, again grasp the two sides, and quickly invert. The timbale will be right side up on your platter and ready for slicing.

Our Gardens

For Tavern's staff horticulturist, there's no down time or slow season. There are five gardens: the Rafters, Crystal, and Chestnut gardens form a horseshoe around the glass-enclosed Crystal Room, while the Terrace and Park gardens provide private outdoor spaces adjacent to their eponymous rooms. All of them, as well as the surrounding grounds, are actively tended twelve months a year. When not planting, the gardening staff is always cleaning up fall leaves or keeping the grounds free of debris.

Since 2000, Tavern has designed gardens that are considered to be some of the finest in New York City. Prior to that year, during the blooming season impatiens filled the gardens in planters and baskets. Though the profusion of them had a colorful visual impact, the lack of variety was out of sync with what was happening in garden circles. Now, the hanging baskets alone feature several dozen different kinds of plants (somewhat to the chagrin of Regis Philbin, who is a big fan of impatiens and has lamented that they no longer rule the Tavern landscape).

The restaurant works very closely with the Central Park Conservancy to maintain the beauty New Yorkers have come to expect in the park. Tavern's horticulturist keeps a particularly close eye on the London plane trees that form a canopy over the outdoor terraces, as trees of all kinds are among the park's most valuable assets. In fact, one of the rarest, an eighty-year-old American elm, grows in a spacious niche in the hallway between Tavern's Park and Chestnut rooms. Indeed, the rooms were built around it!

SPRING

Easter marks the beginning of the season for the keepers of the gardens. One week before Easter Sunday, two staff gardeners, along with the horticulturist, begin planting those icons of the Easter holiday, daffodils. Nine thousand plants in full bloom, having been started by an outside horticulture concern, are divided among the five gardens. As the mercury rises, red tulips—fifty thousand in all over the spring season—join the daffodils and eventually overtake them, resulting in a jaw-dropping monochromatic display throughout Tavern's grounds. It's not the end for all those daffodils, though; they are dug up and distributed to gardens throughout the city where they'll continue to bloom year after year. By the end of April, the gardeners are planting tulips at the rate of five thousand every other week! Fragrant light-purple hyacinths are added to the gardens next. These fragrant blooms are also combined with showy foxglove, tulips, and daffodils in the fifty outscale pots that dot the terraces and announce the entrance to Tavern. The sixty-plus baskets filled with cool-season plants such as argyranthemum, hebe, and ivies are moved to the perimeter of the gardens at this time, signaling the transformation of the outdoor dining spaces from winter to spring. The appearance of the brimming pots and baskets and blooming flower beds entices guests to eat outside as early as mid-April. So lush and colorful are the gardens already that diners often overlook the outsize topiaries that are cleverly tucked into the beds.

SUMMER

The exuberant summer gardens are installed around May 15. They include many different annuals and tropicals in combination with perennials such as aquilegia, dicentra, euphorbia, hosta, and phlox. The 120 baskets feature sixteen different combinations of plant material; Lysimachia, coleus 'India frills,' cissus, alternanthera, and helichrysum are just a few on display.

Tavern's gardens are planted rather tightly, since natural light is at a premium. In fact, each garden varies according to the amount of light it receives. For example, the Terrace Garden is very shady, so tropical plants are installed for their foliage, which can tolerate the deep shade. In the spring, however, perennials can be planted because they come into bloom before the trees have their leaves. To compensate for the lack of light, light-colored flowers are the blooms of choice; chartreuse and off-white buds combined with darker colors give much-needed depth to the patio gardens.

Summer is spent maintaining the gardens by weeding, fertilizing, pruning, and—most important—watering them vigilantly. Quenching the thirst of so many plants is the most challenging task for the gardeners, since every plant is hand-watered and the

task must be completed before the restaurant opens at 11:30 A.M. It requires a staff of three, who arrive at 6 every morning to lug around five hundred feet of hose to get the job done.

Tavern's gardens are the scene of great revelry and celebration, which can lead to unintentional damage to the flower beds. Whether someone dances among the flowers or a carriage horse makes lunch of the hanging baskets, the damaged goods are immediately replaced; a duplicate of each garden grows in a holding area adjacent to the restaurant, allowing the gardeners to change out a few flowers or the entire garden in no time.

FALL AND WINTER

Tavern's fall gardens are simpler but no less enchanting than the flamboyant spring and summer displays. Purple, orange, ivory, and gold mums, purple and white kale, and purple asters are installed in all the planter boxes and pots throughout the restaurant. At the same time, the summer baskets are being diligently nursed as the shorter days and decreased light take their toll. There are three changeovers of the fall plants; after the last, the winter season begins. In early November, assorted evergreen plants, such as gold thread cypress, holly, fir trees, and red and yellow twig dogwoods are planted in those same planter boxes and pots.

MACARONI
WITH WILD MUSHROOMS AND THREE CHEESES

*N*o matter how many friends, chefs, acquaintances, or guests suggested to Warner that he replace the macaroni and cheese on the menu at Maxwell's Plum with a more fashionable dish, the comfort-food lover insisted it stay. Sometimes, it's just a macaroni and cheese kind of night. But that doesn't mean you can't refine the standard version a bit: Here, wild mushrooms and top-quality cheeses give an unconventional twist that both traditionalists and nonconformists will love.

To lend the dish an even earthier flavor, substitute 4 ounces of grated smoked fontina for half of the plain fontina. • SERVES 8 TO 10

---

12 tablespoons (1½ sticks) unsalted butter, plus additional, softened, for greasing

1 large shallot, finely chopped

1 pound assorted wild or cultivated mushrooms, stemmed and quartered

Salt and freshly ground black pepper

½ medium onion, thinly sliced

⅓ cup plus 1 tablespoon flour

4½ cups whole milk

1 bay leaf

1 sprig of thyme

9 black peppercorns

⅛ teaspoon ground nutmeg

⅛ teaspoon ground allspice

½ pound (2 cups) finely shredded fontina cheese

½ pound (2 cups) whole-milk, low-moisture mozzarella, shredded

5 ounces (1¼ cups) grated Parmigiano-Reggiano or other *grana padana* cheese

Kosher salt

1 pound dried imported elbow macaroni, gemelli, or penne rigate

1½ cups Garlic Bread Crumbs (page 105)

In a large skillet, heat 4 tablespoons of the butter over medium-high heat. Add the shallot and mushrooms and sauté, stirring frequently, until tender, about 6 minutes. Season to taste with salt and pepper and set aside.

Use the softened butter to generously grease a 9 x 14-inch or similar-size earthenware, ceramic, or glass baking dish. Put a very large pot of water on to boil, for the pasta. Preheat the oven to 375°F.

In a large saucepan, melt the remaining 8 tablespoons butter over medium-low heat and add the onion. Cook until softened, stirring occasionally, about 5 minutes. Sprinkle the flour evenly over the onion and stir constantly for 2 minutes, but do not allow the flour to brown. Stir in the milk a little at a time at first, stirring constantly, until you have added about 1 cup. Stir until smooth, then add the bay leaf, thyme, peppercorns, and the remaining 3½ cups milk. Increase the heat to medium-high and keep stirring frequently until the liquid reaches a boil (watch carefully so that it does not boil over). Boil for 1 minute, then lower the heat so the milk barely simmers and continue to cook, stirring frequently, for 10 minutes more.

continued

Remove from the heat and let stand for 5 minutes. Strain the sauce through a fine-mesh sieve into a very large bowl, working the onion back and forth with a rubber spatula to extract all the liquid. Immediately stir in 2 teaspoons salt, about 1 teaspoon pepper, the nutmeg, allspice, and all the cheeses, stirring until the cheese is just melted.

Add 2 tablespoons kosher salt to the pasta water and add the pasta. Cook until al dente, according to package directions. Drain the pasta in a colander, shaking well.

Stir the pasta into the sauce, add the sautéed mushrooms, and stir thoroughly until all the ingredients are evenly distributed. Spoon the mixture into the prepared baking dish and scatter the top with an even layer of the garlic bread crumbs.

Bake for 20 minutes. Transfer to a hot broiler (or turn on the broiler in your oven) and brown for 1 to 3 minutes, watching carefully, until sizzling and golden. Let stand for 5 to 10 minutes before serving.

MAINTENANCE TIDBIT

Tavern has its own off-site workshop, where eight employees, including seamstresses, upholsterers, and woodworkers, make tablecloths, rehabilitate chairs, and build armature for special parties. The workshop is but a tiny part of Tavern's huge warehouse, where hundreds of spare chairs, dozens of tables, and boxes of holiday decorations are stored. Twice a day, tired Tavern furniture is trucked to the warehouse to be refreshed and replaced by newly upholstered and repaired pieces.

PENNE WITH
SPICY VODKA-TOMATO SAUCE

*T*his classic pasta dish became all the rage in New York City in the 1970s, and its popularity has never flagged. You will encounter it in old-fashioned and new-fashioned Italian restaurants alike, so beloved is the vodka-spiked tomato cream sauce.

♦ SERVES 8; MAY BE HALVED

⅓ cup extra-virgin olive oil

2 large yellow onions, very finely chopped

8 garlic cloves, very finely chopped or pushed through a press

One 28-ounce can crushed Italian tomatoes (preferably San Marzano), with their juices

2 teaspoons dried thyme

2½ tablespoons finely chopped oregano leaves

1½ teaspoons crushed red pepper flakes

1 cup vodka

¾ cup chicken stock or broth (low-sodium canned is fine)

1½ cups heavy cream

Salt and freshly ground black pepper

Kosher salt

1½ to 2 pounds dried imported penne

1 cup grated Parmigiano-Reggiano or other *grana padana* cheese

¾ cup coarsely chopped flat-leaf parsley

Place a very large sauté pan, skillet, or saucepan over medium-low heat and add the oil. When it is hot, add the onions and sauté, stirring frequently, until tender and golden, about 10 minutes. Add the garlic and cook for 30 seconds more, then add the crushed tomatoes and simmer for 2 to 3 minutes, to thicken slightly. Add the thyme, oregano, red pepper flakes, vodka, and chicken stock, and bring to a gentle simmer. Cook for about 30 minutes, regulating the heat so the liquid continues to simmer gently, until the liquid is reduced by about one third.

Meanwhile, put a very large pot of water on to boil, for the pasta (if you don't have a pot that holds more than 8 quarts of water, use two pots).

Stir the cream into the reduced sauce and add ¾ teaspoon salt and about ¼ teaspoon pepper; increase the heat to medium. After the sauce comes to a brisk simmer, cook about 2 minutes until thickened to a nice coating consistency. Remove the sauce from the heat and cover the pan.

Add 2 tablespoons kosher salt to the pasta water and add the penne. Cook until al dente, according to the package directions. Drain the pasta in a colander, shaking well. Turn into the skillet with the sauce. (If everything will not fit in the skillet, transfer the sauce to the empty pasta-cooking pot and then add the drained pasta.)

Over low heat, toss the penne with tongs until all the quills are evenly coated with the creamy sauce. Mound the pasta into a warmed serving bowl and add three quarters of the Parmigiano and parsley. Toss until evenly blended, then top with any remaining sauce, Parmigiano, and parsley. Serve at once.

POLENTA "NAPOLEON"
WITH PORCINI-SAUSAGE RAGÙ

*T*avern chefs have long adapted the classic dessert technique of layered puff pastry to savory dishes for other courses of the meal. On the summer brunch menu, for example, a stack of red and yellow heirloom tomatoes layered with ricotta salata and topped with a pesto crouton is a favorite of guests. This main-course winter offering deserves pride of place as the centerpiece for an extra-special occasion. It has all the flavors and colors of the Italian kitchen, presented in a slightly unconventional form: Here, thin layers of golden yellow polenta take the place of lasagna noodles, and the rustic sausage ragù is as gutsy as they come. • SERVES 6 TO 7

POLENTA LAYERS
1 tablespoon extra-virgin olive oil

2 garlic cloves, finely chopped

3 cups chicken stock or broth
(low-sodium canned is fine)

3 cups water

Kosher salt

1½ cups polenta or coarsely ground yellow cornmeal

3 tablespoons butter

PORCINI-SAUSAGE RAGÙ
1 ounce dried porcini mushrooms

2 tablespoons extra-virgin olive oil

1 medium white or yellow onion,
coarsely chopped

12 ounces hot or sweet Italian sausage,
casings removed

Salt and freshly ground black pepper

1 tablespoon tomato paste

One 14-ounce can peeled Italian plum
tomatoes (preferably San Marzano),
drained well

¼ cup heavy cream

2 tablespoons finely chopped oregano leaves

Softened butter, for the baking dish

1¼ cups (10 ounces) whole-milk ricotta
cheese, at room temperature

½ cup grated Parmigiano-Reggiano or
other *grana padana* cheese

¼ pound Italian fontina, slivered

Freshly ground black pepper

TO MAKE THE POLENTA
Place a large, heavy saucepan over very low heat and add the oil. Add the garlic and sauté, stirring constantly, for about 3 minutes, or until softened. Do not let the garlic burn.

Add the chicken stock, water, and 1 teaspoon kosher salt and bring to a boil. Reduce the heat and, when the liquid is simmering, gradually sprinkle the polenta in a very slow, thin stream, whisking constantly in the same direction until all the grains have been incorporated and no lumps remain. Reduce the heat to very low, and use a wooden paddle to stir every 1 or 2 minutes for 20 to 25 minutes, or until the mixture pulls away from the sides of the pan and the grains of polenta have softened. Stir in the butter; the mixture will be very thick.

continued

Rinse a 12 x 17-inch rimmed baking sheet with cold water. Mound the polenta on the baking sheet and, using a rubber spatula repeatedly dipped in hot water, spread the polenta evenly until it is just over ¼ inch thick. Cover with a clean kitchen towel and allow to rest for 1 hour at room temperature, or up to 24 hours in the refrigerator.

TO MAKE THE FILLING

Soak the dried porcini in very hot water to cover for 20 minutes. Squeeze as dry as possible and chop fine.

Place a large skillet over medium-low heat and add the oil. Add the onion and sauté for 4 to 5 minutes, stirring, until softened. Add the porcini and sausage and cook, breaking up the sausage with a wooden spoon into small pieces, until no more pink remains. Stir in ½ teaspoon salt, a generous grinding of black pepper, and the tomato paste. Add the peeled tomatoes one at a time, squeezing out and discarding some of the seeds and crushing the tomatoes with one hand as you do so. Partially cover the pan and cook at a low simmer for 8 to 10 minutes, stirring occasionally, until the tomatoes have almost completely melted.

Stir in the cream and the oregano and cook for about 2 minutes, until nicely thickened. Remove from the heat. (If desired, make the ragù the day before, cool to room temperature, and refrigerate overnight.)

TO FINISH

Preheat the oven to 375°F.

Use the softened butter to grease the bottom and sides of a large, deep earthenware, ceramic, or glass baking dish, either a 10 x 14 x 2-inch rectangular dish or a 13 x 9-inch oval dish.

Cut the polenta into 2 x 4-inch rectangles. Layer the ingredients in the following order: polenta rectangles, a scoop of ricotta sprinkled with a pinch of Parmigiano, another layer of polenta, a spoonful of porcini-sausage ragù, ricotta sprinkled with fontina, and another layer of polenta (you should have three layers of polenta). Continue layering until you have used up all the ingredients, finishing with a final layer of polenta topped with a thin layer of the ragù and sprinkled with Parmigiano and a bit of black pepper. Tap the baking dish gently on the counter to settle the ingredients.

Bake for 35 minutes, or until the top is golden brown. Let stand for about 10 minutes, and serve.

ASPARAGUS
AND PARMESAN RISOTTO

*T*his can be a first course or a side dish with equally spectacular results (the portions are approximately the same in either case). If you want to serve it as a side dish, choose a main course that requires very little last-minute attention, such as Grilled Butterflied Leg of Lamb with Red Wine–Shallot Butter (page 192). • SERVES 8 TO 10

2½ pounds asparagus, woody ends trimmed

Salt

2 quarts (8 cups) chicken stock or broth
(preferably homemade, but low-sodium
canned is fine)

¼ cup extra-virgin olive oil

3 shallots, very finely chopped

3 garlic cloves, very finely chopped or
pushed through a press

3½ cups (1 pound) Arborio or Carnaroli rice

¾ cup dry white wine

1 tablespoon butter

1¼ cups (about 4 ounces) grated Parmigiano-
Reggiano or other *grana padana* cheese

Freshly ground black pepper

Cut off the asparagus tips and set them aside. Peel the bottom 2 inches of the stalks with a vegetable peeler and snap the stalks in half. In a large saucepan of lightly salted boiling water, cook the tips just until tender, about 2 minutes. Transfer to a colander and refresh with cold running water; set aside. Add the asparagus stalks to the still-boiling water and cook until very tender, about 10 minutes. Reserve ⅓ cup of the cooking water. Drain the stalks; puree in a food processor or blender until very smooth.

In a medium saucepan, bring the chicken stock to a slow simmer. Preheat the oven to its lowest setting. If serving as an appetizer, place 8 to 10 shallow bowls inside to warm. If serving as a side dish, place a platter inside to warm.

Place a large saucepan over low heat and add the oil. Add the shallots and sauté, stirring occasionally, for about 4 minutes or until softened but not browned. Add the garlic and cook for 2 minutes. Add the rice, increase the heat to medium, and cook, stirring, for 1 to 2 minutes to coat the grains with the oil and toast them slightly. Add the wine and keep stirring until almost all the liquid has evaporated. Add 1 cup of the simmering stock and stir fairly frequently until almost all the stock is absorbed.

Continue adding stock 1 cup at a time and stirring until it's absorbed; regulate the heat so the stock simmers actively. After about 15 minutes, the rice should be just tender but with a little bite at the center of each grain. Stir in the asparagus puree and continue cooking for 1 minute, so the bright green color will not be lost.

Add the asparagus tips and stir gently for another minute to heat through. Remove the pan from the heat and fold in the butter, Parmigiano, ¾ teaspoon salt, and a generous grinding of pepper; taste for seasoning. Spoon into the warmed bowls and serve at once. (Or, mound on a warmed platter and serve as a side dish.)

MARATHON PASTA
FOR A CROWD

Nothing brings out the spirit of New Yorkers quite like the New York City Marathon. Every November, more than twenty thousand runners gather on the Verrazano Narrows Bridge at sunrise in anticipation of the start later that morning. New Yorkers come out in droves, lining the twenty-six-mile course that winds through the five boroughs to cheer friends and foreigners alike.

The night before the race, Tavern plays host to the marathoners for the biggest pasta party on the planet: A line of more than fifteen thousand runners snakes along Central Park West as they await an over-the-top carbo-loading experience. They fuel up on fourteen thousand pounds of pasta, five hundred gallons of sauce, one thousand pounds of ground beef, five thousand pounds of salad, sixteen thousand dinner rolls, twelve thousand apples, an unfathomable amount of water, Gatorade, and, yes, beer.

The next day, when the first world-class athlete crosses the finish line in Central Park—just a stone's throw from Tavern's front door—a collective roar sounds along the Upper West Side.

Soon after the top male and female runners cross the finish line, they are escorted through the restaurant and into the Crystal Room by New York City's mayor and police commissioner to the sound of rousing applause. On the following morning, Tavern hosts a press conference for the winners in the Rafters Room, where representatives of every major and minor news outlet gather to learn the mile-by-mile details of the first-place finishers' races. • SERVES 6; MAY BE INCREASED TO FEED 1,600

---

8 tablespoons (1 stick) butter, plus additional for greasing

¾ cup flour

6 cups whole milk

Salt and freshly ground white pepper

2 cups grated Parmigiano-Reggiano or other *grana padana* cheese

2 tablespoons extra-virgin olive oil

1 large shallot, thinly sliced

1 pound spicy Italian sausage, casings removed

One 8-ounce bag of frozen baby peas, thawed

Kosher salt

1 pound dried elbow pasta (macaroni)

Place a large, heavy saucepan or soup pot over medium-low heat and add the 8 tablespoons butter. When it has melted, add the flour and whisk until a smooth paste forms. Keep cooking, stirring frequently, for about 3 minutes; do not let it brown. Whisk in the milk, ¾ teaspoon salt, and a generous grinding of white pepper. Whisking occasionally, regulate the heat to bring the liquid to a gentle simmer (watch carefully; it can boil over in a heartbeat). After the liquid comes to a simmer, cook for about 1½ minutes, stirring with a wooden spoon around the base and corners of the pan, until just slightly thickened. Remove from the heat and stir in about three-quarters of the cheese.

Preheat the oven to 375°F. Put a very large pot of water on to boil, for the pasta.

In a medium skillet, warm the oil over medium-high heat. Add the shallot and stir for 1 to 2 minutes, then add the sausage and cook, breaking it into small pieces with a wooden spoon, until no pink remains. Add the peas and cook for 1 minute more, then add the sausage mixture to the white sauce, scraping the pan to get every last bit of flavor into the sauce.

Add 2 tablespoons kosher salt to the pasta water and add the elbows. Cook for a little more than half the recommended cooking time in the package directions. Drain the pasta in a colander, shaking well.

Use the softened butter to generously grease a 9 x 13 x 2-inch or similar-size earthenware, ceramic, or glass baking dish. In it, combine the white sauce and the pasta and mix well. Scatter with the remaining cheese. Bake, uncovered, for 25 to 30 minutes, until bubbling and golden brown on the top. Let stand at room temperature for 15 minutes to firm slightly, then transfer to a buffet or serve at once.

BLACK PEPPER ORZO
WITH LAMB SAUSAGE, FETA, AND MINT

*B*ecause this main-course pasta dish is so easy to make, it's ideal for an impromptu celebration. It also makes a lovely side dish for six if you omit the sausage.

If you find precooked lamb sausages, by all means substitute them for the fresh sausages called for below. Omit the precooking step and simply slice them as described.

◆ SERVES 8

1½ to 2 pounds lamb sausage, or lamb-and-beef sausage (merguez)

Kosher salt

12 ounces orzo pasta

⅓ cup extra-virgin olive oil, plus additional as needed

14 ounces French or Greek feta cheese, crumbled (about 2½ cups)

Finely grated zest of 2 scrubbed lemons (see Note, page 41)

⅓ cup coarsely chopped mint leaves

Freshly ground black pepper

Put a large pot of water on to boil, for the orzo.

In a large skillet or sauté pan, combine the sausages with ½ cup water and place over medium heat. Cook, uncovered, turning occasionally, until all the water has evaporated and the sausages start to brown, about 12 minutes.

Continue cooking for 10 to 12 minutes more (depending on the thickness of the sausage), until the sausages are firm and deep golden brown all over (regulate the heat so the sausages sizzle but don't burn, and add a few drops of oil if necessary).

Cool slightly and slice about ½ inch thick on the diagonal. Transfer to a large serving platter and set aside.

Add 2 tablespoons kosher salt to the pasta water and add the orzo. Cook until al dente, about 9 minutes. Drain the pasta in a colander and rinse under cold running water, then drain again, shaking the colander gently.

Transfer the orzo to the platter with the sausage and drizzle with the ⅓ cup oil; mix well to stop the pasta from sticking. Let stand for at least 10 and up to 20 minutes.

Add the feta, about two thirds of the lemon zest, and about two thirds of the mint to the pasta; season quite generously with black pepper. Fold together gently, then drizzle with a little more olive oil, if desired, and scatter with the remaining lemon zest and mint. Place on a buffet or serve.

CREAMY CRAB LINGUINE
WITH FRESH BASIL

*T*he sparkling and romantic dining rooms and patios at Tavern are frequently the scene of marriage proposals, but your own home could be the perfect setting, too. This dish may be a labor of love, but it yields spectacular results: Make it for someone *you* love.

Cutting up the whole crab takes muscle and can be a bit messy, but do persevere (or get a fishmonger to persevere for you): 100 percent of the flavor from the shell *and* meat will end up in the creamy sauce. If you allow plenty of time to prepare the sauce, it can wait for up to forty-five minutes, just enough time to attend to other romantic details—and perhaps take a relaxing bath! • SERVES 2

---

1 small, shell-on crab, cleaned

Salt and freshly ground white pepper

3 tablespoons unsalted butter

2 small shallots, coarsely chopped

1 small carrot, peeled and coarsely chopped

1 small leek, white part only, well washed and coarsely chopped

½ teaspoon tomato paste

1 bay leaf

1 sprig of thyme

2 sprigs of tarragon

2 teaspoons Cognac or brandy

½ cup dry white wine or vermouth

1½ cups heavy cream

TO SERVE

Kosher salt

½ to ¾ pound dried imported linguine

2 teaspoons unsalted butter

6 ounces jumbo lump or backfin crabmeat, coarsely chopped

About 6 basil leaves, stacked rolled, and slivered (chiffonade)

With a large, heavy knife, cut the whole crab in half, then chop each half into 3 or 4 rough pieces. Season the pieces generously with salt and pepper.

Place a large sauté pan or skillet over medium-high heat and add the butter. When it has melted, add the crab pieces and sauté, stirring frequently, for 2 to 3 minutes, until golden brown and aromatic. Add the shallots, carrot, leek, tomato paste, bay leaf, thyme, and tarragon and reduce the heat to medium. Sauté, without browning further, for 2 minutes, stirring frequently.

Add the Cognac and cook for 1 minute (this is too small a quantity to flame, but the alcohol will evaporate quickly). Add the wine and cook, stirring occasionally. for 8 minutes, until the liquid has almost completely evaporated. Stir in the cream, ½ teaspoon salt, and about ¼ teaspoon pepper. Bring to a simmer, then reduce the heat to low, cover the pan, and simmer gently for about 15 minutes, stirring occasionally; the sauce will be slightly thickened.

Strain through a fine-mesh sieve into a bowl or measuring cup, pressing down hard on the solids to extract all the flavor. Discard the solids. Wipe the pan with a paper towel to remove any bits of shell, and return the sauce to the pan. Taste for seasoning and set aside for up to 45 minutes at the back of the stove. Warm through gently just before serving.

TO SERVE

Put a large pot of water on to boil, for the pasta. When the pasta water boils, add 1 tablespoon kosher salt and the linguine. Cook the pasta until al dente, according to the package directions.

Meanwhile, in a small skillet over low heat, melt the butter. Warm the crabmeat gently in the butter, about 3 minutes.

Drain the pasta in a colander, shaking once or twice. Immediately add the pasta to the pan of warm sauce and toss thoroughly. Add half the basil and toss briefly. Serve in warmed bowls, scattering the warm crabmeat and the remaining basil over the top.

BROADWAY ROYALTY

Over the years, Tavern has been pleased to serve the legendary stars who grace the stages of Broadway theaters a few blocks south. Jessica Tandy and Hume Cronyn appeared in many great plays together during their long professional and personal partnership—they had been married for fifty-two years when Ms. Tandy, an Oscar winner for *Driving Miss Daisy*, died in 1994. When one of our staff asked them how they managed to stay married for so long, Hume replied, "We give each other space. I go to a hotel for the weekend and call my wife to tell her I'm there."

6

FISH

SALT-CRUSTED SWORDFISH
WITH MOJITO BUTTER

*Y*ou will need to be great friends with your fishmonger to get the piece of sword-fish called for here; it's worth buddying up to him or her for it! Substitute Pacific cod or sustainable sea bass if swordfish is simply not available. • SERVES 6 TO 8 • *photograph on page 126*

One 4-pound, skin-on, center-cut piece of
   swordfish (about 3 inches thick),
   patted dry with paper towels
5 tablespoons butter, melted
¾ cup fine sea salt

MOJITO BUTTER
10 tablespoons (5 ounces; 1¼ sticks)
   unsalted butter

¼ cup white rum
2 tablespoons dark rum, such as Mount Gay
¼ cup fresh lime juice
2 teaspoons very finely chopped mint leaves
Mango Salsa (recipe follows, or use store-
   bought), for serving (optional)

Place the fish on a small, rimmed baking sheet and brush the top surface with about half of the melted butter. Scatter with half of the salt, pressing it down gently. Refrigerate for 20 minutes, to chill the butter.

Take the sheet out, carefully turn the swordfish over, brush with the remaining melted butter, and coat with the remaining salt. Return to the refrigerator for 20 minutes more.

Meanwhile, begin making the mojito butter: Cut the butter into 10 pieces, place on a plate, and put in the freezer for 10 minutes. In a small nonreactive saucepan, combine the white and dark rums and the lime juice, place over medium heat, and simmer until reduced and slightly thickened, about 6 minutes (there will be about 2 tablespoons liquid remaining).

Place an oven rack about 6 inches from the source of heat and preheat the oven to broil. Remove the reduced liquid from the heat and whisk in one piece of the chilled butter. Return to *very* low heat and continue whisking in the butter, one piece at a time, until the sauce is creamy and emulsified. Don't let it get too hot, or the butter will melt and the sauce will become oily; move the pan back and forth to keep the sauce just lukewarm. Whisk in the mint and set aside at the back of the stove, covered, while you broil the fish (don't try to re-warm the sauce, or it may separate).

Place the baking sheet under the broiler and broil the swordfish without moving or disturbing it for 14 minutes, or until golden brown.

With a flat-ended metal spatula, turn the fish over and broil for about 12 minutes more, until firm and only just cooked through to the center. Slice and serve on warmed plates. Drizzle the slices with a little of the (very rich) mojito butter and place a little mound of mango salsa on top.

MANGO SALSA

2 cups diced ripe mango
  (½-inch dice)

1 small serrano chile,
  stemmed, seeded,
  and minced (about
  1 teaspoon), or to taste

6 green onions, white and
  light green parts only,
  thinly sliced on the
  diagonal

1 cup loosely packed cilantro
  leaves, coarsely chopped

¼ red bell pepper, cored,
  seeded, and finely diced

3 tablespoons fresh lime
  juice

1 teaspoon salt

In a glass or ceramic bowl, combine all the ingredients. Toss together gently, then let rest for about 30 minutes in the refrigerator, for the flavors to marry. Do not keep longer than 1 hour or the fruit will get mushy. • MAKES ABOUT 2½ CUPS

A LITTLE BIT OF PROVENCE IN CENTRAL PARK

Every August, in the two weeks leading up to Labor Day, Tavern touches down in southern France. Indoors and out, sunflowers spring up to the tune of 3,000 blooms. Every planter box outside is filled to bursting, and 150 arrangements fill the interior. Even the kitchen gets into the act, incorporating sunflower oil and seeds into several dishes.

SOLE MEUNIÈRE

Virtually all the luminaries in the food world have graced Tavern's tables, but perhaps no arrival was more anticipated than that of the woman who served as an inspiration to so many chefs: Julia Child. Through her groundbreaking book, *Mastering the Art of French Cooking*, and her TV show, Child brought classic French cooking to America's home cooks in her breezy, unintimidating style. She came to Tavern to attend star-studded culinary fetes, and on one memorable occasion was the guest of honor at a benefit to raise money for public television. Child has said that her first bite of sole prepared in this classic French style was a relevation when she tasted it in France; it inspired her to turn her talents to the stove.

This is a luxurious yet simple, last-minute, hands-on dish, so it serves only four people; feel free to halve it for a romantic dinner. You can easily substitute turbot or halibut, but flounder and cod tend to be too delicate. • SERVES 4

---

4 sole fillets, about 6 ounces each

1 cup whole milk

¾ cup flour

Salt and freshly ground black pepper

6 tablespoons (¾ stick) unsalted butter, melted

4 ounces clarified butter (see Note)

2 tablespoons fresh lemon juice

2 tablespoons finely chopped flat-leaf parsley

Place the fillets in a shallow baking dish and pour the milk over them. Let them soak for at least 5 minutes and up to 20 minutes (no need to refrigerate).

On a large plate, stir the flour together with ½ teaspoon salt and about ¼ teaspoon pepper. Place the melted butter (not the clarified butter) in a very small, heavy-bottomed saucepan. Place over a burner but do not yet turn it on.

Near the stove, assemble the soaking fish, the plate of flour, the clarified butter, several paper towels, and the lemon juice and parsley, so that you will be able to move quickly. (Set the table, warm the plates, and open the wine, too.)

In one very large (say, 14-inch) skillet or two smaller ones, heat the clarified butter over medium-high heat. When the butter is very hot but not smoking, lift a fillet from the milk and blot both sides quickly on the paper towels; coat in the seasoned flour, gently shake off the excess, and then slide it into the hot clarified butter. Repeat with the remaining fillets. Adjust the heat to keep the butter sizzling gently but not burning while you cook the fillets for about 2 minutes on the first side, until the bottom is golden. Very gently use a wide fish spatula to flip the fish over (use a helper spatula too, if necessary). When the second sides of the fillets are golden brown, use the wide spatula to transfer each fillet to a warmed plate.

Working very quickly, heat the small pan of melted butter over medium-high heat, swirling, until the solids at the bottom turn golden brown (not dark). Remove the pan from the heat; quickly drizzle ½ tablespoon lemon juice over each fillet, and sprinkle each with ½ tablespoon parsley. Immediately pour the hot butter over each fillet, dividing it evenly. It will sizzle! Serve at once.

NOTE · **To make about 4 ounces of clarified butter, place 12 tablespoons (6 ounces; 1½ sticks) unsalted butter in a small, heavy saucepan over low heat; do not stir and do not allow the butter to sizzle. When the butter has melted, use a wide spoon to skim off the foam that has risen to the top. Carefully pour the clear yellow liquid into a Pyrex measuring cup or other heat-proof container, leaving all the milky solids behind on the base of the pan; discard the solids. Store the clarified butter, covered, in the refrigerator for up to 3 months.**

THE PERFECT PLACE TO CELEBRATE

We've hosted all kinds of celebrations, from a party for Sean Connery after his gala tribute from the Film Society of Lincoln Center to the premiere of Clint Eastwood's *Mystic River*, starring Sean Penn. But among our proudest nights was Hillary Clinton's fifty-ninth birthday party. It was an elaborate black-tie affair with some of the most influential people in the world. All had a great time, including former president Bill Clinton, who wandered all over the restaurant and shook hands with everyone who wanted to meet him. He was incredibly charming and considerate, even if he probably drove his security detail crazy that night.

MUSTARD·GLAZED SALMON
ON BUTTERY SAVOY CABBAGE

*S*almon has a rich and fatty flavor that is unique and comforting, but it does benefit from the balance of an acidic and piquant element, here provided by mustard. The luscious cabbage would make a nice partner for roasted chicken or lamb as well.

Place the salmon, arranged on a large platter with a decorative serving spatula, in the center of the table so that guests can serve themselves. • SERVES 8; MAY BE HALVED OR DOUBLED

---

1 small head of Savoy cabbage, quartered, cored, and sliced crosswise about ¾ inch thick

⅓ cup Dijon mustard

4 teaspoons sugar

Salt and freshly ground black pepper

8 center-cut skinless wild salmon fillets (6 to 7 ounces each, about 1¼ inches thick)

3 teaspoons canola oil

1 large yellow onion, halved lengthwise, then sliced thick

3 garlic cloves, finely chopped

½ cup dry white wine or vermouth

1 teaspoon sherry vinegar

4 tablespoons (½ stick) salted butter (see Note, page 178), cut into small pieces

---

Place a large bowl of ice and water near the sink.

In a large pot of lightly salted boiling water, immerse the cabbage and cook for 3 minutes. Drain in a colander, immediately transfer to the ice water, and swirl to cool, to stop the cooking and ensure that the cabbage stays bright green. Drain in the colander, removing the ice, and shake a few times to remove most of the water.

Preheat the oven to 375°F.

In a bowl, whisk together the mustard, sugar, ¼ teaspoon salt, and ¼ teaspoon pepper. Brush both sides of the fillets generously with the mustard glaze, and place skin side down on a rack over a roasting pan. Set aside.

Meanwhile, finish the cabbage: Place the canola oil in a large skillet over low heat, add the onion, and sauté gently for about 7 minutes more, until translucent. Add the garlic and cook for 1 minute more. Add the cabbage, wine, and ½ teaspoon salt.

At this point, place the salmon in the oven. Roast for 10 minutes.

Cover the pan of cabbage and braise for 5 minutes, stirring occasionally. Remove the lid and cook for 1 to 2 minutes more, to dry out slightly. Season generously with pepper, remove from the heat, and stir in the vinegar and butter until creamy; taste for seasoning. Remove the salmon from the oven.

Spread the cabbage in an even layer on a warm platter and top with pieces of salmon. Serve at once.

HALIBUT AND TOMATO GRATIN,
FOR A CROWD

*T*his is an excellent oven-to-table fish dish and a good choice when there are non-meat-eaters in the group. It's as hearty as fish gets.

You can make the gratin in advance, then cover with plastic wrap and refrigerate for up to two hours before baking. If you do this, add five to ten minutes to the baking time, and check to be sure the fish is cooked through before serving. • SERVES 8; MAY BE DOUBLED

Softened butter, for greasing

½ cup extra-virgin olive oil

3 large white or yellow onions, coarsely chopped

9 large garlic cloves, 6 finely chopped, 3 pushed through a press

3 tablespoons coarsely chopped flat-leaf parsley

4 small sprigs of thyme

Salt and freshly ground black pepper

2½ pounds halibut or other white fish fillets, skinned, boned, and cut into 1½-inch chunks

One 28-ounce can Italian plum tomatoes (preferably San Marzano), drained, seeded, and halved (or quartered, if large)

½ lemon

2 tablespoons dry white wine

2 cups fresh bread crumbs (preferably made from croissants, challah, or other rich bread or rolls)

3 ounces (about 1½ cups) coarsely grated Gruyère cheese

Preheat the oven to 400°F. Butter a 9 x 12-inch or similar-size earthenware, ceramic, or glass gratin dish.

In a large skillet, heat ¼ cup of the oil over medium-low heat. Add the onions and sauté for about 10 minutes, stirring occasionally, until softened but not browned. Add the chopped garlic and cook for 1 minute more. Transfer half of the onion mixture to the prepared baking dish and spread evenly in the base. Scatter half the parsley, 2 sprigs of thyme, ½ teaspoon salt, and about ¼ teaspoon pepper over the onion layer, then create a layer with all the fish and tomatoes, distributing them evenly. Squeeze the half lemon over the fish, then scatter with the remaining parsley, sprigs of thyme, another ½ teaspoon salt and ¼ teaspoon pepper. Top with the remaining onion mixture. Drizzle 2 tablespoons olive oil and the white wine over the top and around the edges.

In a bowl, toss the bread crumbs with the pressed garlic, cheese, and ¼ teaspoon salt until evenly mixed. Top the gratin with the bread crumbs, packing them down firmly. Drizzle the remaining 2 tablespoons oil evenly over the top and bake for 25 minutes, or until the top is golden brown. Let stand for 5 minutes before serving.

Tavern's Topiaries

*H*ollywood was in Warner's blood, so no wonder it would sometimes inspire him. In 1990, he was enchanted by *Edward Scissorhands*, the movie in which Johnny Depp starred as an eccentric boy with, yes, scissors for hands. As soon as Warner heard a store in Manhattan had some of the topiaries fashioned by Depp's character in the film, he bought them for Tavern's gardens.

Not long afterward, he was in the Beverly Hills Hotel exuberantly telling a friend about this recent coup. A man sitting nearby who overheard the conversation challenged Warner's claim that he owned the *Edward Scissorhands* topiaries. Warner began defending the provenance of his new treasures, but he was stopped dead in his tracks when the stranger introduced himself as Dan Ondrejko, the greensman for the film. (In Hollywood, a greensman creates the foliage used on movie sets, greenery that is usually fake.) Ondrejko went on to maintain that he knew exactly where the topiaries he'd made for the film were, and it wasn't New York.

Ondrejko invited Warner to see his work, and as soon as Warner did, he knew Tavern's topiaries hadn't been created for *Edward Scissorhands* Ondrejko's work was noticeably superior, more lifelike in every respect, from the quality of the plastic greens to the skeletal structures supporting them.

To replace the fakes that he had bought, Warner commissioned Ondrejko to make seven one-of-a-kind topiary animals to frolic in Tavern's gardens. Two years later, a truck arrived from Los Angeles and, with the aid of a forklift, the larger-than-life likenesses of a dancing bear, kissing swans, a leaping rabbit, a rearing horse, a standing stag, and a charging elephant were hoisted into place.

It wasn't long before Warner decided his brood wasn't quite big enough. He envisioned mounting a hundred-foot-tall ape on Tavern's roof, positioned to look like it was roaring at entering guests. However, when he was presented with an estimate of $1 million for the creature,

he displayed a rare show of restraint and opted instead for a fourteen-foot replica of King Kong. The new topiary was unveiled in a 1993 ceremony presided over by none other than Fay Wray, star of the 1933 movie. Then in her eighties, she gamely rode a cherry picker up to Kong's face so that she could "feed" him some bananas and give him a kiss!

In 1996, Tavern's topiaries were given another Crystal Garden attraction to keep watch over, a forty-foot bar fashioned from felled and pruned trees from New York City parks. The trees were thus given a new life in the city's greatest park.

Since the moment they were installed, Tavern's topiaries have become a favorite photo-op for park strollers and restaurant guests alike. On special occasions, the gardening crew will move a specific topiary to the front of Tavern—for instance, when the Republican National Convention was held in New York City in 2004, the elephant greeted the guests at more than two dozen events held at Tavern in connection with the convention. And for Easter, the rabbit is the focal point.

BLACK COD
WITH WHITE MISO GLAZE

*T*his is among the most popular banquet dishes in Tavern's repertoire. What's more, cooking it at home is easy and mess-free.

At Tavern the fillets are served over fermented rather than white rice; try to find it at a nearby Asian grocery. If you do use fermented rice, decrease the amount of sake to two tablespoons.

Other favorite accompaniments include thick Asian rice noodles such as chow fun or Japanese udon noodles. • SERVES 6; MAY BE DOUBLED

---

2 tablespoons long- or medium-grain white rice

3 tablespoons sake (Japanese rice wine)

1 tablespoon mirin (Asian sweet wine), or sweet sherry

2 tablespoons sugar

2 teaspoons pickled red ginger

4 tablespoons yellow miso

Butter, for preparing the baking sheet

Six 6-ounce black cod fillets, cut as thick as possible

About 1 pound cooked wheat noodles, warm, for serving

3 green onions, white and light green parts only, very thinly sliced

2 baby bok choy, quartered and steamed until tender, for serving (optional)

In a small saucepan full of rapidly boiling, lightly salted water, cook the rice, partially covered, for 20 minutes, stirring occasionally; drain well in a sieve and set aside.

In the same saucepan, bring the sake and mirin to a simmer over medium-high heat. Stir in the sugar until dissolved, then add the cooked rice. Remove from the heat and let stand for 5 minutes to cool slightly. Transfer to a mini-prep or food processor, add the ginger and miso, and blend until smooth. (If desired, make the glaze up to 2 days in advance and refrigerate; bring to room temperature before proceeding with the dish.)

Preheat the oven to broil and place the oven rack about 4 inches from the heat source.

Butter a large, rimmed baking sheet. Pat the fillets dry with paper towels and place on the baking sheet, brushing both sides generously with the glaze. Broil on one side only for 10 to 12 minutes, until golden brown and firm.

Make a nest of cooked noodles on 6 warmed plates. Using a wide spatula, very gently and carefully transfer a cod fillet onto the top (don't worry if the cod breaks up a little); scatter with the green onions and serve at once, with one or two quarters of steamed bok choy, if desired.

OLIVE OIL–POACHED
TUNA NIÇOISE
WITH CONFIT TOMATOES

*I*f you've never had a tuna niçoise salad prepared with fresh fish, this version, made with chunks of seasoned fresh ahi, will make you swoon. "Poaching" the ahi in a jalapeño- and chipotle-laced paste mixed with ample olive oil makes it meltingly tender.

Preparing and presenting the tuna this way involves very little effort for a restaurant-level payoff. You will be amazed at all the flavors, textures, and colors in this sophisticated take on the niçoise salad. • SERVES 6; MAY BE DOUBLED

1 tablespoon extra-virgin olive oil

2 yellow onions, finely chopped

10 garlic cloves, halved lengthwise

2 jalapeño peppers, stemmed, halved lengthwise, and seeded

About ⅓ of a 7½-ounce can chipotle chiles in adobo (paste and all)

½ cup tomato paste

4 sprigs of rosemary

Freshly ground black pepper

1 small piece of lemon peel, removed with a vegetable peeler

4 bay leaves

3 pounds best-quality ahi tuna, cut into 1-inch chunks

Salt

Pure olive oil (not extra-virgin), as needed, for poaching

TO SERVE

Pale inner leaves from 2 hearts of romaine lettuce, trimmed into 3-inch lengths

Juice of 1 lemon

1 cup niçoise olives, pitted and halved

Confit Tomatoes (recipe follows)

Lemon wedges

Preheat the oven to 200°F.

In a wide, deep ovenproof sauté pan, warm the extra-virgin olive oil on the stovetop over medium heat. Add the onions and cook, stirring occasionally, until golden brown, about 5 minutes. Add the garlic, jalapeños, chipotles and their paste, tomato paste, rosemary, a generous grinding of pepper, the lemon peel, and bay leaves. Stir to mix evenly; the mixture will be quite chunky.

Season the tuna chunks with salt and pepper and arrange them over the flavoring paste. Add enough pure olive oil to barely cover the tuna. Bring it to a bare simmer over medium-low heat. Cover the pan and transfer to the warm oven for 1 hour.

Remove from the oven and allow to cool completely at room temperature. If desired, transfer to a perfectly clean and dry glass container. Be sure the fish is fully covered by the oil, and refrigerate for up to 2 days.

TO SERVE

Bring the tuna confit, in the oil, to room temperature (allow 1 hour for this). Fish out and discard the jalapeño halves, rosemary sprigs, lemon peel, and bay leaves.

Place the romaine leaves in a large bowl and, using tongs, gently toss with about 3 tablespoons of the olive oil from the confit, just to coat lightly. Drizzle with the lemon juice and toss again. Spread the lettuce evenly on a large platter. With a slotted spoon, retrieve the chunks of tuna from the olive oil, scooping up some of the flavoring paste with each chunk. Arrange the tuna over the romaine. Scatter with the olives and the Confit Tomatoes, place a few lemon wedges around the edges of the platter, and place on a buffet or serve.

CONFIT TOMATOES

2 pounds plum tomatoes, peeled, cut into eighths lengthwise (through the stem end), and seeded

24 small sprigs of thyme

3 garlic cloves, thinly sliced

2 tablespoons extra-virgin olive oil

Salt and freshly ground black pepper

Preheat the oven to 350°F.

Line a rimmed baking sheet with parchment paper and put the tomatoes on it, rounded sides down. Scatter evenly with the thyme and garlic, and drizzle with the oil. Season liberally with salt and pepper, and roast for 50 to 60 minutes, until the tomatoes soften and are slightly shriveled and the garlic is golden.

Discard the thyme sprigs before serving.

WHITE FISH ESCABECHE
FOR A CROWD

*S*ummer nights on Tavern's terraces provide a cool refuge from the city heat. Guests sip icy drinks there, and tend to order more seafood than anything else on the menu. This popular Spanish dish is ideal for such balmy nights; it is typically served at room temperature or slightly chilled.

If a few extra diners show up at the last minute, cut the fish into smaller pieces and increase the amount of couscous. • SERVES 6 TO 8

---

1 tablespoon extra-virgin olive oil

2 tablespoons coriander seeds

7 garlic cloves, sliced

1 large red onion, finely chopped

2 red bell peppers, cored, seeded, and finely chopped

¼ cup sherry vinegar

¼ cup red wine vinegar

2 tablespoons tomato paste

2 cups tomato juice

2 cups dry white wine or vermouth

5 sprigs of cilantro

4 sprigs of thyme

2 bay leaves

Salt and freshly ground black pepper

1 teaspoon Tabasco sauce

6 or 8 fillets of delicate white fish, such as sole, flounder, or pollock, about 6 ounces each

Orange Couscous (recipe follows)

12 or 16 live mussels, steamed just until they open, for garnish (optional)

In a large nonreactive skillet, warm the olive oil over medium-low heat and sauté the coriander seeds for 1 minute. Add the garlic and cook for 30 seconds more, then stir in the onion and cook gently for 5 minutes. Add the bell peppers and cook, stirring occasionally, for about 3 minutes, until wilted. Stir in the sherry vinegar and red wine vinegar, and stir to deglaze. Bring the liquid to a simmer and cook for 5 minutes, to reduce slightly. Stir in the tomato paste, tomato juice, and wine and bring to a boil over high heat, then lower the heat so the mixture simmers gently. Add the cilantro, thyme, and bay leaves and simmer, uncovered, for about 40 minutes.

Remove the herb sprigs and bay leaves, and discard. Pour the mixture into a large shallow bowl or baking dish suitable for serving. Stir in ½ teaspoon salt, about ½ teaspoon pepper, and the Tabasco. Taste for seasoning and set aside.

Season both sides of the fish fillets with salt and pepper and place in an oiled steamer basket over lightly salted, slightly simmering water. Cover and steam for 5 minutes, or until firm. Place the fish in the serving dish, spoon some of the sauce over the top, and cover with plastic wrap. Let stand at room temperature for at least 1 hour before serving, or place in the refrigerator for up to 3 hours; return to room temperature for 30 minutes before serving. Place the dish on a buffet or serve at the table, with the couscous on the side and garnished with the mussels, if desired.

ORANGE COUSCOUS

1 cup quick-cooking,
medium couscous

1½ cups chicken or
vegetable stock or broth
(low-sodium canned is
fine), simmering

2 tablespoons extra-virgin
olive oil

2 teaspoons fresh lemon
juice

2 tablespoons finely chopped
flat-leaf parsley

Finely grated zest of half a
scrubbed orange
(see Note, page 41)

Salt and freshly ground
black pepper

Place the couscous in a metal bowl and pour the hot chicken stock over the top. Stir with a fork, cover with a plate, and let stand for 5 minutes. Fluff with the fork, then add the olive oil, lemon juice, parsley, and orange zest. Season with salt and pepper and toss to combine.

✦ MAKES ABOUT 3 CUPS

PAN·ROASTED COD
WITH OLIVE·CAPER SAUCE

*T*he sauce in this dish has been so popular among Tavern visitors that a bottled variety, Central Park Dipping Oil, made with garlic and a mix of secret spices, is now available at our gift shop to take home. It's inspired by *bagna cauda*, the warm Italian dipping sauce, and also incorporates the flavors of southern of France.

Serve this delightfully uncomplicated dish for a light summer supper with a delicate green salad and fruit sorbet for dessert. • SERVES 6

FOR THE SAUCE

1½ cups extra-virgin olive oil

15 kalamata olives, pitted and slivered

15 green olives, pitted and slivered

15 oil-cured black olives, pitted and slivered

2 shallots, very finely chopped

2 tablespoons capers, rinsed and drained

⅓ cup finely chopped sage

2 tablespoons finely chopped flat-leaf parsley

10 large basil leaves, stacked, rolled, and slivered (chiffonade)

¾ cup finely grated Pecorino Romano cheese

¾ cup fine, toasted fresh bread crumbs or panko

6 cod fillets, about 8 ounces each

2 large egg whites, lightly beaten with a pinch of salt

5 tablespoons extra-virgin olive oil

3 tablespoons unsalted butter

3 tablespoons pine nuts, toasted until golden and finely chopped (see Note, page 102; optional)

In a small saucepan, combine the 1½ cups oil, the pitted olives, shallots, capers, and sage. Place over very low heat and let warm through gently for 20 to 30 minutes.

Meanwhile, dredge and sauté the fish: On a large plate, combine the Pecorino and bread crumbs and blend together. Brush both sides of each fillet with some of the egg white, then dredge both sides in the crumb mixture, patting to help them adhere.

Place a 12- or 14-inch nonstick skillet over medium-high heat and add the 5 tablespoons oil and the butter. (If you do not have a large skillet, use 2 smaller nonstick pans.) When the foam from the butter has subsided, carefully slide the fillets into the pan and leave undisturbed for 2½ minutes, so the crust has a chance to firm. With a wide spatula, carefully turn the fillets side and cook for 2 minutes. Reduce the heat to very low and cook for 2 to 4 minutes more, depending on the thickness of the fish, until golden brown and quite firm to the touch.

Add the parsley and basil to the olive-caper sauce and stir well. Cover the base of 6 shallow bowls with the sauce and place a fillet on top of each. Scatter with the toasted pine nuts, if desired, and serve at once.

ROASTED PROSCIUTTO·WRAPPED SCALLOPS

Since Tavern's opening day in 1936, scallops have remained on the menu without interruption. They've been seared, sautéed, broiled, baked, and, as in this dish, roasted to concentrate their sweetness.

This is a last-minute dish that is nevertheless suitable for a dinner party because the unwrapped scallops can be refrigerated for up to 1 hour before going directly into the hot oven. This leaves plenty of time to create an interesting side dish, such as the Asparagus and Parmesan Risotto on page 119. · SERVES 8

GREMOLATA

1 tablespoon minced garlic

1 tablespoon finely grated zest from a scrubbed lemon (see Note, page 41)

1 tablespoon finely chopped flat-leaf parsley

24 large scallops, preferably diver-caught, side adductor muscle pulled off, if necessary

12 slices prosciutto, halved lengthwise

Freshly ground black pepper

In a small bowl, combine the ingredients for the gremolata. Cover with plastic wrap and refrigerate for up to 2 hours before serving time, if desired.

Line a baking sheet with paper towels and place all the scallops on the towels, flat sides down. Place another layer of paper towels over the top and top with another baking sheet. Place in the refrigerator for up to 30 minutes before assembling (this helps to ensure that the scallops are perfectly dry, so they will sear to an attractive and tasty golden brown).

If planning to cook right away (see headnote), preheat the oven to 425°F.

Lay the prosciutto strips on a work surface and place a scallop in the center of each one. Season the scallops sparingly with pepper, and roll up in the prosciutto, enclosing them completely. Transfer the scallop bundles to a dry baking sheet (nonstick is fine) and cook right away, if desired, or hold in the refrigerator (no need to cover) for up to 1 hour before roasting.

Roast the scallops for 7 to 10 minutes, until the prosciutto is crisp and golden and the scallops are cooked through. Transfer to warm plates, serving 3 scallops per person. Scatter with the gremolata, and serve immediately.

GRILLED AND HERB·MARINATED GIANT SHRIMP
ON COLD SESAME·PEANUT NOODLES

*B*egin preparing the shrimp anywhere from 2½ to 4½ hours before serving time. The noodles may also be prepared up to 4 hours ahead. All that's left at serving time is to assemble, garnish, and dig in. This incredibly bright and refreshing dish is even better when served on chilled plates. • SERVES 6; MAY BE DOUBLED

FOR THE HERB PASTE

5 green onions, white and green parts only, coarsely chopped

8 garlic cloves, coarsely chopped

4-inch-long piece of peeled fresh ginger, coarsely chopped

8 ribs of celery, coarsely chopped

Zest of 2 scrubbed oranges, removed with a vegetable peeler in pieces (try to leave all the white pith behind)

2 tablespoons sesame oil

½ cup mirin wine or sweet sherry

1 small bunch of cilantro, coarsest stems removed

1 small bunch of basil, coarsest stems removed

2 pounds large shrimp (11 to 15 count), peeled and deveined, tails left on

¼ cup canola oil

Salt and freshly ground black pepper

Cold Sesame-Peanut Noodles (recipe follows)

1 red bell pepper, cored, seeded, and cut into small dice

2 tablespoons finely chopped unsalted roasted peanuts

Coarsely chopped cilantro leaves, for garnish

Slivered green onions, for garnish (optional)

In a food processor, combine the green onions, garlic, ginger, celery, orange zest, sesame oil, mirin, cilantro, and basil. Pulse once or twice to make a thick, but not perfectly smooth, paste. Transfer the paste to a large, rimmed metal baking sheet and spread into an even layer. Cover the paste with a single layer of cheesecloth and refrigerate while you grill the shrimp.

In a large bowl, toss the shrimp with the oil until evenly coated, then season generously with salt and pepper and toss again. Preheat a gas or charcoal grill to medium-high heat, or preheat a ridged cast-iron griddle on the stovetop.

Grill the shrimp for 1½ to 2 minutes on each side, turning over with tongs, until pink and firm. Immediately transfer them to the baking sheet, arranging them in a single layer over the cheesecloth and pushing them down slightly into the juicy mixture. Cover tightly with plastic wrap and refrigerate for at least 2 and up to 4 hours, turning the shrimp over once halfway through the marinating time.

To serve, place some sesame-peanut noodles on each plate, top with the marinated shrimp, and garnish with the bell pepper, peanuts, cilantro, and, if desired, green onions.

1 pound dried soba noodles
  or angel-hair pasta

2 tablespoons sesame oil

2 tablespoons peanut oil

1-inch piece peeled fresh
  ginger, finely chopped

3 garlic cloves, finely
  chopped or pushed
  through a press

1 teaspoon red chili paste

Juice of 1 large lime

½ cup creamy peanut butter

¼ cup rice vinegar

2 tablespoons brown sugar

3 tablespoons low-sodium
  soy sauce

5 tablespoons hot water

In a large pot of boiling, unsalted water, cook the noodles until just tender (2 minutes for soba; 3 to 4 minutes for angel hair). Drain immediately in a colander and rinse thoroughly with cold water; shake the colander vigorously to drain, and transfer the noodles to a large shallow bowl. Immediately drizzle with the sesame oil and toss well, so the noodles won't stick together.

In a blender or a small food processor, combine the peanut oil, ginger, garlic, chili paste, lime juice, peanut butter, vinegar, brown sugar, and soy sauce. Add the hot water and blend until smooth. Add the sauce to the noodles and toss together thoroughly. Cover the bowl and refrigerate for at least 30 minutes and up to 4 hours.

TAVERN'S PAELLA

*I*n Spain, paella is a celebration dish that can include any of the following ingredients: rabbit, clams, mussels, lobster, chicken, squid, cured sausage, air-dried ham, and snails. It was traditionally cooked (by men only!) over an outdoor fire made of driftwood or vine cuttings. This version is, luckily, simpler, but just as festive.

If you have a large enough pan, this dish is perfect for feeding a crowd, and we especially like to cook it outdoors on the barbecue, just as the Spanish cowboys and fishermen used to do. Note that Spanish and Mexican chorizo are quite different and are not interchangeable. Spanish chorizo is cured and requires very little cooking, while Mexican chorizo is fresh, with a substantial fat content, and requires full cooking. • SERVES 8

---

1 pound jumbo shrimp, deveined through the back of the shell (substitute shelled shrimp, if desired)

3 large garlic cloves, coarsely chopped

¼ cup extra-virgin olive oil

1 tablespoon finely chopped flat-leaf parsley

Freshly ground black pepper

Dash of cayenne pepper, or to taste

2 tablespoons dry white wine or vermouth

1 tablespoon fresh lemon juice

1½ to 2 pounds cured Spanish chorizo sausage or other cured smoked sausage (see headnote)

RICE

2 tablespoons white wine

1 generous teaspoon saffron threads

6 cups chicken stock or broth (low-sodium canned is fine)

3 cups fish stock (use a bouillon cube, if desired)

2 cups water

¼ cup pure olive oil

1 large red onion, finely chopped

4½ cups short-grain rice, such as Arborio

Salt and freshly ground black pepper

One 10-ounce package frozen baby peas, thawed

½ pound small green beans, trimmed and blanched for 5 minutes in boiling water

⅔ cup jarred fire-roasted red peppers, drained and cut into strips (optional)

3 large lemons, cut into wedges

In a large bowl, combine the shrimp, garlic, olive oil, parsley, a generous grinding of black pepper, cayenne, wine, and lemon juice. Cover and refrigerate for at least 30 minutes and up to 2 hours. Slice the sausages into 2- or 3-inch lengths on the diagonal and set aside.

FOR THE RICE

In a small saucepan or a microwave oven, heat the wine until hot. Place the saffron threads in a small bowl, add the hot wine, and set aside for 15 minutes. In a medium saucepan, combine both stocks and water and bring to a simmer. Drain the shrimp from their marinade; pick out and discard any garlic from the shrimp.

continued

Place a paella pan (about 18 inches is ideal, or use two 12-inch skillets) over medium-high heat and add the pure olive oil. When it is quite hot, add the shrimp and sauté for about 3 minutes, tossing and stirring frequently. With a slotted spoon, transfer the shrimp to a plate, draining as much oil as possible back into the pan. Set the shrimp aside.

Reduce the heat to medium-low, add the onion, and sauté for about 5 minutes, stirring occasionally, until softened. Add the rice and the saffron-wine mixture to the pan and stir for about 5 minutes, or until the rice is well coated with the liquid and a few grains have begun to turn golden. Add the simmering stock mixture, 1½ teaspoons salt, and a generous grinding of pepper. Jiggle the pan carefully to level the rice, reduce the heat to low, and cook the rice for 18 to 20 minutes, without stirring. (Ideally, *all* the rice should be cooking at a very slow simmer, so rotate the pan and gently smooth the top of the rice with the back of a large spoon once or twice to submerge any grains of rice standing above the liquid.)

Stir the peas and green beans into the rice and nestle the sausage on the top. Tent the pan loosely with foil (or cover with a lid, if available) and cook for about 5 minutes more. When the rice is just tender, distribute the shrimp and red peppers, if using, attractively over the top. Cover again and continue cooking for about 2 minutes more just to heat through. Remove from the heat and place lemon wedges all around the edges. Serve directly from the pan.

What a Guy!

*W*arner LeRoy had high expectations for his employees. He had read every newspaper, including *The New York Times*, from front to back before 6:00 A.M. It wasn't unusual for him to call a manager at 6:30 A.M. to review the news of the day. Here are some of his other quirks, which sometimes made him a challenging man to work for.

• Tavern has long been noted for its flamboyant tablecloths; they're all custom made from top-quality fabrics and in some cases from fabrics designed specifically for the restaurant. Warner had suits and ties made from his favorite tablecloth fabrics, most notably an exuberant cabbage-rose pattern that announced his presence the minute he walked into any room!

• In the early days of the Food Network (back then it was TVFN), when the fledgling venture was produced out of a tiny brownstone on Manhattan's West Side, Warner was booked for a show hosted by Robin Leach. It was around Thanksgiving, so he showed up on the set in a velvet tuxedo embroidered with pumpkins and turkeys.

• Warner's fixations weren't limited to Tavern's decor; he had very specific ideas about the food, too. He insisted the menu offer essential comfort foods such as mashed potatoes, chocolate brownie desserts, crab cakes, and crème brûlée. The gourmand, who was as well known for his gregarious restaurants as for his girth, used three different vendors for ice cream alone. Baking chocolate was strictly Valrhona. Guests never saw cauliflower, broccoli, cantaloupe, honeydew melon, or monkfish on the menu; Warner disliked them.

• Warner was emphatic that Tavern use no prepared products. He once sent back shrimp that was labeled "fresh" because he was sure it had once been frozen. He was right.

SIMPLE BOUILLABAISSE
WITH MONKFISH AND FENNEL,
FOR A CROWD

*F*rance's most revered fish soup and a hugely popular rustic summer dish, bouilla-baisse can contain myriad kinds of fish and shellfish, but many of the traditional ingredients are not available very far from the shores of the Mediterranean. This version has plenty of flavor but requires far less work.

If you can't find fish on the bone, ask the fishmonger for eight ounces of assorted fish bones, preferably not from salmon. If no bones are available, use a small, whole fish, chopped, for the simple stock. • SERVES 10 TO 12

4 pounds monkfish or cod, preferably on the bone (see headnote)

¼ cup extra-virgin olive oil, plus additional for toasts

20 garlic cloves, peeled

2 teaspoons fennel seeds

1 bouquet garni (see Note)

Salt

¼ cup tomato paste

¼ cup Pernod

One 28-ounce can peeled Italian plum tomatoes (preferably San Marzano), with their juice

1 teaspoon Spanish smoked paprika (*pimentón*)

3 quarts (12 cups) water

4 small fennel bulbs, quartered, cored, and cut into 1-inch wedges (reserve feathery green tops for garnish)

10 to 12 (½-inch-thick) slices country bread

1 cup Saffron Aioli (recipe follows) or Smoked Paprika Mayo (page 87) (optional)

1 tablespoon zest from a scrubbed orange (see Note, page 41)

Cut the fish into approximately 2-inch pieces, reserving the bones for the stock. Cover the fish pieces and refrigerate.

Heat a large, heavy-bottomed stockpot over medium heat and add the ¼ cup olive oil. Wait 10 seconds, then add the fish bones, garlic, fennel seeds, bouquet garni, and 1 tablespoon salt. Reduce the heat to low and sweat the mixture without letting it brown, stirring occasionally, for 10 minutes. Add the tomato paste, Pernod, canned tomatoes with their juices, paprika, and water. Bring the mixture to a boil, partially cover the pan, and regulate the heat to maintain a slow simmer for 45 minutes.

Uncover the pan. Retrieve and discard the fish bones and the bouquet garni, then use an immersion blender to puree the liquid. (Or, pass the liquid through the coarse disk of a food mill. Don't worry if it is not perfectly smooth. Return to the pan.) Add the fennel wedges, cover the pan, and simmer gently for 20 minutes, until the fennel is tender. Taste for seasoning and adjust with salt and paprika as necessary.

At this point, the tomato broth may be set aside for several hours, or cooled to room temperature and refrigerated overnight, before finishing the dish.

Preheat the oven to 350°F.

Brush the bread on both sides with a little olive oil, place on a baking sheet, and toast for 10 minutes, turning over once, until just golden.

To finish, bring the broth back to a gentle simmer and add the fish pieces. Simmer the soup gently for 5 minutes, to just cook the fish. Finely chop a few of the feathery fennel fronds. Ladle the soup into wide warmed bowls, distributing the fish, fennel wedges, and broth evenly. If desired, place a dollop of saffron aioli in the center of each bowl; scatter a little orange zest and some chopped fennel greens over the top. Serve at once, with a slice of toasted bread on the side.

NOTE · **To make a bouquet garni, use fine kitchen twine to tie together 2 sprigs of flat-leaf parsley, 1 celery top with leaves, 2 bay leaves, and 2 sprigs of thyme.**

SAFFRON AIOLI

Tiny pinch of saffron threads, about 20 strands

1½ tablespoons warm water

1 cup Mayo/Aioli (page 42, made with 3 garlic cloves) or store-bought mayonnaise (mixed with 3 pressed garlic cloves)

2 teaspoons fresh lemon juice

Freshly ground black pepper

In a very small bowl, soak the saffron threads in the warm water for 20 minutes. In a larger bowl, combine the mayo with the saffron and its soaking water. Swirl the lemon juice in the saffron-soaking bowl to catch any remaining saffron essence, and add it to the mayo. Add a few grinds of pepper and whisk to blend evenly. · MAKES 1 CUP

GARLICKY PROVENÇAL BOURRIDE

*F*or some odd reason, this soup is little known outside of Provence and the Côte d'Azur, but in those regions of France it's almost as popular as bouillabaisse. The two are only distantly related, and this elegantly pale and creamy soup (which contains no cream) is the choice for a more formal occasion. Topping the finished stew with parsley does add a bright flavor note, but it also interrupts the perfect paleness of the smooth garlicky sauce; use your own judgment.

Instead of frozen artichoke hearts, you can also use well-drained canned hearts packed in brine. (Do not use marinated hearts, which are too oily.) • SERVES 8 TO 10

---

12 very small new potatoes, washed

3 quarts (12 cups) fish stock (best-quality bouillion cubes are fine), or, in a pinch, chicken stock or broth (low-sodium canned)

Salt

One 10-ounce package frozen artichoke hearts, completely thawed

2 pounds Pacific cod or Alaskan pollock, cut into 2-inch chunks

2 cups Mayo/Aioli (page 42, made with 3 garlic cloves), or store-bought mayonnaise (mixed with 3 pressed garlic cloves) (see Note)

2 large egg yolks (see Note, page 231)

Freshly ground white pepper

12 small Garlic Croûtes (page 206)

½ cup coarsely chopped flat-leaf parsley, for garnish (optional)

In a large saucepan, cover the potatoes with lightly salted cold water. Bring to a rapid boil over high heat, cover the pan, and remove from the heat. Let the potatoes stand in the hot water for 45 minutes; they will cook gently in the residual heat. Remove and, if desired, hold for up to 4 hours at room temperature or up to overnight in the refrigerator (return to room temperature before finishing the dish).

In a very large sauté pan, a large enameled cast-iron casserole, or a covered flameproof gratin dish, combine the fish stock and ½ teaspoon salt. Over medium-high heat, bring the stock to a boil, then lower the heat so the liquid barely simmers. Add the artichokes and the fish, cover the pan, and cook for 6 minutes, until the fish is firm and opaque. With a slotted spoon, carefully transfer the artichokes and fish to a wide, shallow serving bowl, add the cooked potatoes (halve them if they seem large), and cover with aluminum foil. Place the bowl in an oven set to its lowest temperature.

Place a heat-proof mixing bowl next to the stove and, in it, combine 1¼ cups of the mayo/aioli with 2 egg yolks; whisk until smooth. Using a soup ladle, add about 1 cup of the hot fish stock to the mayonnaise mixture, whisking constantly until smooth. Add this mixture to the pan with the fish stock and place over medium-high heat. (Do not leave the stove during the remainder of this operation.) Continuing to whisk constantly, cook the sauce mixture until it thickens slightly, to the consistency of heavy cream. Do not let it boil. This will take about 8 minutes but is mainly a matter of judging the texture carefully. Remove from the heat, whisk in about ½ teaspoon ground white pepper, and taste for seasoning.

Immediately pour the hot stock mixture over the potatoes, artichokes, and fish; cover with foil and let stand for about 5 minutes to heat through. Serve the fish stew with a bowl of garlic croûtes and the remaining ¾ cup mayo/aioli on the side. Guests place one or two croûtes in the base of their own wide, shallow soup bowl, then ladle in the stew—with an equal amount of vegetables and fish—and top the mixture with a spoonful or two of the garlicky mayo/aioli. Garnish with parsley, if desired.

NOTE · **If store-bought mayonnaise is used in place of the Mayo/Aioli on page 42, bump up the flavor by whisking in 3 minced or pressed garlic cloves and 1 tablespoon fresh lemon juice. You will also need to whisk an extra egg yolk into the 1¼ cups mayonnaise that is used for thickening the broth, making a total of 3 yolks for the recipe.**

· for two ·

OYSTER PAN ROAST

*O*ld-fashioned but oh-so romantic. This dish must be put together at the last minute for best results. In other words, after the Champagne is already icy cold, the flutes are chilled, and Tony Bennett is cued up on the iPod.

For seamless presentation, be sure to shuck the oysters and whiz the croissant, measure out all the ingredients, and assemble everything near the stove before the significant other arrives. ◆ SERVES 2

---

12 large, shell-on oysters, scrubbed clean with a stiff brush

3 fresh or slightly stale croissants

1 large egg

1 tablespoon whole milk

Salt and freshly ground white pepper

Butter, for frying

Canola oil, for frying

1 small garlic clove, pushed through a press

¾ cup dry white wine

¾ teaspoon Worcestershire sauce

3 tablespoons very cold unsalted butter, cut into small pieces

2 teaspoons fresh lemon juice

1 tablespoon finely snipped chives

Shuck the oysters (see page 52) and pat them dry gently. Cut one of the croissants into large chunks, then whiz it into slightly coarse crumbs in a food processor. Spread the crumbs on a dinner plate.

Carefully cut the other two croissants in half, crosswise, and place the bottom half of each in the center of a dinner plate; place the two croissant tops on the rims of the plates and place the two plates in a very low oven.

In a shallow bowl, beat the egg until frothy. Whisk in the milk, ¼ teaspoon salt, and a pinch of white pepper.

One by one, roll the oysters in the croissant crumbs, then dip in the egg mixture, then roll again in the crumbs.

In a medium sauté pan, combine enough butter and oil, in equal quantities, to reach just under ¼ inch in depth. Place over medium-high heat and, when the foam from the butter has subsided, swirl the pan and gently add the oysters. Sauté for about 1 minute, just until pale golden. Gently turn over and continue cooking for 1 to 1½ minutes. Mound the oysters over the croissant bases in the oven; don't worry if some tumble over onto the plate.

Turn off the oven and immediately finish the sauce: Discard all but about 2 teaspoons of the fat in the sauté pan and add the garlic. Stir for 30 seconds, then add the wine and Worcestershire; increase the heat to high and simmer until reduced by half, 2 to 3 minutes.

Remove the pan from the heat and add the pieces of cold butter all at once, swirling the pan constantly. Keep swirling and whisking until all the butter has melted and the sauce is only just creamy. Quickly whisk in the lemon juice and chives, then divide the sauce among the two plates, drizzling the oyster-topped croissants generously. Top each "sandwich" with the top half of the croissant and serve at once.

REGULARS

Like almost every other restaurant, we have a number of regulars who love coming back. The only difference is that many of our regulars are familiar faces from movies or television. For example, Robert DeNiro loves to have brunch in the garden. Al Pacino, who lives nearby, stops in for hot chocolate or espresso from time to time. And talk-show host Regis Philbin is invariably both gracious and gregarious! Fran Drescher and Tommy Tune love to sit in the gardens. Just as Tavern is part of the glorious tapestry of New York, famous New Yorkers are part of the tapestry of Tavern.

7

POULTRY,
MEAT,
and
GAME

ROASTED TURKEY
WITH BRIOCHE-APRICOT DRESSING
AND CALVADOS GRAVY

*T*urkey's not *just* for Thanksgiving, but it's certainly one day of the year no one wants to be without a glistening bird on the table. Indeed, Tavern roasts more than 200 turkeys to serve to almost 4,000 guests who visit the restaurant on the big day. Many who have spent the morning watching the Macy's parade just outside on Central Park West warm up first with a mug of piping hot cider or nutmeg-laced eggnog.

America's love affair with the national bird gets stronger every year, especially now that heirloom breeds and free-range birds are becoming quite widely available. The improvement in flavor is so surprising that almost everyone who tries an heirloom breed never returns to supermarket standards.

Here, we've provided all the fixings for a festive and sensational feast! Serve this with Comforting Mashed Potatoes (page 243), Parmesan-Roasted Onions (page 255), and Braised Escarole (page 254). • SERVES 15 • *photograph on page 156*

---

1 fresh 18- to 20-pound turkey, preferably free-range or an heirloom breed

4 tablespoons (½ stick) unsalted butter

2 tablespoons honey

Salt and freshly ground black pepper

Brioche-Apricot Dressing (recipe follows)

Calvados Gravy (recipe follows)

Cranberry-Pear Chutney (page 210; optional)

Remove the neck and the giblets from the turkey and save for the gravy; discard the liver and kidney(s), if included. Rinse the turkey inside and out with cold water and pat dry all over with plenty of paper towels. Let stand for 2 hours, to come to room temperature and dry out the skin slightly.

Preheat the oven to 375°F.

Tie the turkey legs together with kitchen twine and place the turkey on a rack inside a large roasting pan.

In a small saucepan, melt the butter with the honey over low heat. Brush all sides of the turkey generously with the butter-honey mixture, and season very generously with salt and pepper, concentrating the seasoning over the breast.

Place the turkey in the oven with the legs toward the rear, and roast for 35 to 45 minutes, until the breast has begun to brown. Lower the oven temperature to 250°F, add 1 tablespoon water to the bottom of the roasting pan, and cover the turkey with aluminum foil. Cook for 2 to 2½ hours more, basting the turkey with the pan juices every 30 minutes. The internal temperature of the turkey at the thickest part of the breast should reach 165°F on an instant-read thermometer; 12 minutes per pound total cooking time is a good guideline.

Place the pan of dressing in the oven for the last 45 minutes of roasting time.

When the turkey is done, remove from the oven, transfer to a platter, and let stand, loosely covered with the foil, for 30 minutes. Finish the gravy while the turkey rests. Carve the turkey and serve with the dressing, gravy, and, if desired, the chutney, on the side.

BRIOCHE·APRICOT DRESSING

Be sure to remove the zest of the oranges before squeezing; the zest is called for later in the recipe.

1 pound brioche bread, cut into ½-inch cubes

1 pound dried apricots, halved

1½ cups sweet sherry

¾ cup fresh orange juice

1 tablespoon olive oil

1 pound fresh mild chicken, turkey, or pork sausage, casings removed

2 large yellow onions, finely chopped

1 cup coarsely chopped fresh spinach leaves (firmly packed)

Finely grated zest of 2 scrubbed oranges (see Note, page 41)

1 cup pine nuts, lightly toasted (see Note, page 102)

Salt and freshly ground black pepper

4 large eggs, lightly beaten

4 tablespoons (½ stick) unsalted butter, melted, plus additional, softened, for greasing

Preheat the oven to 350°F.

Spread the brioche cubes on a rimmed baking sheet. Bake the brioche for 20 minutes, until slightly golden. Set aside.

In a small saucepan over medium heat, combine the apricots, sherry, and orange juice and simmer, covered, for 10 minutes. Remove from the heat, cool to room temperature, then coarsely chop. (Drain off any excess liquid and add it to the gravy.)

In a medium skillet, heat the oil over medium heat and sauté the sausage and onions for about 7 minutes, breaking the sausage into small pieces with a wooden spoon, until the onions are softened and no pink remains in the sausage. Add the spinach and cook for 3 minutes, stirring, until the spinach has wilted. Cool the mixture to room temperature.

In a large bowl, combine the sausage mixture, apricots, orange zest, pine nuts, 2 teaspoons salt, about 1 teaspoon pepper, the toasted brioche, and the eggs. Mix thoroughly and pack firmly into a buttered 14 x 9-inch or similar-size shallow earthenware, ceramic, or glass baking dish.

Cover with aluminum foil and bake alongside the turkey for the final 45 to 50 minutes of cooking time. While the turkey is resting and being carved, remove the foil from the dressing and drizzle evenly with the melted butter. Place under a hot broiler for 2 to 3 minutes, to create a crisp and golden crust. • SERVES 8

The giblet stock may be made up to two days ahead.

Giblets and neck, reserved from an 18- to 20-pound turkey

Salt and freshly ground black pepper

2 teaspoons extra-virgin olive oil

1 carrot, coarsely chopped

1 rib of celery, coarsely chopped

1 small yellow onion, coarsely chopped

1 quart (4 cups) chicken stock or broth (low-sodium canned is fine)

1 cup water

2½ tablespoons butter

¼ cup finely chopped shallots

3 sprigs of thyme

¼ cup flour

½ cup Calvados

½ cup dry white wine

½ cup heavy cream

Coarsely chop the reserved giblets and neck and season with salt and pepper. In a saucepan, heat the oil over medium-high heat. When it's very hot, add the giblet pieces and sauté until deep golden brown and crusty, stirring occasionally. Add the carrot, celery, and onion, and cook, stirring frequently, for 7 to 8 minutes, until slightly browned.

Add the chicken stock and bring to a boil. Lower the heat so the liquid simmers gently, partially cover the pan, and simmer for 1 hour. Add the water and simmer for 1 more hour.

Remove from the heat and cool to room temperature, then strain through a fine-mesh sieve. You should have about 3 cups of liquid. Refrigerate until the turkey comes out of the oven.

Pour all the juices from the turkey-roasting pan into a fat separator or Pyrex measuring cup. Skim off and discard the fat.

Place the empty roasting pan over medium-low heat and add the butter. When it has melted, add the shallots and thyme. Cook, stirring, for 3 minutes. Add the flour and stir into a smooth paste; cook, stirring frequently, until the flour is slightly browned, 3 to 4 minutes.

Whisk in the Calvados and wine. Stir to deglaze, then add the reserved pan juices, the reserved giblet stock, 1 teaspoon salt, a generous grinding of pepper, and the cream. Increase the heat to medium-high and bring to a fast simmer; cook until slightly thickened, stirring frequently to dislodge all the tasty bits from the base and sides of the roasting pan. Discard the thyme sprigs and pour the gravy into a sauceboat. (If you'd like a perfectly smooth gravy without little flecks of brown from the pan drippings, strain again through the fine-mesh sieve.) • MAKES ABOUT 4½ CUPS

HOW TO CARVE A TURKEY

Our chefs know a thing or two about turkey—about cooking it and carving it so that every ounce of meat comes off its bones. There really is a way to carve elegant slices without wasting a bit of meat. Once the turkey has cooled for at least 30 minutes:

1. Begin by removing the whole leg by pulling it away from the body and cutting loose the joint that holds the thigh to the body. Repeat with the other leg.

2. After the legs have been completely removed, begin removing the breast meat by holding the turkey firmly on the cutting board with a fork. Using a sharp knife, make a cut along the backbone (keel).

3. Next, make a horizontal cut from near the location of the wing, at the bottom of the turkey, toward the ribs. Repeat on the other side.

4. Place the knife in the incision made at the backbone and carve each breast lobe away from the rib cage by slowly cutting under and around the contour of the body next to the ribs. Carefully pull the entire lobe of breast meat away from the bone with your hands (a feat that is much easier after the legs have been removed).

5. To carve the dark meat, place the leg flat on the cutting board and cut through the joint to separate the drumstick and thigh.

6. Hold the thigh firmly with a fork and cut slices evenly and parallel to the bone. If you want to carve the drumstick, tilt it slightly and slice downward toward the cutting board.

GRILLED BUTTERFLIED CHICKEN
WITH A GREEK FLAVOR

*T*his succulent chicken dish is a perfect choice for an al fresco meal with the boss or new neighbors. Butterflying a chicken has the effect of bringing more of the bird into contact with the heat, thereby allowing it to cook much faster than a whole one. Because the flattened pieces remain intact, the chicken retains its juiciness (much of which is lost when a chicken is cut into individual serving pieces). • SERVES 4; MAY BE DOUBLED

One 3½- to 4-pound kosher or free-range chicken

⅓ cup finely chopped oregano, plus 4 sprigs of oregano for garnish

6 large garlic cloves, very finely chopped or pushed through a press

Zest of 2 scrubbed lemons (see Note, page 41)

Salt and coarsely ground black pepper

¼ cup extra-virgin olive oil

1 lemon, quartered, for serving

1 cup pitted kalamata or other brine-cured olives, for serving

---

Rinse the chicken inside and out with cool water and pat thoroughly dry with paper towels. Remove any excess fat from around the vent of the chicken and remove the wishbone from between the top of the breasts with a small, sharp knife (this makes it much easier to carve). Remove the backbone by cutting along either side with sharp kitchen shears and, with the chicken breast side up, push down to flatten with the palm of your hand, breaking some of the rib bones.

In a small bowl, make a paste with the oregano, garlic, lemon zest, 1½ teaspoons salt, 1 teaspoon pepper, and the oil. Smear the paste all over the chicken, gently loosening the skin of the breast and thigh to push some of the paste underneath. Place on a platter and refrigerate, uncovered, for 2 to 4 hours.

Clean and oil the grill grate to prevent sticking, if necessary, and prepare an outdoor charcoal or gas grill for medium-high indirect grilling. Place a drip pan between the two piles of coals, under the center of the grate.

Bring the chicken back to room temperature for about 30 minutes.

Grill, covered, for 20 minutes, then turn over and grill for 20 to 25 minutes more, until the juices from the thigh run clear and the internal temperature of the thigh is 160°F on an instant-read thermometer..

Transfer to a clean platter, tent loosely with foil, and let rest for 10 minutes. Carve with kitchen shears by cutting between the breasts and along the edges to make 2 breast-wing portions and 2 thigh-drumstick portions. Serve with a wedge of lemon, a sprig of oregano, and a few olives.

FIG BALSAMIC–GLAZED DUCK
WITH PLUM MOJO

*W*hen serving whole duck, it's generally wise to allow at least two pounds per person, since so much of the duck is bone and the legs don't deliver a lot of meat. If you have a very large roasting pan or two ovens, by all means roast three or even four ducks. Adding water to the roasting pan stops some of the energetic spattering that roasting ducks always create, but you still might want to be prepared to clean the oven the next day!

As a light and bracing appetizer for this mahogany-brown, sweet-sour duck, serve the Belgian Endive and Roasted Beet Salad with Citrus Vinaigrette (page 203).

✦ SERVES 4 TO 6

Two 4- to 5-pound ducks

About ⅓ cup balsamic vinegar, preferably fig balsamic

Salt

1 tablespoon plus 1 teaspoon five-spice powder

1 sprig of parsley (optional)

Plum Mojo (recipe follows)

Preheat the oven to 425°F.

Remove the giblets and necks from the duck cavities; discard or reserve for another use. Cut off excess fat from the cavities; rinse inside and out with cool water and pat dry thoroughly with plenty of paper towels.

Place the ducks, breast side down, on a rack inside a large roasting pan; add about 1 inch of water to the roasting pan. Brush the backs with a little balsamic vinegar, season generously with salt, and sprinkle with half of the five-spice powder.

Roast the ducks for 35 minutes. Prick the backs all over with the point of a sharp knife and turn over. Brush the breasts with more balsamic, season with salt, and sprinkle with the remaining five-spice powder.

Add a little more water to the pan if the juices are spattering. Roast for 20 minutes, then prick the breasts all over and brush with more balsamic. Roast for 10 minutes more and brush again. Roast for 5 or 10 minutes more if necessary, until the ducks are deep golden brown all over, an instant-read thermometer inserted into the inner thigh below the leg joint (but not touching the bone) registers at least 155°F, and the juices run clear.

Remove from the oven and tent loosely with aluminum foil. Let rest for 10 minutes, and garnish with parsley, if carving at the table. Carve and serve with the plum mojo on the side.

PLUM MOJO

4 purple or black plums, washed, halved and pitted, and cut into ¼-inch dice

5 green onions, white and light green parts only, thinly sliced

1 tablespoon seasoned rice vinegar

1 tablespoon mirin (Asian sweet wine), or sweet sherry

1 tablespoon Thai or Vietnamese fish sauce

1½ teaspoons low-sodium soy sauce

¾ teaspoon sesame oil

¾ teaspoon fresh lemon juice

Combine all the ingredients in a glass or ceramic bowl. Serve immediately or cover and refrigerate for up to 1 hour.

SLICED DUCK BREASTS
WITH SHALLOT-GINGER GLAZE

*T*o get the best golden-crisp skin when sautéing duck breasts, high heat is imperative. Unfortunately, this results in quite a bit of smoke before the ducks go into
the oven to finish cooking, so turn up the exhaust fan or open a window.

Duck breasts vary greatly in size. Use the weight as your guideline (three pounds
could be anywhere from two to five breasts). Slice the breasts before serving to make
even portions. ◆ SERVES 6

⅓ cup ginger preserves, preferably Tiptree

2 large shallots, very finely chopped

¼ cup fresh lemon juice

3 tablespoons extra-virgin olive oil

3 tablespoons low-sodium soy sauce

3 pounds individual boneless duck breasts,
 skin on

Salt and freshly ground black pepper

2 teaspoons canola or vegetable oil

Preheat the oven to 400°F. Place a small, heavy roasting pan inside to heat up.

In a small saucepan, whisk together the ginger preserves, shallots, lemon juice,
olive oil, and soy sauce; set aside.

Using a very sharp knife, score the skin of the duck breasts in several places; do
not cut into the flesh. Season both sides generously with salt and pepper.

In a large, heavy sauté pan, heat the canola oil over medium-high heat. When it
is very hot, place the duck breasts, skin side down, into the pan—do not move them
for at least 1 minute. Cook for 9 to 10 minutes, pouring off some of the rendered fat
halfway through; the skin should be brown and crispy.

Transfer the breasts to the hot roasting pan with the flesh side down. Roast for
8 to 10 minutes, depending on how pink you like your duck, and then transfer to a
cutting board. Loosely cover with foil and let rest for 5 minutes. Warm the ginger
glaze over medium-high heat just until bubbling.

Slice the duck breasts across the grain ¾ inch thick, and place the slices on
warmed dinner plates; spoon some of the ginger glaze over each portion of duck and
serve at once.

A Holiday Spectacle

Few places in New York radiate as much magic during the holiday season as Tavern on the Green. After all, what could be more enchanting than 750,000 lights twinkling in the trees outside? Stretched end to end, that's more than ten miles of holiday sparkle!

For the 30,000 guests who visit the restaurant during the holidays—6,000 of them on Christmas Eve and Christmas Day alone—stepping through the cranberry-canopied doors anytime between Thanksgiving and the new year is a childhood holiday fantasy come alive. The lobby immediately announces that this is no ordinary Christmas scene. One year, you might find yourself mesmerized not only by the huge chandelier overhead, but by forty more surrounding it and fitted out with red bulbs. Another year, fifty snow-covered trees welcomed guests, and yet another holiday season was announced by a captivating gaggle of flying gold angels. Inside, two fifteen-foot trees boasted more than 3,000 assorted European glass ornaments, each depicting bells, Santas, reindeer, snowmen, or stags.

There's never a plain round ornament to be found on the trees; Warner thought such balls were boring. Therefore, anything perfectly round has to be studded, painted, or glittered. The blown-glass beauties bask in the glow of 15,000 tiny colored lights strung one quarter inch apart around each tree.

. . .

The two Christmas trees are set up in the Crystal Room and the Chestnut Room, but the other dining areas are by no means neglected. Every room at Tavern, in fact, is decorated to the hilt for the holidays. Anywhere from thirteen to thirty wreaths—the smallest is four feet in diameter, the largest, a whopping seven feet—decorate the walls. Some weigh up to one hundred pounds. Wherever glass walls span parts of the space, the wreaths are double-sided so that they can be enjoyed from outside, too. More than fifty swags of glass balls, in the traditional holiday colors of green, red, silver, and gold, flounce along the ceiling moldings in the Crystal and Terrace rooms. In the Crystal Room, 150 red poinsettias fill the flower boxes. Throughout the season, as plants are damaged or die, they're replaced, so that by the time the holidays are over, some 500 plants have graced the room.

And the ribbon! Seven miles of it wind their way around the trees, the wreaths, and the five miles of garland—layers of mixed greens, apples, strung cranberries, and lights—that dash along the walls of the restaurant. The garland? More than one thousand feet of it snake along the mirrored corridors, with a custom-made bow punctuating every three feet (see page 171).

No opportunity is missed to make a splashy display of the season. Even the ceilings are decorated: The beams in the Rafters and Chestnut rooms are wrapped with thick garlands and lights. The bronze bear hovering outside the Park Room gets into the holiday spirit, donning a plush Santa suit custom made for quadrupeds. Every table in the restaurant—nearly five hundred in all—is draped with custom-made overlays and an arrangement of evergreens and red roses.

Visitors to New York from all over the world clamor for reservations during the holiday season. The season officially begins on Thanksgiving, when more than four thousand guests, many of them having spent the morning at the Macy's Thanksgiving Day Parade (another fabulous only-in-New-York spectacle), land a coveted spot on the reservation list.

To make room for everyone during these special weeks, some patios are tented and, as if by magic, transformed into rooms that mimic the permanent dining rooms. The floors are carpeted, the ceilings and walls are covered in white voile, and, of course, crystal chandeliers hang from the ceiling. On any given day, guests may be treated to costumed carolers, a brass trio, toy soldiers, elfettes, or a roaming Santa Claus.

OH CHRISTMAS TREE, OH CHRISTMAS TREE

You don't have to have soaring ceilings and a warehouse full of decorations to do your own take on Tavern's trees. The secret is in striking the right balance between ornaments and lights. Paul Brummer, Tavern's resident Kris Kringle, uses the divide-and-decorate method. Divide the tree in thirds horizontally. Next, divide your ornaments and lights in thirds. Arrange the lights and ornaments for the middle third of the tree on it. Halve one remaining pile of lights and ornaments and add this half to the other pile. Arrange this larger group of decorations on the bottom third of the tree. The remaining lights and ornaments should hang on the top third of the tree.

Paul suggests using assorted shapes and sizes of ornaments on the tree and tucking the larger ones farther in on the branches, leaving the tips for the more refined, smaller pieces. At Tavern, the indoor trees feature colored lights so as not to compete with the white lights wrapped around the trees outside. If you prefer white lights, add strands of light green or chartreuse lights to give depth.

IT'S THE MOST WONDERFUL TIME
OF THE YEAR, ALL YEAR

For Tavern's interior design staff, planning for the year's Christmas décor begins in January. As they pack up the previous holiday's trees, wreaths, garlands, and ornaments, they make a list of which items need to be replaced. New ribbon is ordered every year. Invariably some of the blown-glass ornaments, which are always double-wired to the tree, are broken—or are lost to nervy guests apparently wielding wire cutters—and need to be replaced. Garlands lose their heft over time. As early as the first month of the year, the decorators determine the theme for the coming season; it is often centered on a color or a material such as nuts, fruit, or pine cones. Over the years, the decorations have become more stylized and more sophisticated; red and green are not the only colors used at Tavern.

Up until Labor Day, the design team orders supplies and materials to realize that year's vision. This might include miles of pine cones on a rope, new ornaments, bolt after bolt of special fabric—there's no decorative item they've not considered. On Labor Day, a team of two people begins installing the tiny white lights in the trees outside. It takes them two full months, working out of a cherry picker, to wrap the strands a half inch apart from the base of the trunk to the tip of every branch. No nails, staples,

or fasteners of any kind are used. (The following April, this duo goes back up in the cherry picker night after night for a full month to remove the lights and replace them with a thousand lanterns.) Meanwhile, the interior designers are in Tavern's Long Island City warehouse using a color coding system to mark each box of holiday decorations according to the room in which they will go and the evenings on which they must arrive at Tavern.

On the ten nights before Thanksgiving, two fourteen-foot trucks pull into Tavern's parking lot to unload the designated boxes of decorations. In all, 510 outsize cartons are dropped off over the course of those nights; it takes

Tavern's bows are made in tiers using three different ribbons in a variety of patterns, textures, and widths—and never out of sheer or paper satin ribbon. Some ribbons were custom-made from fabric Warner picked out himself.

forty to fifty people working an overnight shift to unpack, unwrap, and hang or mount the contents. One employee works full-time for two weeks making Paul Brummer's bows, while for five nights running a team of three people is dedicated solely to the task of fluffing the garland.

By Thanksgiving, the restaurant is impeccably—and festively—turned out. Each morning throughout the season, the decorations are inspected: Broken ornaments are replaced, and thinned garlands are fattened up. The place looks as impeccable on January 3, the day the design staff begins dismantling the decorations, as it did on Thanksgiving. Those same delivery trucks bring back the empty color-coded boxes and the removal process begins; overnight the dining rooms are full of bows, bubble wrap, and packing peanuts! A master list of every single item in the boxes is drawn up, the boxes are loaded back onto the trucks, and they go off to the warehouse until next year.

VENISON MEDALLIONS
WITH CRANBERRY POLENTA

*T*his dish is perfect for a special occasion in the winter. The Chestnut Room, with its autocratic hunting lodge feel—copper stags crowning the entry and hulking beams spanning the room—is certainly the ideal place in which to serve it.

Make the polenta the night before and toast it just before guests are expected; assemble everything you need to finish it near the stove. ◆ SERVES 8

CRANBERRY POLENTA

1 tablespoon extra-virgin olive oil

1 ounce pancetta, coarsely chopped

½ red onion, finely chopped

1 garlic clove, finely chopped

Finely grated zest of 1 scrubbed orange
   (see Note, page 41)

3 cups water

1 cup beef consommé or rich beef stock

Juice of 1 orange

Coarse sea salt (kosher is fine)

1 cup polenta or coarsely ground yellow
   cornmeal

4 tablespoons (½ stick) unsalted butter,
   cut into ½-inch cubes

½ cup dried cranberries

TO SERVE

2 tablespoons unsalted butter, melted

Salt and freshly ground black pepper

8 venison loin slices, or medallions
   (about 3½ ounces each)

3 tablespoons clarified butter
   (see Note, page 131)

2 tablespoons Cointreau or Grand Marnier

1 cup beef consommé or rich beef stock

¾ cup pinot noir or other dry, fruity red wine

3 paper-thin slices of orange, halved crosswise
   to make 6 semicircles

¼ cup dried cranberries

FOR THE POLENTA

In a large, heavy saucepan, combine the oil and pancetta and cook over low heat for about 8 minutes, until the pancetta has rendered its fat. Add the onion and garlic and cook, stirring occasionally, for 4 to 5 minutes, or until softened. Add the orange zest and cook, stirring, for 1 minute more.

Add the water, consommé, orange juice, and 1 teaspoon sea salt to the pan; bring the liquid to a boil. Reduce the heat and, when the liquid is simmering, gradually sprinkle in the polenta in a very slow, thin stream, whisking constantly until no lumps remain. Reduce the heat to very low, switch to a wooden spoon, and stir every 1 or 2 minutes for 25 to 30 minutes, or until the mixture pulls away from the sides of the pan and the grains of polenta have softened. Stir in the butter and the ½ cup cranberries. The mixture will be very thick.

Rinse an 8 x 12-inch roasting pan with cold water and shake it dry. Mound the polenta in the pan and, using a rubber spatula repeatedly dipped in very hot water, spread the polenta evenly in the pan until it is just over ¼ inch thick. Cover the pan with a clean kitchen towel and set aside for 1 hour at room temperature or up to 24 hours in the refrigerator.

TO SERVE

Preheat a grill or broiler to high heat.

Cut the polenta in the pan into 8 squares or rounds, brush them with the melted butter, and season generously with salt and pepper. Brown under the hot broiler for about 6 minutes on each side, or until golden and glazed.

Turn off the broiler and place 8 plates and a platter in the oven to warm.

Season the venison medallions generously with salt and pepper. In a large, heavy skillet, heat the clarified butter over medium-high heat. When it is very hot, add the medallions and sauté for 2 to 3 minutes on each side (be careful not to overcook; the meat should still be slightly rosy at the center). Transfer to the platter in the oven. Increase the heat under the skillet to high and add the Cointreau; deglaze the pan, stirring with a wooden spoon to scrape up all the delicious brown bits. Add the consommé and the pinot noir and simmer rapidly to reduce, until there is only about ¾ cup of just barely thickened liquid remaining. Taste for seasoning and adjust with salt.

Place a piece of polenta in the center of each warmed plate and top with a venison medallion. Drizzle the sauce over the top and garnish each plate with half a slice of orange topped with a few dried cranberries. Serve at once.

EVEN STARS HAVE TO KILL TIME

From Harrison Ford to Tom Hanks, from Matt Damon to Will Smith, Hollywood's biggest stars have come to Tavern to have a wonderful meal and enjoy the drama of the place. One of our most memorable star moments was the afternoon that Tom Cruise spent here while he waited for his wife, Katie Holmes, to finish running the New York City Marathon. He carried his daughter Suri in his arms from room to room, admiring the grand chandeliers and the magnificent murals.

About 2½ hours before serving time, remove the steaks from the refrigerator, pat them dry with paper towels, and rub both sides with the oil. Let stand at room temperature for 1 to 1½ hours.

In a small saucepan, cover the green peppercorns with cold water and bring to a boil. Boil for 1 minute, then drain. Set the peppercorns aside.

Place a heavy, 14-inch, ovenproof sauté pan over high heat. Sprinkle one side of each steak generously with salt and a little pepper. When the pan is very hot, after about 4 minutes, place the steaks in the pan with tongs, seasoned side down, without touching one another. *Do not move or press down on them* (this makes it important to get the placement in the pan right the first time).

Cook for 2½ minutes. Season the tops of the steaks with salt and pepper and turn over, again watching your placement. Cook, again without touching or moving, for 2½ minutes more. Transfer the steaks to a rack set over a plate and let stand at room temperature for 30 minutes. Do not wash the pan.

Preheat the oven to 425°F.

When the oven is fully heated, return the steaks to the pan in which they were seared and finish cooking in the oven for 8 minutes for medium-rare, or 12 minutes for medium. (Cooking to the well-done stage is not recommended.)

Let rest for 10 minutes on the rack while you make the sauce. In the same sauté pan you used for the steaks, over medium heat, melt the butter and add the shallot. Cook, stirring, for 2 minutes, until softened. Add the peppercorns and stir for 1 minute, then add the brandy. Stand back and ignite the brandy by tipping the pan to the flame, or with a long match. Flambé until the flames die down, shaking the pan gently. Add the cream and consommé, increase the heat to medium-high, and swirl to combine, then cook for 2 minutes more.

Return the steaks to the pan and spoon the sauce over the top, then remove from the heat and taste the sauce for seasoning. Serve on warm plates, with a pot of the blue cheese butter on the side, if desired.

BLUE CHEESE BUTTER

⅓ cup unsalted butter,
  at room temperature
⅓ cup crumbled blue cheese,
  such as Maytag blue

In a small bowl, combine the butter and cheese using a fork. The mixture will still have crumbles of cheese. Cover and refrigerate overnight, but be sure to return to room temperature before serving.

SIRLOIN BURGERS
WITH CHIMICHURRI SAUCE

*M*axwell's Plum offered a mix of humble and haute dishes. In its more-than-twenty-year run, offerings came and went, but hamburgers remained a fixture. They were always formed very gently by hand, as the best burgers are.

If you don't want to make the chimichurri sauce—a tangy condiment as popular and ubiquitous in Argentina as our ketchup is here—substitute a nice garlicky aioli. Either way, assemble everything you need for serving. • SERVES 6

---

6 onion slices, each about ⅓ inch thick

1¾ pounds ground sirloin (20% fat content)

3 small shallots, minced or grated

1 tablespoon finely chopped flat-leaf parsley

Salt and cayenne pepper

6 soft buns, split and toasted until golden

Chimichurri Sauce (recipe follows)

Preheat a gas or charcoal grill, a broiler, or a large ridged stovetop griddle pan to medium-high heat (if using a broiler, place the rack about 6 inches from the heat source and set to the highest heat).

Grill the onion slices for about 2 minutes on each side, until lightly charred. Set the onion aside and leave the grill on.

In a mixing bowl, combine the ground beef with the shallots, parsley, 1 teaspoon salt, and ⅛ teaspoon cayenne. With a fork, toss quickly to mix evenly and then bring the meat together into loose, flattened patties.

Grill the burgers for 4 to 6 minutes on each side, to the desired degree of doneness. Transfer the bottom half of each bun to a warmed plate and drizzle with a generous tablespoon of chimichurri. Top each with a burger and an onion slice, drizzle with a little more sauce, top with the top half of the toasted bun, and serve at once.

CHIMICHURRI SAUCE

---

1 cup firmly packed flat-leaf parsley, leaves and tender stems only

4 garlic cloves, quartered

1½ tablespoons oregano leaves

½ cup extra-virgin olive oil

2 tablespoons white wine vinegar

Salt and freshly ground pepper

¼ teaspoon crushed red pepper flakes

In a food processor or by hand, combine and finely chop the parsley, garlic, and oregano. Transfer the mixture to a small bowl and stir in the oil, vinegar, 2 teaspoons salt, about ¼ teaspoon pepper, and the red pepper flakes. Use at once or cover and refrigerate for up to 12 hours. •

MAKES 1 SCANT CUP

UPTOWN CHILI CON CARNE

*A*nother favorite of the smart set who frequented Maxwell's Plum, this chic chili was good enough for Warren Beatty and Bill Blass. Using beef consommé gives it a smooth and glossy texture, very dark red color, and gloriously beefy flavor. This chili never saw a ranch or a cowboy (unless he was wearing alligator boots); it's pure, unadulterated sophistication. • SERVES 6 TO 8; MAY BE DOUBLED IF YOU HAVE A LARGE POT

¼ cup canola oil

4 pounds beef chuck, cut into ½-inch cubes

Salt and freshly ground black pepper

2 large onions, coarsely chopped

8 garlic cloves, finely chopped

¼ cup best-quality chili powder

2 teaspoons ground cumin

1 teaspoon dried Mexican oregano

1 teaspoon crushed red pepper flakes

1 cup tomato paste

1½ quarts (6 cups) canned beef consommé

2½ cups grated sharp Cheddar cheese

2½ cups sour cream

¾ cup coarsely chopped cilantro leaves

Place a very large, heavy Dutch oven or wide-bottomed soup pot over medium-high heat and add the oil. Season the beef cubes on all sides with salt and pepper. When the oil is very hot, add half the beef. Brown for about 5 minutes, turning over the cubes occasionally with tongs to help them brown evenly.

Transfer the browned beef to a platter with a slotted spoon, letting the oil drain back into the pot, and brown the second batch in the same way; transfer to the platter. Lower the heat to medium. Add the onions and garlic and sauté, stirring occasionally, for about 6 minutes, until softened.

Remove from the heat and add the chili powder, cumin, oregano, red pepper flakes, and tomato paste. Stir together to make a paste, then stir in the consommé, 1½ teaspoons salt, and a generous grinding of black pepper. Stir to blend, add the cubed beef, and return to the heat.

Bring the mixture to a boil, stirring once or twice. Lower the heat so the liquid is just simmering and partially cover the pot. Simmer for 1¼ hours, until the meat is tender.

Ladle the hot chili into shallow bowls and pass the cheese, sour cream, and cilantro at the table.

BRINED AND ROASTED
LOIN OF PORK
WITH SHERRY-DIJON SAUCE

*A*lthough this dish requires some advance planning, brining is really the only way to enjoy supermarket pork. Supermarket pork shoulder (or Boston butt) has enough marbling to remain moist when gently cooked, leaner cuts such as this loin are very often unpleasantly dry after roasting. Two to three days in a flavored brine allows the meat to absorb the salt and other flavorings, resulting in a tender, juicy roast that is reminiscent of the way pork used to taste twenty or thirty years ago. Of course, if you can obtain an heirloom breed of pork from a local farm or farmers' market or via the Internet, there is no need for the brining process.

Serve this with Warm Fingerling Potatoes with White Wine–Chive Sauce (page 246). • SERVES 6 TO 8

½ cup sugar

½ cup kosher salt

3 garlic cloves

2 bay leaves

2 tablespoons juniper berries

1 tablespoon dried thyme

½ tablespoon black peppercorns

5 allspice berries or ⅛ teaspoon ground allspice

One 4- to 5-pound boneless pork loin, trimmed

1 tablespoon extra-virgin olive oil

Freshly ground black pepper

SHERRY-DIJON SAUCE

3 tablespoons butter

3 tablespoons flour

⅔ cup sweet or off-dry sherry

1 cup chicken stock or broth (low-sodium canned is fine)

⅓ cup heavy cream

2 to 3 tablespoons Dijon mustard

Freshly ground black pepper

Two to three days before serving, put 2 quarts (8 cups) of cold water in a tall and narrow, or oval, nonreactive container that will hold the meat and all the brine (about 4-quart capacity) and also will fit inside your refrigerator. In a small saucepan, combine another ½ quart (2 cups) water with the sugar and salt. Cook over low heat, stirring, just until the salt and sugar dissolve, then remove from the heat and cool slightly. Add to the cold water.

Using a mortar and pestle or in a bowl, slightly crush together the garlic cloves, bay leaves, juniper berries, thyme, peppercorns, and allspice. Add to the brine mixture, and then add the pork. Put a plate on top to keep the meat completely submerged, if necessary, and refrigerate for 48 to 72 hours.

About 4½ hours before serving time, remove the pork from the brine, rinse under cold running water, and pat dry thoroughly with paper towels. Discard the brine.

Place the loin on a rack in a roasting pan and let it come to room temperature, loosely covered with a clean kitchen towel; this should take about 2 hours.

Preheat the oven to 400°F.

Brush the roast evenly with the oil and season generously with pepper *only*. Place in the oven and roast for 20 minutes.

Reduce the heat to 325°F and cook for a total time (including the first 20 minutes) of about 19 minutes per pound, until the internal temperature at the thickest part of the meat reaches 155°F on an instant-read thermometer. When the roast is done, transfer to a serving platter, turn off the oven, and place the roast inside with the door ajar while you make the sauce.

Set the roasting pan over medium heat and add the butter to melt it. When the foam has subsided, whisk in the flour to form a paste. Whisk for 2 to 3 minutes (don't worry if it browns—this will just improve the flavor). Drizzle in the sherry and the chicken stock and scrape up the flavorful bits from the sides and bottom of the pan. Bring to a simmer and cook for 2 to 3 minutes, until thickened. Whisk in the cream and simmer for 1 minute. Remove from the heat.

Whisk in the mustard to taste and a little pepper. Taste for seasoning and adjust (because of the brine, it will probably not need any additional salt).

Cut the pork into ½- to ¾-inch-thick slices and serve on warmed plates with a generous drizzle of the sauce. Pass the remaining sauce at the table.

ALWAYS READY TO REPORT

New York being the headquarters of the national news media, we've had the pleasure of serving many of the world's most recognizable journalists, including one of our favorite regulars, Barbara Walters. Another favorite was Peter Jennings, who loved coming in. One day, though, not long after he sat down to lunch, he abruptly excused himself from the table and rushed out of the restaurant. We didn't know what had happened, but later learned that he had just been informed of the tragic Columbine shooting, and he needed to go on the air. He was the consummate professional and a consummate gentleman, and we miss him.

COWBOY BABY BACK RIBS

*C*hef Patrick Clark, one of the culinary world's shining stars, brought his innovative regional American cooking to Tavern in 1992 to great acclaim. When he died in 1998, Warner spoke for all when he said, "His spirit and inspiration lifted the lives of all who knew him." His cooking, a fusion of his French culinary training and his love of southern cuisine, lives on in these lip-smacking ribs. Serve them piled high on a platter with lots of napkins, accompanied by coleslaw and buttermilk corn muffins for the true Patrick Clark experience.

You have to make the rub the day before. If you double this recipe, increase the rub and the sauce by one and a half times only, not two. The ribs may also be crisped under a broiler. ◆ SERVES 6; MAY BE DOUBLED

RUB AND RIBS
¼ cup sweet paprika
2 tablespoons Old Bay seasoning
2 tablespoons chili powder
1 to 3 teaspoons cayenne pepper, to taste
2 teaspoons garlic powder
Salt and freshly ground black pepper
1 tablespoon sugar
½ cup cider vinegar
6 pounds baby back ribs

BARBECUE SAUCE
1 large onion, sliced
2 cups fresh orange juice
4 cups ketchup

½ cup fresh lime juice
½ cup cider vinegar
¼ cup firmly packed brown sugar
2 tablespoons dry mustard
2 tablespoons sweet paprika
1 tablespoon crushed red pepper flakes
1 teaspoon garlic powder
1 teaspoon chili powder
1 to 2 tablespoons Tabasco sauce
2 tablespoons tamarind paste
2 tablespoons honey
1 tablespoon salt
1 tablespoon freshly ground black pepper
12 tablespoons (6 ounces; 1½ sticks) unsalted butter

PREPARE THE RUB FOR THE RIBS

Sift all the spices into a large bowl and add 1 tablespoon each of salt and pepper, and the sugar. Add the vinegar and whisk together with a fork, to make a paste. Rub the paste into the meat and wrap thoroughly in plastic wrap. Place in a large roasting pan to contain any leakage, and refrigerate overnight.

MAKE THE BARBECUE SAUCE

In a blender or a food processor, combine the onion and ½ cup of the orange juice and puree for 1 minute, until very smooth. Combine the remaining orange juice and all the remaining ingredients, in a large, nonreactive saucepan over medium heat. Stir in the onion puree. Bring the mixture to a slow simmer and cook for 25 minutes. Remove from the heat and let cool.

Preheat the oven to 250°F.

Unwrap the ribs and place them on a large, aluminum-foil-lined, rimmed baking sheet. Bake for 3½ hours without turning the meat. Remove the ribs from the oven and allow them to rest for 10 minutes to 1 hour, until just before serving time.

Preheat a gas or charcoal grill until very hot. Place the ribs on the grill, meaty side down, for 2 to 3 minutes, or just until the fat starts to sizzle. Turn over and cook for 2 to 3 minutes more. Remove the meat from the grill and slice between the ribs to separate.

Mound on a platter and drizzle with plenty of the barbecue sauce, or serve the ribs dry and pass large bowls of warm sauce at the table.

GRILLED BUTTERFLIED
LEG OF LAMB
WITH RED WINE–SHALLOT BUTTER

To make fast work of preparing this classic grilled specialty, ask your butcher to butterfly the lamb for you. The result is shaped roughly like a butterfly with a surface that resembles the Himalayan mountain range. The plus side of the odd-shaped piece of meat is that it slices like a dream and provides very tasty well-done, medium-rare, and pink slices all at the same time, serving pretty much everyone's tastes. Unlike the Standing Rib Roast of Beef (page 180), this is best sliced in the kitchen as its appearance is a bit odd!

In very hot weather, substitute a simple cucumber–sour cream raita-style sauce for the red wine–shallot butter, and serve the lamb and sauce at room temperature. ◆

SERVES 8

¾ cup dry red wine

¾ cup fruity olive oil

1 well-trimmed leg of lamb,
    about 6 to 7 pounds, butterflied

Salt and freshly ground black pepper

6 small sprigs of thyme

Red Wine–Shallot Butter (recipe follows)

About 5½ hours before serving time, combine the wine and oil in a baking dish or roasting pan just large enough to hold the lamb in an even layer. Place the lamb in the marinade with the uneven, meaty side down; cover and marinate for 2 hours in the refrigerator. Turn the lamb and marinate for 2 to 3 hours more. Bring to room temperature for 30 to 40 minutes before grilling.

Preheat a gas or charcoal grill, or a broiler, to medium-high heat.

Dry the lamb well with paper towels and season all the nooks and crannies generously with salt and pepper. Tuck the thyme sprigs in here and there, and grill with the uneven side facing the heat source for 15 minutes.

Turn over and grill for an additional 15 minutes. Reduce the heat to medium-low or raise the grill several inches away from the heat source, and cook for an additional 5 to 10 minutes, until done to your liking. (Because of the irregular thickness of the meat, there will be some rare pieces and some well done.)

Let the lamb rest for 10 to 15 minutes, loosely covered with aluminum foil. Slice across the grain into long, thin slices and serve on warmed plates with a large nugget or two of the red wine–shallot butter.

RED WINE–SHALLOT BUTTER

This classic butter sauce is known as *marchand de vin* ("wine merchant's sauce") in French.

2 cups dry red wine

2 small shallots, minced

¾ pound (3 sticks) unsalted butter, cut into 12 pieces and softened to room temperature

2 tablespoons fresh lemon juice

2 tablespoons finely chopped flat-leaf parsley

Salt and freshly ground black pepper

In a small nonreactive saucepan, combine the wine and shallots and place over medium-high heat. Boil, uncovered, for 15 to 18 minutes, until the liquid is reduced to about ¼ cup. Set aside to cool for 10 minutes.

In a mixing bowl, combine the butter, lemon juice, and parsley. Gradually whisk in the reduced wine and shallot mixture, adding ½ teaspoon salt and a good pinch of pepper. The texture should be creamy.

Store the butter in the refrigerator for up to 1 week, or in the freezer for up to 3 months. Bring to room temperature before serving. • MAKES 1¾ CUPS

LIGHTING TIDBIT

Cleaning the Tavern's renowned chandeliers is a full-time job for a team of four people. For each of the sixty fixtures, three members of the quartet lower the fixture and the fourth cleans it with a vinegar-and-water solution and a microfiber cloth. They begin in the lobby and make their way through the six dining rooms and the labyrinthine hallways. By the time they polish the last crystal and lightbulb on the last chandelier, it's time to head back to the lobby and start over again.

VEAL PAILLARD
WITH ARUGULA-TOMATO SALAD

*H*ere's a refined version of the always popular American favorite—steak and salad. This dish makes a delicate dinner for two, yet still maintains a satisfyingly meaty undertone. The veal scallop is topped with a brightly flavored salad of spicy greens and luscious tomatoes. This is a pan-seared dish, but it is of course best in the summer when baby arugula and tomatoes are at their peak. • SERVES 2

Two 6- to 7-ounce veal scallops, preferably cut from the top round

1 ripe beefsteak-style tomato, halved, seeds squeezed out, and finely diced

Finely grated zest of 1 small, scrubbed lemon (see Note, page 41)

1 tablespoon fresh lemon juice

Salt and freshly ground black pepper

4 cups baby arugula (about 4 ounces), washed and spun dry

½ cup extra-virgin olive oil

1 tablespoon unsalted butter

Place each scallop between large sheets of plastic wrap on a work surface. Use the flat side of a meat mallet to pound lightly from the center outward, gently easing the veal to an even thickness of about ¼ inch. The paillards should be roughly 4 x 8 inches. (This step may be done up to 4 hours in advance; refrigerate the paillards on a baking sheet, still sandwiched between sheets of plastic wrap, until 10 minutes before you are ready to cook them.)

In a bowl, combine the diced tomato, lemon zest, lemon juice, ¼ teaspoon salt, and a good grinding of pepper; toss well. Add the arugula and ¼ cup of the oil to the tomato mixture, toss gently, and taste for seasoning.

Place a 13- or 14-inch heavy skillet or sauté pan over medium-high heat and add the remaining ¼ cup oil and the butter. Season both sides of each paillard generously with salt and pepper.

When the butter has melted, the foam has subsided, and the fat is very hot, quickly but carefully add the paillards to the pan, without overlapping. Do not move them for 1½ minutes. Turn them over and sauté for 1 minute more, until firm.

Place a paillard on each of 2 warmed plates and mound half the salad on top of each one. Serve at once.

8

SALADS

and

SANDWICHES

SMOKED CHICKEN, WILD RICE, AND APRICOT SALAD

*I*n early autumn, when Central Park is brilliant and the air is still warm enough for city folk to soak up some sun, they head to the Sheep Meadow, the vast expanse of green on view from Tavern's Crystal Terrace. Frisbees fly, soccer balls roll, and picnic baskets hold an astonishing array of gourmet delights. This tasty, make-ahead salad is an excellent portable dish for a picnic on a glorious day: It's a meal in itself. • SERVES 6 • *photograph on page 196*

2½ cups chicken stock or broth
    (low-sodium canned is fine)

Salt

1 cup wild rice, picked over and well rinsed

One 10-ounce package chopped frozen
    spinach, completely thawed

¼ cup extra-virgin olive oil, plus additional
    for drizzling

1 small red onion, finely chopped

⅓ cup pine nuts, coarsely chopped

1 cup diced dried apricots (about 12 ounces)

Freshly ground black pepper

1 teaspoon fresh lemon juice

10 ounces smoked chicken or turkey,
    cut into ¼-inch dice

3 tablespoons coarsely chopped tarragon

In a saucepan, bring the stock to a boil and add ½ teaspoon salt. Add the rice and return to the boil. Reduce the heat so the rice simmers gently, partially cover the pan, and simmer for 50 to 60 minutes, until some of the rice grains burst. Remove from the heat and drain off any excess liquid; let stand for 10 minutes.

While the rice is cooking, squeeze the spinach very firmly in small handfuls to extract as much water as possible.

In a large skillet over medium heat, heat the oil. Add the onion and sauté, stirring, for about 3 minutes, until just tender. Add the pine nuts and stir for about 2 minutes, until slightly golden. Stir in the squeezed spinach, the apricots, ¼ teaspoon salt, and a generous grinding of black pepper. Remove the pan from the heat and stir in the drained wild rice, lemon juice, diced chicken, and tarragon, mixing well. Taste for seasoning and drizzle with a little good olive oil.

The salad may be cooled to room temperature, covered, and refrigerated overnight. If you do this, be sure to return it to room temperature before serving, to reawaken the flavors.

SPINACH, BACON, AND MUSHROOM SALAD

*T*his salad is one of those classic American dishes that simply never go out of style. It has crunch, saltiness, the earthy flavor of mushrooms, and that quintessentially American dressing, ranch. The greens will wilt quickly if the salad sits on a buffet spread, so it's best to serve it plated. • SERVES 6

12 slices thick-cut bacon, preferably smoked
½ large red onion
¼ cup pure olive oil
1 tablespoon red wine vinegar
Salt and freshly ground black pepper

8 small white button mushrooms, brushed clean, stems removed, and thinly sliced
1 pound baby spinach, well washed, well dried, and stemmed
1 cup Ranch Dressing (recipe follows)

In a large, heavy skillet, preferably cast iron, cook the bacon over medium-low heat until done to your liking. Drain on a doubled layer of paper towels, then cut or crumble into large pieces and set aside.

Chill 6 plates in the refrigerator.

Slice the onion half in half again lengthwise through the root end. Place the 2 onion quarters cut side down, and slice lengthwise into very thin julienne.

In a very large bowl, whisk together the oil, vinegar, ½ teaspoon salt, and a few grinds of pepper. Add the mushrooms and toss thoroughly. Add the onion and spinach and toss again.

Using tongs, transfer an equal amount of the spinach salad to each of the plates and divide the bacon among the salads. Drizzle each salad with about 2 tablespoons of ranch dressing, and serve at once.

RANCH DRESSING

½ teaspoon garlic salt
⅓ cup buttermilk
1 tablespoon fresh lemon juice
2 teaspoons finely chopped cilantro
2 teaspoons finely snipped chives
1 teaspoon finely chopped flat-leaf parsley
Freshly ground white pepper

3 tablespoons mayonnaise
Salt, as needed

In a mixing bowl, whisk together the garlic salt, buttermilk, lemon juice, cilantro, chives, parsley, and a scant ¼ teaspoon white pepper. Whisk in the mayonnaise. Taste for seasoning and adjust with salt and white pepper, if necessary.

Use immediately, or cover tightly and refrigerate for up to 3 days. The flavor of the dressing will improve after 1 day in the refrigerator. • MAKES ¾ CUP

BUFFALO CHICKEN SALAD
WITH MAYTAG BLUE DRESSING

*I*t's hard to say whether New Yorkers take their sports teams or their food more seriously. Over the years, Tavern has been tapped to celebrate some of the most exciting victories in the city's history, including the Mets' pennant victory in 1986 and the Yankees' World Series win in 1997. Both banquets featured a version of this special take on classic American spectator-sport fare, Buffalo chicken wings. Here, the wild-hot flavors are tamed a little by the addition of cool, crisp iceberg lettuce and juicy cherry tomatoes. • SERVES 6

1½ pounds boneless, skinless chicken breasts or chicken tenders, halved crosswise and cut into large bite-size pieces

⅓ pound Maytag or other blue cheese, crumbled

⅔ cup mayonnaise

1½ cups plus ⅔ cup buttermilk

2 tablespoons cider vinegar

4 green onions, white and light green parts only, thinly sliced

2 tablespoons coarsely chopped flat-leaf parsley

Salt and freshly ground black pepper

About 1 quart vegetable oil, for deep-frying

2 teaspoons garlic powder

2 cups flour

1 small head of iceberg lettuce, quartered and torn into bite-size pieces

1 pint cherry tomatoes, quartered

1 small red onion, halved lengthwise and sliced crosswise paper-thin

Spicy Butter, for serving (recipe follows)

Pat the chicken pieces dry with paper towels, then spread on a rack to dry thoroughly.

In a large bowl, combine the blue cheese, mayonnaise, the ⅔ cup buttermilk, the vinegar, green onions, parsley, ½ teaspoon salt, and a generous grinding of pepper. Scoop out about a quarter of this dressing and place in a sauceboat or small serving bowl. Set both aside.

Place a deep, heavy saucepan or Dutch oven, preferably enameled cast iron, over high heat and add enough oil to come about a third of the way (no more) up the sides of the pan. Line a large baking sheet with a layer of brown paper or slightly crumpled newspaper and place in a low oven.

In a shallow bowl, combine 2 teaspoons salt, 2 teaspoons pepper, and the garlic powder. In a large resealable plastic bag, combine the flour and half this seasoning mixture. Stir the remaining 1½ cups buttermilk into the bowl with the remaining seasoning mixture.

When the oil reaches 360°F on an instant-read thermometer, dip and swirl half the chicken pieces in the buttermilk mixture, then add them to the bag of flour, seal, and toss until evenly coated. With tongs, add the chicken pieces to the hot oil and fry for about 4 minutes, until golden and quite firm. Transfer the first batch to the oven and return the oil to 360°F before coating and frying the second batch.

To serve, add the lettuce, tomatoes, and red onion to the large bowl with the dressing. Toss to coat evenly and divide among 6 plates. Top with pieces of fried chicken and pass the remaining dressing on the side. Provide ramekins of the spicy butter, for dipping, and serve at once.

SPICY BUTTER

4 tablespoons (½ stick) butter

¼ cup hot sauce of your choice

¾ teaspoon kosher salt

In a small saucepan over low heat, combine all the ingredients and stir to melt the butter. Keep barely warm until serving time.

A $100 COKE

Working the long hours necessary to keep a successful operation running smoothly can be challenging, so the Tavern staff is grateful for our really generous patrons. But there are big tippers, and then there's Victoria Gotti, daughter of the late mob boss John Gotti and star of her own television show. One time she tried to give a waiter a hundred-dollar bill for a Coke. The waiter politely declined the huge tip, but then Ms. Gotti no longer wanted the Coke.

BELGIAN ENDIVE AND ROASTED BEET SALAD
WITH CITRUS VINAIGRETTE

*A*lmost unknown a decade ago, the pairing of crisp white endive, ruby-red beets, and walnuts has quickly become a new American classic. Be sure to buy your walnuts from a purveyor with a high turnover; nothing will spoil this salad quite like stale nuts. • SERVES 6

---

6 small beets, ends trimmed

2 small shallots, finely chopped

3 tablespoons balsamic vinegar

About 1 tablespoon zest from a scrubbed orange (see Note, page 41)

1 tablespoon fresh orange juice

1 tablespoon fresh lemon juice

1 tablespoon fresh lime juice

Scant 1 teaspoon ground fennel (optional)

⅓ cup best-quality extra-virgin olive oil

Salt and freshly ground black pepper

3 small or 2 large heads of Belgian endive, root ends trimmed, cored, and slivered lengthwise

3 cups mâche or baby spinach leaves

¾ cup coarsely chopped walnuts

Preheat the oven to 350°F.

Wash the beets, wrap each one in aluminum foil, and place on a baking sheet. Bake for 35 to 45 minutes, until tender when pierced with a knife.

Cool the beets. If desired, the roasted beets may be wrapped and refrigerated overnight before continuing with the recipe. Wearing an old pair of rubber gloves, peel the beets and cut into ½-inch cubes.

At least 30 minutes and up to 1 hour before serving time, in a large bowl, whisk together the shallots, vinegar, orange zest, citrus juices, ground fennel (if using), and oil. Whisk in ¾ teaspoon salt and a generous grinding of pepper. Add the beet cubes and toss to coat. Let the mixture marinate, stirring every 10 minutes, for 30 minutes to 1 hour.

Add the endive to the bowl with the beets and toss together thoroughly. Fold in the mâche and about half of the walnuts. Transfer to a platter or plates and scatter with the remaining walnuts. Serve at once.

OPEN-FACED TUNA NIÇOISE
ON GARLIC CROÛTES

*T*hese savory *tartines*, the French equivalent of open-faced sandwiches, make a lovely lunch offering. If you plan to make them part of a buffet, arrange them on large platters; crowding them will look messy.

The cooked tuna and potatoes may be covered and refrigerated overnight; just bring them back to room temperature before combining with the other ingredients. Or, you can prepare the entire niçoise mixture, then cool, cover, and refrigerate for up to six hours. Bring to room temperature before topping the croûtes. Spoon the niçoise onto the croûtes just before guests arrive. • SERVES 6

---

6 small red or fingerling potatoes, scrubbed and cut into scant ½-inch dice

1 or 2 ahi tuna steak(s), 12 to 14 ounces total

¼ cup extra-virgin olive oil

Salt and freshly ground black pepper

1 large yellow onion, coarsely chopped

4 garlic cloves, very finely chopped or pushed through a press

8 olive oil–packed anchovy fillets, soaked for 5 minutes in warm water, drained, patted dry, and chopped

8 plum tomatoes, seeded and diced

2 bay leaves, crumbled

1½ teaspoons chopped oregano leaves, plus a few small sprigs for garnish

One 6-ounce can tomato paste

⅓ cup capers, rinsed and drained

⅓ cup white wine vinegar

⅓ cup niçoise or other brine-cured black olives, pitted and quartered

Garlic Croûtes (recipe follows)

⅓ cup drained caperberries, for garnish

Place the potatoes in a steamer basket over simmering water. Cover and steam until tender but not mushy, about 5 minutes. Transfer to a bowl.

Preheat the broiler and position a rack about 4 inches from the heat source.

Brush both sides of the tuna with about 1 tablespoon of the oil, then season generously with salt and pepper. Place on a broiler pan and put under the broiler. Cook, turning once, until just opaque throughout, about 6 minutes on each side. Transfer to a plate and let cool.

Place a large sauté pan over medium-low heat and add the remaining olive oil. Add the onion, stir to coat with oil, and cover the pan. Cook gently, stirring occasionally, until very soft, about 20 minutes.

Add the garlic, anchovies, tomatoes, bay leaves, and chopped oregano. Cover and cook for 5 minutes to blend the flavors. Stir in the tomato paste, capers, vinegar, olives, and potatoes and cook, uncovered, until slightly thickened, about 5 more minutes.

Cut the tuna into generous ¼-inch chunks and stir into the tomato mixture. Remove from the heat and let stand while you make the garlic croûtes.

continued

Place two garlic croûtes on each plate or arrange them all on a large platter. Top each croûte with about ¾ cup of the tuna mixture. Garnish with the oregano sprigs and whole caperberries, and serve at once.

GARLIC CROÛTES

Twelve ½-inch-thick slices rustic country French or Italian bread, 5 to 6 inches across, or six 5-inch lengths of baguette, halved

2 to 3 tablespoons pure olive oil

4 garlic cloves, halved crosswise

Preheat the oven to 350°F.

Place the bread slices on a baking sheet and brush both sides lightly with the oil. Bake until golden, 10 to 15 minutes. Immediately rub one side of each slice firmly back and forth several times with the cut sides of the garlic cloves.

Store cooled croûtes in an airtight container at room temperature for up to 24 hours. Recrisp in a low oven if necessary. • MAKES 12 CROÛTES

WHAT A LIFE

Among the many celebrities who have frequented Tavern on the Green, one of our favorites was John F. Kennedy Jr. He was here for various events, but he also made a habit of just dropping by when he was Rollerblading through Central Park. "I'd always give him a bottle of water," recalls Rodney Shepherd, a longtime banquet captain at Tavern. "One night, when we were hosting a benefit for the Robin Hood Foundation, I was standing next to him while the cameras were flashing, literally blinding us. He muttered, 'What a life, Rodney.'" Indeed, he was truly a special man, and his was truly a special life, sadly cut short.

WARM POTATO SALAD
WITH DOUBLE-SMOKED BACON AND FRESH ROSEMARY

*F*or even the most hard-to-impress New Yorkers, a summer meal on one of Tavern's terraces is as enchanting an experience as you can get. Some might argue that the food simply tastes better when eaten *en plein air*. No matter where you eat it, this version of the classic potato dish will make you feel as if you're dining in sunny France, where cooks have a way with potatoes. This aromatic offering takes advantage of the gentle warmth of the just-cooked spuds, which helps to release the flavors of fragrant rosemary and olive oil. Serve these alongside grilled meats, poultry, or fish. • SERVES 6

4 slices thick-cut smoked, or double-smoked, bacon (3 to 4 ounces)

2 pounds small red potatoes

Coarse sea salt

2 tablespoons Champagne vinegar

1 tablespoon dry white wine

1 teaspoon Dijon mustard

1 teaspoon very finely chopped rosemary leaves

Freshly ground black pepper

⅓ cup extra-virgin olive oil, preferably French

3 tablespoons coarsely chopped baby arugula leaves

1 large shallot, minced

Place a large, heavy skillet over medium-low heat. Add the bacon and cook until crisp, turning occasionally. Drain on a paper towel, crumble, and set aside.

Scrub the potatoes and, if they are larger than a golf ball, cut them in half. Bring a large saucepan of water to a boil and add 1 tablespoon sea salt. Add the potatoes and simmer for about 15 minutes, until they are tender but not mushy. Drain in a colander. Set the potatoes aside until just cool enough to handle.

In a large serving bowl, whisk together the vinegar, wine, mustard, rosemary, ½ teaspoon salt, and pepper to taste. Drizzle in the oil in a thin stream, constantly whisking until the dressing has emulsified. Stir in the arugula.

As soon as the potatoes are just cool enough to handle, cut them into quarters and place them in the bowl with the dressing (if you wait too long before cutting them, the potatoes will lose their shape and won't absorb the flavors of the dressing as well). Toss gently to coat the potatoes; add the crumbled bacon and the shallot, toss again briefly, and taste for seasoning. Adjust with salt and pepper as necessary, and serve.

SMOKED TURKEY
CLUB SANDWICHES
WITH CLASSIC SLAW

*T*he club sandwich is another of the classics that Tavern does so well. It's an especially American classic: Visitors to this country often remark how big everything is, and here's a sandwich with not two but *three* slices of bread!

We like to serve coleslaw as the accompaniment—true coleslaw, tossed with boiled dressing, not a mayonnaise-based concoction. Make it the old-fashioned way once, and you'll never reach for the mayo again. • SERVES 8; MAY BE HALVED OR DOUBLED

---

16 slices smoked, thick-cut bacon

1 large red onion, sliced about ¼ inch thick

Olive oil

Salt and freshly ground black pepper

24 wide slices (⅓-inch-thick) of sourdough, potato, or other fluffy bread, crusts removed if desired

⅔ cup Smoked Paprika Mayo (page 87), or store-bought mayonnaise

4 small, ripe tomatoes, cored and sliced ¼ inch thick

2 ripe avocados, pitted and thinly sliced

About 24 large basil leaves

1½ pounds thinly sliced smoked turkey

Classic Slaw (recipe follows)

In a skillet over medium heat, cook the bacon until crisp and brown, 5 to 7 minutes. Drain on paper towels.

Preheat a broiler, outdoor grill, or a cast-iron griddle pan to medium heat.

Brush the onion slices lightly with a little oil, season lightly with salt and pepper, and broil or grill until charred and softened. Set aside.

Toast the bread slices until pale golden on both sides, turning over once; let cool slightly. Keep 8 slices aside.

Working with 16 slices of bread, spread each slice with some mayo, then top 8 of the slices with sliced tomatoes and top the other 8 with sliced avocado. Season lightly with salt and pepper. Place a layer of bacon on top of the tomatoes, and a layer of grilled onions and basil leaves on top of the avocado. Divide the smoked turkey among the 16 pieces of bread. Stack the onion- and basil-topped slices on top of the bacon-topped slices, filling upward. Top each stack with a final slice of bread, then press down firmly with the palm of your hand to compact, and slice in half on the diagonal. Secure each half with a toothpick, and serve with a big spoonful of slaw on the side.

CLASSIC SLAW

2 teaspoons flour

Scant 2 teaspoons dry mustard powder

¼ cup sugar

Pinch of cayenne pepper

Salt

⅔ cup apple cider vinegar

⅔ cup heavy cream

2 large egg yolks

1½ tablespoons poppy seeds

1½ tablespoons prepared horseradish

1½ pounds white cabbage, core and tough outer leaves removed, very finely sliced

2 medium carrots, grated

In the top of a double boiler (off the heat), combine the flour, mustard powder, sugar, cayenne pepper, and 1 generous teaspoon salt and whisk together to blend.

In a small saucepan, combine the vinegar and the cream and bring to a boil over high heat. Whisk the hot vinegar mixture into the dry ingredients, then place the double-boiler insert over a pan of simmering water. Whisk in the egg yolks and stir the mixture until it thickens slightly, 3 to 4 minutes. Remove from the heat and stir in the poppy seeds and horseradish. Cool to room temperature, cover, and refrigerate until chilled.

In a large serving bowl, combine the white cabbage and carrots. Add the dressing and toss until well mixed. Taste for seasoning and serve at once, or refrigerate, covered, for up to 2 days. • SERVES 8

DÉCOR TIDBIT

Each year, Tavern buys three thousand dinner plates to replace those lost, chipped, or stolen. Every week, two hundred glasses and two hundred to three hundred pieces of silverware are replaced.

ROASTED PORK SANDWICH
WITH BLUE CHEESE AND CRANBERRY-PEAR CHUTNEY,
FOR A CROWD

*M*ake this sandwich with leftover roasted pork or purchased roasted pork from your deli. If you're hosting a crowd, make our Brined and Roasted Loin of Pork (page 188) exclusively for creating these tall and impressive sandwiches.

The chutney recipe yields three cups, so if you double the sandwich recipe, there's no need to increase the amount of chutney. You can substitute any rustic bread that's about eight by three inches for the focaccia; each pound of bread should yield about twelve large slices. • SERVES 6; MAY BE DOUBLED OR TRIPLED

---

6 squares of plain focaccia bread, each about 3½ by 3½ inches

1½ cups Cranberry-Pear Chutney (recipe follows)

1¼ to 1½ pounds roasted pork, thinly sliced

8 ounces firm domestic blue cheese, sliced

1½ cups loosely packed watercress, tough stems removed

Split the focaccia squares horizontally. Lay the bottom 6 slices on the counter and spread about ¼ cup of the chutney on each one. Top with some of the sliced pork, then top the pork with slices of blue cheese. Loosely top each one with about ¼ cup watercress leaves and cap with the remaining slices of focaccia, pressing down gently.

Slice each sandwich in half and skewer each half with a decorative toothpick. Serve immediately, or wrap and transport for a picnic.

CRANBERRY-PEAR CHUTNEY

---

2 large, unripe pears

12 ounces (about 3 cups) fresh or frozen cranberries

1 tablespoon white wine vinegar

¾ cup firmly packed light brown sugar

1 teaspoon ground ginger

Peel, quarter, stem, and core the pears. Cut each quarter into 4 thin wedges, then chop fine. In a large, heavy, nonreactive saucepan, combine the pears, cranberries, and vinegar. Cook over low heat, stirring frequently, until the cranberries burst, about 15 minutes.

Remove from the heat and add the brown sugar, stirring until it has dissolved. Add the ginger and return the pan to the heat. Cook, stirring frequently, until the mixture is deep scarlet and very thick, about 10 more minutes.

Cool to room temperature, cover, and refrigerate for up to five days. • MAKES 3 CUPS

A Day in the Life of Tavern

4:00 A.M.   The housekeeping team starts cleaning every nook and cranny of the landmark building. Carpets are vacuumed (or shampooed, depending on what day it is in the cleaning rotation), the copper and brass fixtures are buffed, the mirrors and windows are washed and the chandeliers, valued in excess of $10 million, are polished.

5:00 A.M.   The receiving crew arrives to organize the 4,000 square feet of walk-in coolers in preparation for the delivery of thousands of pounds of beef, fish, chicken, produce, etc., from more than fifty suppliers.

    The morning prep sous chef fires up the steam kettles in which the day's stocks, soups, and sauces will be made. Meanwhile, the rest of the prep crew begins cutting, clipping, peeling, and cleaning hundreds of pounds of potatoes, haricots verts, onions, asparagus, and other fresh ingredients that will be utilized over the next seventeen to twenty hours.

6:00 A.M.   The horticulture team arrives to prune, water, plant, and spruce up the more than 22,000 square feet of grounds surrounding the building.

    A maintenance crew of three to fifteen, depending on the season, arrives. They will tend to either the more than ten miles of tiny white lights wrapped around the limbs of Tavern's elegant London plane trees or the three-hundred-plus chintz-covered Japanese lanterns that hang in their branches. They also paint, stain, adjust, or repair the furnishings, wood paneling, doors, and window frames, addressing all of the constant wear and tear on the 140-year-old building.

6:30 A.M.   The chef whose sole responsibility it is to make the two daily family (staff) meals arrives to begin cooking.

7:00 A.M.   The morning brigade of sous chefs and cooks, some twenty-five in all, set up their stations—pasta, broiler, fish, hot appetizers, sauté, bread and coffee, dessert, garde-manger (cold appetizers, salads, and sandwiches), butcher, banquet, and pastry.

7:30 A.M.   The executive pastry chef and four of eight pastry culinarians arrive to fashion the day's desserts. All sweet goods served at Tavern are house-made, requiring at least a case each of walnuts, pecans, and pistachios, as well as twenty cases of chocolate, a week.

The wine director begins a day that will include placing orders with at least six vendors, educating waitstaff about which wines to suggest with which dish, attending wine tastings throughout the city, planning wine-related events at Tavern, and creating seasonal cocktail menus.

8:00 A.M.   Ten to twelve dishwashers and porters begin polishing all the china, glass, and silver. Meanwhile, the executive steward inspects the kitchen, checking to make sure the previous night's crew left it spic and span; he then reviews the inventory of kitchen supplies and service equipment.

The purchasing director arrives to examine the daily receiving log, before preparing his orders for the day. He updates the multiple bids from Tavern's more than seventy food vendors; from these, he will purchase $50,000 worth of goods.

8:30 A.M.   The reservationists take their places in the second floor call center. Their first order of business is to organize the paperwork associated with VIP guest reservations, cake orders, and travel/theater package vouchers. By 9:00, calls will begin streaming in—as many as two thousand a day, despite an online reservations system that handles about 20 percent of Tavern's reservations.

Downstairs, the in-house florist opens his workshop. He methodically replaces any damaged flowers in the several magnificent displays throughout the restaurant. Meanwhile his staff starts preparing centerpieces and other décor elements contracted for the day's events.

Before the chief operating officer settles in for a day of dealing with financial, branding, and future expansion issues at Tavern's corporate offices (located a block away from the restaurant), he takes a tour of the property, inquiring with staff members about any operational or personnel concerns they may have.

9:00 A.M.   The general manager and catering director take their morning walks through the premises, as a precursor to drafting their daily to-do lists. The GM assesses the staff's progress with their preparations for the day and checking on even the most minute details, like ensuring all the more than 50,000 lightbulbs are working. The catering director surveys the private dining rooms to make sure they are properly set for the day's bookings, before hitting the phones to finalize plans on more of the 800 events he oversees each year.

The private dining sales team joins their boss on the phones contacting current clients to review details of upcoming events, as well as soliciting potential new clients.

10:00 A.M.   The executive chef walks the 13,000-square-foot kitchen, inspecting each station and working with the sous chefs and cooks to assess the best presentations for the day's specials and the private event menus. Then he turns to scheduling, payroll, and menus.

Restaurant floor managers, front desk, host, bar, waitstaff, and banquet waitstaff report for duty. The floor managers determine what dining rooms they will open and prepare them for guests; they also collect the day's contracts for large groups and paperwork for special orders and VIP reservations.

The Tavern Store manager and staff work on displays, review inventory, and stock new merchandise.

First staff meal of the day.

Jennifer checks in for one of two daily conference calls with chief operating officer, general manager, and catering director, often sharing observations about operational issues and food from a recent meal.

10:30 A.M.   The three dining room hostesses and two front desk greeters take their places, while the liveried doorman assumes his post at the brass-handled double doors.

11:00 A.M.   The floor managers gather the waitstaff in one of the dining rooms for roll call.

11:30 A.M.   Doors open for lunch. Tavern Store opens for business.

11:40 A.M.   The first order, deployed from a captain in the dining room via computer, spits out of the printer mounted in the kitchen. The orders dribble in at first, but they very quickly come in droves. The kitchen kicks into gear and is firing on all cylinders by 12:30 with the expediter—sometimes the executive chef—orchestrating the flow of preparation at each station, so that all orders for a single table are ready at the same time.

12:00 NOON	The general manager strolls through the dining rooms to make sure service standards are being upheld. He stops to chat with regular diners or to meet clients being entertained by the sales managers.
12:30 P.M.	The director of catering conducts a tasting with clients to evaluate suggested menu items for an upcoming event.
2:30–3:30 P.M.	During this relative "down" period, weekly managers, banquet event orders, and sales meetings generally take place. It is also prime time for the executive chef's ongoing series of tastings of new dishes with Jennifer, the general manager, and the chief operating officer.
3:00 P.M.	Last diners for lunch are seated. As the day cooks begin to leave, the night crew trickles in. By 4:00 P.M., the kitchen will be fully turned over to the night crew, who will repeat the tasks of their predecessors.
	Porters begin turning rooms for the evening set-up.
3:30 P.M.	Evening banquet waitstaff arrive to set tables, bars, and buffets for the evening's events.
	Jennifer conducts the second conference call of the day.
4:00 P.M.	The day reservationists pass the phones over to their evening counterparts, who will take calls until 10:00 P.M.
	The night bartenders and doorman arrive.
	Second staff meal of the day.
4:30 P.M.	Dinner waitstaff gather for roll call, at which a sous chef explains the evening's specials while the wine director makes pairing suggestions for these dishes.
5:00 P.M.	Dinner service begins.
5:05 P.M.	First dinner order shoots out of the printer; tickets continue to flood the kitchen until 11:00 P.M. (midnight during the holidays). On an average night, the kitchen will serve 800 dinners (up to 2,500 during the holidays).
6:00 P.M.	First of the private functions begins. Sales managers and banquet staff station themselves in lobby and hallways to direct guests.

7:00 P.M.   During the summer, a DJ cranks up the sound system in the garden for dancing. There is a different musical theme every night.

8:00 P.M.   The night kitchen cleaning crews arrives for their eight-hour shift, during which they will mop, scrub, wash, and steam every inch of the facility, including the walk-ins.

11:00 P.M.   The last order hits the kitchen. Cooks clean their stations. The store's lights are turned off (the store itself closed when the last diner was seated).

11:30 P.M.   Ten overnight porters arrive to move furniture to accommodate the next day's set-ups.

CHILLED ROMAINE
WITH A PARMESAN TUILE AND
WHITE ANCHOVY DRESSING

*T*avern's holiday lunch menu always features a version of this variation on the Caesar salad. If you're short on time, you can float a few wide, thinly shaved planks of Parmesan atop the greens rather than making the Parmesan tuile (*tuile* is the French term; in Italy, these crisps are called *frico*).

Avoid using pre-grated Parmesan; it's way too dry. Instead, use the best-quality Parmigiano you can find. Taking the time to wash and chill the romaine makes the difference between a mundane and a show-stopping salad; this step makes the lettuce beautifully crisp. If you know your guest well, eat the deliciously salty leaves of romaine with your fingers, the way California's food elite do. ◆ SERVES 2

PARMESAN TUILES

Olive or vegetable oil, for preparing the pan

¼ cup coarsely grated Parmigiano-Reggiano or other *grana padana* cheese, firmly packed (1 to 1½ ounces)

SALAD

2 to 3 hearts of romaine lettuce, very small and pale inner leaves only

Salt and freshly ground black pepper

1 tablespoon egg yolk (half a large egg yolk)

2 garlic cloves, very finely chopped or pushed through a press

4 marinated white anchovies (*boquerones*; see Note)

1½ teaspoons Dijon mustard

1½ tablespoons fresh lemon juice

½ teaspoon Worcestershire sauce

½ teaspoon red wine vinegar

½ cup extra-virgin olive oil

½ cup finely grated Parmigiano-Reggiano or other *grana padana* cheese (about 2 ounces)

FOR PARMESAN TUILES

Preheat the oven to 350°F (do not use the convection feature).

Lightly oil a nonstick baking sheet. Using half the coarsely grated cheese, make a circle about 4 inches in diameter. Pat and spread the cheese gently into a thin, even layer—there will be a few tiny gaps, but they'll fill in when the cheese melts. Make a second circle in the same way and bake the tuiles for 4 to 5 minutes, until bubbling, lacy, and still pale. Do not overcook, or the tuiles will be bitter and brittle. Remove from the oven and let stand for 1 minute, then loosen the edges with a nonstick spatula and transfer gently to a paper towel to harden and remove the excess oil. The tuiles will keep in an airtight container for up to 5 days.

FOR THE SALAD

Chill 2 plates in the refrigerator. Rinse the romaine leaves by immersing in cool water. Drain well and spin dry *thoroughly.* Wrap loosely in a clean kitchen towel and refrigerate for at least 20 minutes, for ultimate crispness.

In a mini-prep or food processor, combine ½ teaspoon salt, a generous grinding of pepper, the egg yolk, garlic, white anchovies, mustard, lemon juice, Worcestershire, vinegar, and oil. Process until completely smooth, about 20 seconds.

In a large bowl, combine the whole romaine leaves and the dressing and toss until evenly coated. Add the Parmigiano and a generous grinding of pepper, and toss again. Divide the leaves between the chilled plates and top each salad with a Parmesan tuile. Serve at once.

NOTE · **If you can't find the lusciously mild and juicy white anchovies known as *boquerones*— often available in Italian markets and at good deli counters—substitute two oil- or salt-packed anchovies, gently rinsed, patted dry with a paper towel, and finely chopped.**

A FAVORITE DESTINATION
FOR ROCKERS

Tavern has been the place of choice for rock and pop stars since it first opened. We've been fortunate to host some of the biggest names in music, including Mick Jagger, Elton John, Mariah Carey, and Cyndi Lauper. One of our favorite moments was when Jon Bon Jovi, who came for a great party, silenced the room with an amazing rendition of the Simon and Garfunkel ballad "Bridge over Troubled Water."

9

BRUNCH

BREAKFAST BERRY STRATA

*T*his strata has a nice, light sweetness, perfect for breakfast or brunch. There's really no way to hurry the drying of the brioche by putting it in the oven; it has a tendency to dry out so much that it will not absorb the custard. If you can buy stale brioche or if you have some left over from another gathering, skip the overnight drying step. • SERVES 8 • *photograph on page 220*

One 8-inch loaf of brioche or other rich egg
    bread such as challah, crusts trimmed,
    cut into ½-inch chunks (about 1 pound)

3 large eggs

2 large egg yolks

¼ cup Baker's, or superfine, sugar

1¼ cups whole milk

⅔ cup heavy cream

2 teaspoons best-quality vanilla extract

Finely grated zest of 1 scrubbed lemon
    (see Note, page 41)

Softened butter, for greasing the baking dish

1½ pounds assorted whole berries such as
    blueberries, blackberries, raspberries,
    or halved strawberries

½ cup slivered, blanched almonds

Confectioners' sugar, for serving

Spread the chunks of brioche on a large baking sheet and leave at room temperature overnight to dry out.

In a large bowl, thoroughly whisk together the eggs and egg yolks, sugar, milk, cream, vanilla, and lemon zest. Stir in the brioche chunks and turn several times to coat. Place a small plate over the top and put a large, heavy can on the plate to weight it down, so the brioche stays submerged; let soak for 45 minutes, stirring again once or twice.

Preheat the oven to 350°F.

Place the rack in the center of the oven; place a large baking sheet on the rack, to catch the berry juices. Use the softened butter to thoroughly grease a 9 x 9-inch or similar-size earthenware, ceramic, or glass baking dish.

Stir the berries into the brioche-custard mixture until evenly distributed, reserving a few of the more attractive ones. Spoon the mixture into the prepared dish. Scatter the almonds over the top, place the dish on the baking sheet, and bake for about 1 hour, until the custard is set in the center and the top is golden brown (poke with a spoon to be sure no uncooked custard comes bubbling up).

Serve warm or, if serving within 2 hours, let the strata stand at room temperature until serving time. If desired, reheat in a 325°F oven for 10 minutes. Garnish with the reserved berries.

HOMEMADE MUESLI
WITH WARM FRUIT SALAD

The Swiss are very exact about many things, such as clocks, train schedules, and confidentiality. So naturally, the Swiss national breakfast, muesli, has been refined to perfection.

Note that the mixture must be started the night before you plan to serve. For the fruit salad, choose a combination of any of the following: strawberries, raspberries, pears, plums, figs, apples, blueberries, and rhubarb. • MAKES 1½ QUARTS

MUESLI

4 medium Granny Smith apples

Juice of ½ lemon

2 cups rolled or old-fashioned oats

½ cup shelled sunflower seeds

2 cups whole milk, at room temperature

Scant ¼ cup honey

¼ cup coarsely chopped hazelnuts

Tiny pinch of salt

¼ cup raisins

FRUIT SALAD

2 cups ripe fruit (see headnote), cut into approximately 1½-inch slices or chunks

2 tablespoons water, wine, or Champagne

1 to 2 tablespoons sugar

Juice of ½ lemon

Peel, quarter, and core the apples the night before you plan to serve. Grate them into a very large bowl or airtight container, and sprinkle with the lemon juice. Add the oats, sunflower seeds, milk, honey, hazelnuts, salt, and raisins. Toss until all the ingredients are evenly moistened. Cover and refrigerate overnight.

For the fruit salad, in a medium nonreactive saucepan, combine the fruit, water, sugar to taste, and lemon juice. Simmer over very low heat, stirring occasionally, for about 10 minutes, until slightly softened and soupy. If any foam rises to the top, remove it with a spoon. Cover and set aside at the back of the stove until serving time.

Serve the muesli straight from the refrigerator, topped with the warm fruit salad.

POTATO LATKES
WITH CHIVE CRÈME FRAÎCHE

Latkes are synonymous with the celebration of Hanukkah, but here in New York we enjoy them year-round. In the traditional Jewish kitchen, latkes are fried in schmaltz, also known as chicken fat. If you have access to schmaltz, by all means substitute it for the canola oil.

Purists prefer their latkes unadorned, so serve them on a platter with the crème fraîche and applesauce in separate vessels. • MAKES ABOUT FORTY 4-INCH LATKES; MAY BE HALVED

---

5 large russet potatoes, about 3 pounds, peeled

2 medium white onions

2 large eggs, lightly beaten

¼ cup matzoh meal or panko

Salt and freshly ground white pepper

2 teaspoons baking powder

Canola oil or schmaltz

Chive Crème Fraîche (recipe follows)

24 ounces chunky applesauce (optional)

Place a large saucepan of water on to boil over high heat. Using the largest holes of a box grater, grate the potatoes and onions into a small-holed colander. As soon as the water boils, pour it slowly over the vegetables (this will partially cook them and stop the potatoes from turning gray).

When cool enough to handle, squeeze out some of the excess liquid and transfer the vegetables to the center of a large, clean kitchen towel. Bring up the corners, twist the towel firmly, and wring out as much liquid as you can; set aside.

In a large bowl, combine the eggs, matzoh meal, 2 teaspoons salt, about ½ teaspoon white pepper, and the baking powder. Add the potatoes and onions and mix together thoroughly.

Place 2 paper-towel–lined platters in a very low oven to warm.

Place a large skillet over medium-high heat and add canola oil to a depth of a little more than ⅛ inch. When the oil is hot but not smoking, drop the mixture by very generous tablespoonfuls into the pan. Quickly flatten the latkes slightly, using a spatula, and cook for 4 to 5 minutes, until crisp and golden brown, turning over once about halfway through the cooking time.

Transfer the finished latkes to the platters in the oven and continue making latkes until you have used all the mixture, adding more oil as necessary and adjusting the heat so the latkes sizzle but don't burn. Remove the paper towels from the platter and serve the latkes warm, with the chive crème fraîche and, if desired, the chunky applesauce on the side.

CHIVE CRÈME FRAÎCHE

1¼ cups (10 ounces) crème fraîche

⅜ teaspoon salt

⅛ teaspoon freshly ground white pepper

¼ cup very finely snipped chives

In a serving bowl, whisk all the ingredients together. If desired, cover with plastic wrap and refrigerate overnight, so the flavors have a chance to marry. Wipe the edges of the bowl clean, and place on the table with the latkes. •

MAKES 1¼ CUPS

WHAT'S THAT IN TONS?

Tavern's menu has changed over the years with the arrival of new chefs, but some dishes, such as Warner's beloved mashed potatoes, are as synonymous with the restaurant as is its Central Park location. No chef would risk customer revolt by taking such classics as prime rib, jumbo shrimp cocktail, or lobster bisque off the menu. To satisfy demand for these and other traditional dishes, Tavern brings in an extraordinary amount of essential ingredients every year. Here's a list of some of the most impressive annual tallies:

Yukon gold potatoes	141,000 pounds
Chicken breast	75,000 pounds
Filet mignon	70,000 pounds
Beef ribeye	65,000 pounds
Haricots verts	32,000 pounds
Jumbo shrimp	15,000 pounds
Jumbo lump crabmeat	12,500 pounds
Strawberries	12,000 pounds
Lobsters	10,000 pounds
Eggs	39,000 dozen (that's 468,000 eggs)

GOAT CHEESE AND
SOUR CHERRY BLINTZES

*I*f you have a crowd for breakfast or brunch, blintzes are a great choice. These are also terrific for an easy after-theater snack, accompanied by lots of good Champagne. Except for the final browning in butter, the filled blintzes can be assembled the night before. • MAKES ABOUT 18 BLINTZES, SERVES 4 TO 6; MAY BE DOUBLED

CREPES

4 large eggs, at room temperature

1 cup whole milk

⅛ teaspoon salt

2 tablespoons unsalted butter, melted

1 cup flour

Melted butter or canola oil

FILLING

8 ounces cream cheese, at room temperature

11 ounces plain fresh goat cheese or farmer cheese, at room temperature

¼ cup sugar

1 large egg

1 teaspoon fresh lemon juice

½ teaspoon best-quality vanilla extract

¼ teaspoon ground cinnamon

2 cups sour cherries in water or syrup, drained and halved

TO FINISH AND SERVE

3 to 4 tablespoons butter

Confectioners' sugar

Ground cinnamon

In a blender, combine the eggs, milk, salt, 2 tablespoons melted butter, and flour. Blend for 10 seconds, then turn off the machine and scrape down the sides with a rubber spatula. Blend for 20 seconds more.

Place a 6-inch crepe pan or a small nonstick skillet over medium heat and brush with a thin film of butter or oil. When the pan is hot, pour in 2 tablespoons of batter (ideally using a 1-ounce ladle so you can work quickly). Immediately swirl the pan to coat the base with a thin film of batter. Cook for about 45 seconds, until the bottom is golden, the top is just set, and the edges of the crepe have begun to come away from the pan. Lift the crepe onto a plate, browned side down (do not flip and cook the other side). Continue making crepes, brushing the pan with a little more butter or oil between each one. You will have about 18 crepes.

In a large bowl, combine the cream cheese, goat cheese, sugar, egg, lemon juice, vanilla, and cinnamon. Whisk with a fork until smooth. Fold in half of the cherries.

Line a large, rimmed baking sheet with parchment paper. Place a crepe in front of you, *browned side up*, and place 2 generous tablespoons of filling in the center. Fold the two outer edges of the crepe in toward the center so that they meet over the filling. Pat gently to flatten slightly. Roll into cylinders and place on the prepared baking sheet. Alternatively, fold the top and bottom in to meet in the center, and place, seam side down, on the baking sheet. Continue making blintzes in the same way.

Either proceed to cooking immediately or cover snugly with plastic wrap and refrigerate overnight (bring to room temperature for 10 minutes before cooking).

Place a large platter in a very low oven to warm.

Place a large skillet over medium-low heat and add 1 tablespoon of the butter. When the butter foams, add 4 or 5 blintzes, seam side down (do not crowd the pan). Sauté for about 5 minutes, until golden. Carefully turn and cook the other side until golden. Transfer to the warm platter in the oven, and cover loosely with aluminum foil while you cook the remaining blintzes, adding more butter as necessary. When all of the blintzes are cooked, scatter the remaining cherries around the edges and, using a sieve, dust the tops of the blintzes with a little confectioners' sugar and cinnamon.

I Do!

*T*avern witnesses more marriage proposals than any other restaurant in the city, averaging at least three each day—and not all of them are accepted! So far we have never lost a ring, nor has anyone swallowed one nestled in a specially ordered dessert or flirting with the bubbles in a Champagne glass. Each year, the restaurant hosts, or, more accurately, produces three hundred wedding receptions, half of which follow onsite ceremonies. We've shared the special day with wedding parties of as few as ten people and as many as two thousand.

Of course, Tavern has enjoyed its share of celebrity weddings, including those of Jaclyn Smith and Dennis Cole (unfortunately it ended in divorce), and Lori Loughlin of the 1990s hit TV sitcom *Full House*. Upon being seated in the Crystal Room for lunch one day, actor Michael Nouri told the captain that he had been married there "a few times, once for real and a couple of times for the camera." Comedian Jeff Foxworthy and his bride, Gregg, said their vows in Central Park, nabbing the groundskeeper to be their witness, and held their reception—a celebratory lunch for two—at Tavern.

Among my fondest childhood memories of visits to Tavern are those days when weddings took place. I would be completely enchanted by the magical setting and by the brides themselves. Never more so than at my sister Carolyn's January 2001 nuptials. After months of planning, the Crystal Room was transformed into a winter wonderland. In a somewhat rare moment of affirmation, my father confided that the room had never looked so good. Working with an apt theme of crystal and candlelight, the ceremony took place under a chuppa festooned with votive candles. While guests—among them Lauren Bacall, Candace Bergen, and Nora Ephron—attended a cocktail reception in the Terrace and Rafters rooms, the Crystal Room was being converted for dinner and dancing, a process that involved the lighting of some two thousand candles. The effect went from spectacular to beyond belief when the centerpieces erupted with fireworks!

My big sister looked like a princess out of one of the fairy tales we loved as children. She walked down an aisle strewn with yellow rose petals to symbolize the Yellow Brick Road, a tribute to our grandfather, Mervyn LeRoy. Under her elaborate silver-embroidered white gown, Carolyn wore sneakers I had decorated with Swarovski crystals, my take on Dorothy's ruby red slippers!

—Jennifer Oz LeRoy

229

Gone Hollywood

A pundit once wrote, "If Oz had a restaurant, this would be it." Indeed, Tavern's movie-set style wasn't lost on Tinseltown. It seems that whenever a film involves a wedding, Tavern's romantic rooms are on the shortlist of locations. It's where Jack Nicholson and Meryl Streep tied the knot in *Heartburn* and Michael Douglas and Jill Clayburgh wed in *It's My Turn*, just to name a few.

The restaurant is featured in more than fifteen films, in some of the most memorable scenes in each. Remember the *Ghostbusters* chase through our Crystal Garden? And the deer-in-the-headlights look on the faces of Goldie Hawn and Steve Martin in *The Out-of-Towners*, when the lights of Tavern's gardens and those in the Crystal Room shone on their amorous moment in the park?

Here are some of the other films that have taken advantage of Tavern's star power:

Arthur (1981) with Dudley Moore, Liza Minnelli, and John Gielgud

Only When I Laugh (1981) with Marsha Mason and Kristy McNichol

Wall Street (1987) with Michael Douglas and Charlie Sheen

Beaches (1988) with Barbara Hershey and Bette Midler

Arthur 2: On the Rocks (1988) with Dudley Moore, Liza Minnelli, and John Gielgud

New York Stories: Oedipus Wrecks (1989) with Woody Allen, Mia Farrow, and
    Julie Kavner

Crimes and Misdemeanors (1989) with Woody Allen, Mia Farrow, and Martin Landau

Stella (1990) with Bette Midler and John Goodman

Whispers in the Dark (1992) with Annabella Sciorra and Jamey Sheridan

The Night We Never Met (1993) with Matthew Broderick and Jeanne Tripplehorn

It Had to Be You (2000) with Natasha Henstridge and Michael Vartan

Hall of Mirrors (2001) with Eric Johnson and Julie Arebalo

Made (2001) with Vince Vaughn, Sean Combs, and Jon Favreau

Alfie (2004) with Jude Law, Renee Taylor, and Jane Krakowski

New York, I Love You (2008) with Natalie Portman, Shia LaBeouf, and James Caan

CREAMY EGGS
WITH SMOKED SALMON AND CAVIAR

With just a few top-quality ingredients at your fingertips, you can make this rich, decadent, and delicious brunch dish. It's also colorful and festive, so it will impress your weekend guests. • SERVES 4

8 large eggs, preferably very fresh

1 cup heavy cream

Salt

1 tablespoon butter

4 ounces thinly sliced smoked salmon

1 ounce imported or domestic caviar

1 tablespoon finely snipped chives

In a bowl, whisk together the eggs, cream, and ¾ teaspoon salt until very smooth.

Place a large nonstick skillet over high heat and add the butter. When the butter has melted and the foam has begun to subside, tilt the pan to distribute the butter evenly. Pour all the egg mixture into the pan and let the eggs cook undisturbed for 30 seconds. Stir gently with a wooden spoon, bringing the partially cooked edges in toward the center. Let stand for 30 seconds more, then stir again. Remove the pan from the heat and let stand for 1 minute more, then stir gently again.

Lay out a quarter of the smoked salmon in an even layer on each of 4 plates. Spoon one quarter of the scrambled eggs in a fairly even layer over the salmon slices. Dollop small spoonfuls of the caviar evenly over the eggs, scatter with the chives, and serve at once.

A NOTE ON EGGS

For dishes in which eggs star, such as deviled eggs, soufflés, emulsified sauces like hollandaise or aioli, and, of course, omelets, choosing cage-free or Omega-3–enriched eggs will lend a deeper yellow color and enhanced flavor to the finished result.

CHICKEN HASH
WITH SAUSAGE, MUSHROOMS, AND BASIL

*A*n absolutely delicious and supremely satisfying dish to serve after a nice long walk in Central Park. Throw it together with a group of friends, assigning the dicing, sautéing, and egg-poaching diplomatically (throw in a Classic Bloody Mary [page 29] or two, and no one will say no). Of course, if you have leftover roasted chicken, perhaps from dinner the night before, there is no need to roast the chicken legs. • SERVES 6

4 chicken leg-and-thigh pieces

Salt and freshly ground black pepper

2 large or 3 medium potatoes

½ cup canola or vegetable oil

1 yellow onion, cut into ¼-inch dice

1 small yellow bell pepper, cored, seeded, and cut into ½-inch dice

1 small red bell pepper, cored, seeded, and cut into ½-inch dice

3 cups small, firm, white button mushrooms (about 8 ounces), brushed clean and sliced ¼ inch thick

8 to 10 ounces fresh chicken or pork sausage, casings removed

15 large basil leaves, julienned

6 large or extra-large fresh eggs, poached to your liking (see Note)

Preheat the oven to 350°F.

Rinse the chicken legs and pat them dry thoroughly with paper towels; season generously with salt and pepper and place on a rack in a roasting pan. Roast for about 45 minutes, or until the juices from the thigh run clear. Cool on the rack and, when cool enough to handle, discard the skin and shred the meat, making sure to remove all the bones and cartilage. Set aside.

Peel the potatoes and cut them into ¼-inch dice (as you cut the potatoes, put them in a bowl of cold water so they will not discolor).

Heat a very large skillet over medium-low heat and add 2 tablespoons of the canola oil. Sauté the onion for 3 to 4 minutes, until slightly softened; add the bell peppers and the mushrooms. Cook for 4 to 5 minutes, until all the vegetables are softened but not mushy. Transfer the vegetables to a large bowl and set aside.

Wipe out the skillet with a paper towel. Add another 2 tablespoons of the oil to the pan and warm over medium heat. Add the sausage and cook, breaking up into small pieces with a wooden spoon, until browned and no longer pink. Add the sausage to the vegetable mixture, and again wipe out the pan.

Drain the potatoes well and pat them dry with a clean kitchen towel. Heat the same skillet over medium-high heat and add the remaining ¼ cup oil. When it is hot, sauté the potatoes, turning them over occasionally with a flat-ended metal spatula, until they are tender but not mushy, about 5 minutes. Add the vegetable-and-sausage mixture and the chicken to the potatoes and toss together gently over low heat until heated through. Add the basil, ¾ teaspoon salt, and pepper to taste. Remove the pan from the heat and set aside, covered, at the back of the stove while you poach the eggs.

To serve, make a generous mound of hash in the bottom of 6 large, warmed bowls; flatten the top of the hash slightly with the back of a spoon. Top each with a poached egg.

NOTE · **Poach eggs for 3 to 3½ minutes for a runny yolk, 5 to 6 minutes for a set yolk; for more detailed instructions, see below.**

HOW TO POACH EGGS

In a large sauté pan with high sides and a tight-fitting lid, bring a generous amount of water to a rolling boil and add ½ teaspoon of white vinegar. Turn off the heat and immediately break the eggs (a maximum of 4) gently just above the surface of the still-just-slightly-shivering water. Quickly cover the pan and leave undisturbed for about 3 minutes if you like the yolk runny, 5 minutes for a set yolk.

10

SIDES

SQUASH CRISP

Not a Thanksgiving passes at Tavern without an inventive squash dish on the menu. This one stands out as one of the most satisfying, if somewhat unconventional. Crystallized, or candied, ginger is added to the bread-crumb-and-cheese topping to lend a welcome bright note. Almonds add that ever-important crunch.

• SERVES 8 TO 10 • *photograph on page 240*

Softened butter, for greasing the baking dish

4 to 5 acorn squash or 2 butternut squash (about 4 pounds total)

Salt and freshly ground black pepper

About ½ cup grated Parmigiano-Reggiano or other *grana padana* cheese

About ½ cup heavy cream

TOPPING

½ cup unseasoned dry bread crumbs or panko

¼ cup coarsely chopped crystallized ginger

½ cup grated Parmigiano-Reggiano or other *grana padana* cheese

½ cup coarsely chopped blanched almonds

Salt

4 tablespoons (½ stick) unsalted butter, melted

Preheat the oven to 350°F.

Generously grease a 2- to 3-quart, 14 x 9-inch earthenware, ceramic, or glass baking dish or gratin with the butter.

Halve the squash lengthwise and scoop out the seeds and fibers. Halve the halves again lengthwise. Peel the quarters with a sharp vegetable peeler; slice the quarters crosswise about ⅛ inch thick. Layer the slices in the baking dish, overlapping slightly and seasoning each layer with about ⅛ teaspoon salt, a few grindings of pepper, a tablespoon or so of the Parmigiano, and about 1 tablespoon of the cream. Press down slightly to compact the layers and cover the dish with aluminum foil. Bake for about 1 hour 15 minutes, until the squash is tender.

In a large bowl, combine the bread crumbs, ginger, Parmigiano, almonds, and ½ teaspoon salt; toss until blended. Add the melted butter and use a fork to blend the mixture until evenly moistened with the butter.

Remove the foil and scatter the topping mixture over the gratin in an even layer. Return, uncovered, to the oven for 10 to 12 more minutes, until the top is browned. Let stand for about 15 minutes to firm slightly before serving.

COMFORTING MASHED POTATOES

*M*ore than seventy tons of Yukon Gold potatoes pass through Tavern's kitchen each year, and most of them are used to make these, a hands-down favorite of Warner's. They are, quite simply, the very best mashed potatoes on the planet. The secret is pushing the cooked potatoes through a food mill or ricer. Also, using an electric stand mixer makes it easy to keep the potatoes warm and frees up your hands for a few extra chores while they whip. A perfect mash is unavoidably a last-minute job, but the results make it worth delegating other pressing preparations to a helper.

✦ SERVES 8

1½ pounds Idaho or other russet potatoes, peeled and cut into 1-inch chunks

1½ pounds Yukon Gold or Yellow Finn potatoes, peeled and cut into 1-inch chunks

10 large garlic cloves, peeled

Kosher salt

1¼ cups heavy cream, or as needed

11 tablespoons (5½ ounces; 1⅜ sticks) unsalted butter, at room temperature

Salt and freshly ground white pepper

¼ teaspoon freshly ground nutmeg

Put all the potatoes and the garlic in a large, heavy stockpot or Dutch oven and add enough cold water to cover the ingredients by 2 inches. Place over high heat and bring just to a boil; add 1 tablespoon kosher salt and regulate the heat to maintain a brisk simmer. Cook until the potatoes are easily pierced with the tip of a knife, about 15 minutes.

Warm the bowl of an electric stand mixer fitted with the paddle attachment by filling it with very hot water and letting it stand for about 10 minutes (be sure to pour out the water and dry the bowl before adding the potatoes).

Drain the potatoes and garlic and return them to the original pan. Place over medium heat and shake back and forth for a minute to dry thoroughly. Immediately pass the mixture through the fine disk of a food mill or press through a potato ricer into the completely dried, warm mixer bowl.

In a small saucepan, heat the cream over high heat just until hot (do not allow it to boil). Set the mixer to low speed and begin adding the cream slowly, allowing the potatoes to absorb it gradually. Add just enough cream to give the mixture a soft, mounding consistency, like cream that's been whipped to soft peaks (you may not use all the cream). Add the butter, 1½ teaspoons salt, ½ teaspoon white pepper, and the nutmeg. Continue mixing for 1 to 2 minutes, until fluffy. Taste for seasoning and adjust with salt and pepper if necessary. Serve at once.

CRISPY ROASTED POTATOES,
FOR A CROWD

*T*here may be dozens of roasted potatoes out there, but these are as crisp as it gets. By scoring the cut potatoes before roasting them, you increase the surface area exposed to the high heat, which is the reason behind the extra crunch.

To roast a large amount like this, use two large, rimmed baking sheets and rotate them halfway through the cooking time so that the potatoes cook and crisp evenly. You needn't move them around if using a convection oven. A mix of half bacon fat or strained beef or pork drippings from past cooking and half the olive oil called for below ups the ante just that much more. • SERVES 8 TO 10

---

6 pounds small red potatoes, scrubbed

½ cup pure olive oil

3 tablespoons chopped rosemary (optional)

1½ teaspoons chopped thyme

Salt and freshly ground black pepper

6 large garlic cloves, finely chopped

½ cup grated Parmigiano-Reggiano or other *grana padana* cheese

In a very large steamer—use the pasta insert for your largest pot, if you have one— bring a few inches of water to a boil. Place the potatoes in the steamer, cover, and steam for 20 minutes, keeping the water at an active boil.

Remove the potatoes and, if desired, hold for up to 4 hours at room temperature or overnight in the refrigerator (return to room temperature before finishing the dish).

Preheat the oven to 400°F.

Cut the potatoes in half and use the tines of a fork to lightly score the cut sides. In a large bowl, toss the potatoes with the oil, rosemary (if using), thyme, 1 tablespoon salt, and ½ teaspoon pepper until evenly coated.

Divide the potatoes between 2 large, rimmed baking sheets and roast for 40 to 50 minutes, tossing every 10 minutes or so, until crisp and golden brown.

When the potatoes are done to your liking, mix in the garlic and Parmigiano. Roast for 2 minutes more only, then mound onto a large platter and serve at once.

WARM FINGERLING POTATOES
WITH WHITE WINE–CHIVE SAUCE

*T*here are occasions, such as entertaining the boss or meeting the in-laws, when mashed or roasted potatoes may not seem elegant enough. That's where this delightfully untraditional potato dish comes in. The wine mixture seeps right into the pores of the delicate fingerlings during the cooking time, imbuing them with the fragrance and delicate acidity of the wine. The resulting dish, with its winey-shalloty-buttery "sauce," is light, refreshing, *and* soul satisfying. Yet it's polished and will impress your guests. • SERVES 8; MAY BE HALVED

---

3 pounds fingerling potatoes, scrubbed

3 cups dry white wine

½ cup white wine vinegar

6 shallots, very finely chopped

4 tablespoons (½ stick) unsalted butter

Salt and freshly ground black pepper

¼ cup finely snipped chives

Prick each potato in two places, with a fork. Place the potatoes in a tall, narrow nonreactive saucepan and add the wine, vinegar, shallots, butter, 2 teaspoons salt, and a generous grinding of pepper. Cover the pan and place over medium-high heat; bring to a boil, then reduce the heat to very low so the liquid is barely simmering. Cook for 20 to 25 minutes, until the potatoes are tender but not falling apart.

With a slotted spoon, transfer the potatoes to a shallow serving bowl and keep warm in a very low oven while you reduce the sauce.

Return the pan to high heat, and simmer briskly, uncovered, until the liquid is the consistency of heavy cream, 5 to 8 minutes.

Stir in the chives, drizzle the sauce over the potatoes, and serve.

POTATO–BLUE CHEESE GRATIN

*Y*ou can't really go wrong when you combine potatoes, heavy cream, and cheese. Gratins are a big crowd-pleaser at Tavern on the Green, where they are made with different cheeses at the whim of the chef; Parmesan, Taleggio, and Gruyère are popular.

To prevent the potato slices from browning, assemble everything in the baking dish first before you begin slicing them. Don't rinse the potatoes: Their own starch is what helps to set this luscious casserole. ◆ SERVES 8 TO 10

Softened butter, for greasing the baking dish

3½ cups whole milk

2 cups heavy cream

Ground nutmeg

Salt and freshly ground black pepper

6 garlic cloves, very finely chopped or pushed through a press

4 pounds Yukon Gold potatoes, peeled

6 ounces Maytag or other blue cheese, crumbled

6 ounces Emmentaler cheese, coarsely grated

Preheat the oven to 400°F.

In a large buttered earthenware, ceramic, or glass baking dish (13 x 10 x 2 inches or larger), combine the milk, cream, a pinch or two of nutmeg, 1 teaspoon salt, ½ teaspoon pepper, and the garlic.

Slice the potatoes about ⅛ inch thick, preferably in a food processor fitted with the slicing blade, or with a mandoline (to make the process faster). With clean hands, add the potatoes to the baking dish and mix thoroughly, making sure they are evenly coated.

Cover the dish tightly with aluminum foil and place on a large, rimmed baking sheet to contain any boil-overs. Bake for 1 hour, or until the potatoes are tender when poked with the tip of a sharp knife.

Uncover the dish and reduce the oven to 350°F. Scatter the two cheeses evenly over the top of the potatoes and cook for about 30 minutes more, until the top is bubbling and golden brown.

Remove from the oven and let stand for 15 to 20 minutes before serving, to firm the "custard" slightly. Reheat for 5 to 10 minutes in a low oven, if desired.

ROASTED GREEN BEANS
WITH SIZZLED HAZELNUTS

*I*t takes one prep cook a full eight hours to top and tail enough green beans for a single day of service at Tavern. In fact, the kitchen prepares 32,000 pounds of them each year. Here, the humble bean becomes a party-worthy dish with a splash of orange juice and white wine vinegar and a crown of crunchy hazelnuts. • SERVES 8

2 pounds green beans, ends trimmed if
   necessary

¼ cup pure olive oil

3 sprigs thyme

Salt and freshly ground black pepper

Finely grated zest of 1 scrubbed orange
   (see Note, page 41)

1 tablespoon fresh orange juice

1 teaspoon white wine vinegar or
   Champagne vinegar

3 tablespoons unsalted butter,
   cut into 3 pieces

½ cup chopped hazelnuts

Preheat the oven to 450°F.

On a large rimmed baking sheet, toss the green beans with the oil, thyme, ¾ teaspoon salt, ¼ teaspoon pepper, and half the orange zest, until evenly coated with the oil.

Spread the beans into an even layer and roast for about 15 minutes, tossing halfway through, until tender and slightly browned. Discard the thyme sprigs and drizzle with the orange juice and vinegar.

Mound the beans on a serving platter with a shallow rim, turn off the oven, and place the platter in the oven to keep warm.

Place a small skillet over medium-high heat and add the butter. When the foam has subsided and the butter is beginning to brown, add the hazelnuts and sizzle for 2 to 3 minutes, until the butter is foamy and pale golden brown and the nuts are aromatic. Quickly drizzle the hazelnuts and all the butter over the beans, scatter the remaining orange zest on top, and serve at once.

LEEK AND BROCCOLI BREAD PUDDING

*B*read pudding—sometimes called strata—is a creative American invention that tastily spans both the savory and the sweet. Countless variations are possible, based on the type of bread used and the choice of complementary ingredients and toppings. This creamy, savory version, made with brioche, is a perfect party dish and makes a great addition to a classic Thanksgiving dinner menu. It could easily make an impressive vegetarian main course, or stand alone as a lunch dish, with a lightly dressed green salad on the side. • SERVES 8 TO 10

Kosher salt

6 tablespoons (¾ stick) butter, plus additional, softened, for greasing

1 pound firm, bright green broccoli

2 large leeks, white and light green parts only, sliced ¼ inch thick and well washed

Salt and freshly ground black pepper

¼ cup dry white wine

1 teaspoon thyme leaves

¼ cup finely chopped flat-leaf parsley

1 pound brioche, challah, or other eggy bread, cut into ¾-inch cubes

4 large eggs

2 cups whole milk

2 cups half-and-half

1 cup chicken stock or broth (low-sodium canned is fine)

1 cup coarsely grated aged white Cheddar cheese

Bring a large pot of generously salted water to a boil.

In a small pan, melt 4 tablespoons of the butter.

Trim off the woody ends of the broccoli and cut off the florets. Using a sharp knife, peel off the coarse outer skins from the stalks. Halve the thick stalks lengthwise and cut crosswise into ½-inch-thick slices. Add the broccoli florets and stalks to the boiling water and cook for 5 to 6 minutes, until bright green and crisp-tender. Drain in a colander and run under plenty of cold water until the steam stops rising. Shake the colander gently, turn the broccoli out onto a clean, thick kitchen towel, and let dry for a few minutes. Coarsely chop the broccoli.

In a sauté pan, warm the remaining 2 tablespoons butter over medium-low heat and add the leeks. Season generously with salt and pepper, cover the pan, and cook for 5 minutes, shaking the pan occasionally. Remove the lid and sauté for about 5 minutes more, then add the wine and cook until it has evaporated; stir in the thyme and parsley and set aside.

Preheat the oven to 350°F.

Divide the brioche between 2 large, rimmed baking sheets and drizzle 2 tablespoons of the melted butter over each one. Toss the brioche until evenly coated. Bake for 20 minutes, until the brioche is crisp and golden. Generously grease a 9 x 14-inch earthenware, ceramic, or glass baking or gratin dish with softened butter.

In a large bowl, combine the eggs, milk, half-and-half, and stock. Whisk to combine, then fold in the broccoli and the leek mixture. Season with ½ teaspoon salt and a generous grinding of pepper. Stir in the brioche cubes and turn into the prepared baking dish. Stir to saturate the bread evenly, then let stand for at least 30 minutes and up to 60 minutes, turning the mixture over occasionally to be sure the brioche soaks up the custard mixture.

Preheat or increase the oven to 375°F before baking.

Cover the dish with a sheet of buttered aluminum foil and bake for 1 hour, until the pudding is just set.

Remove the foil, scatter the cheese on top of the pudding, and bake for 20 to 30 minutes, until golden.

Let stand for 10 minutes, then transfer to a buffet and serve.

NOTE · **If desired, you can finish the bread pudding the night before, then cool to room temperature, cover, and refrigerate. Return to room temperature for about an hour, then cover with aluminum foil and reheat in a 350°F oven for about 35 minutes. Remove the foil and re-crisp the top under a broiler before serving.**

A CREATIVE MUSE

With its many intricate details and Warner's dramatic over-the-top design, Tavern on the Green has been a great muse for all sorts of creative types. The famed artist Leroy Neiman has been coming to Tavern for more than twenty-five years. He often sits at a table in the Crystal Room, sketching on a pad throughout his meal. Copies of his painting of our garden are a bestseller at our gift shop.

BRAISED BABY PEAS
IN VERMOUTH BUTTER

*T*his old-fashioned French side dish adds a lovely note of fresh flavor and bright color to the winter table. • SERVES 8 TO 10

2 to 2½ pounds best-quality frozen petits pois

1 tablespoon canola oil

1 ounce prosciutto or ham, finely chopped (optional)

¼ cup vermouth or dry white wine

2 pale inner hearts of Boston lettuce, cored, cut crosswise ½ inch thick, and washed and spun dry

1 garlic clove, very finely chopped or pushed through a press

3 tablespoons finely chopped flat-leaf parsley

Salt and freshly ground black pepper

2 ounces very cold unsalted butter, cut into small pieces

Half-fill a large metal bowl with cold water and add a few cups of ice. Place near the sink.

In a large saucepan of lightly salted boiling water, blanch the peas for 2 minutes (do not overcook). Drain in a colander and immediately transfer to the ice bath. Swirl for 2 minutes, then use a skimmer or slotted spoon to transfer the peas to a clean kitchen towel. Spread them out in a single layer.

Place a large sauté pan over medium heat and add the oil. Add the prosciutto, if using, and sauté for 2 to 3 minutes, stirring occasionally, until slightly crisp. Tip the pan to one side and spoon off about half of the cooking fat. (If not using the prosciutto, or if the ham was very lean, add 2 teaspoons olive oil to the warm pan before adding the peas.)

Add the peas, vermouth, lettuce, garlic, parsley, ½ teaspoon salt, and a few grindings of pepper to the pan. Stir together, cover the pan, and reduce the heat to low. Let simmer gently for 5 minutes, stirring occasionally, until the vegetables are warmed through and the lettuce is wilted.

Remove the pan from the heat and add the cold butter. Swirl the pan back and forth until the butter has just melted into a creamy emulsion. Serve at once.

BRAISED ESCAROLE

*T*his delightfully green "green" is a bright spot on our winter menu when, despite being tasty and comforting, plates of food can be rather monotone. It also requires very little effort to make. What's more, it will maintain its color if you need to reheat it just before guests sit down at the table. • SERVES 6

---

2 heads of escarole, bruised outer leaves removed

¼ cup extra-virgin olive oil

3 garlic cloves, thinly sliced

3 shallots, thinly sliced

1 sprig of rosemary

¼ teaspoon paprika (*pimentón*), preferably smoked

Salt and cayenne pepper

Cut off the cores of the escarole and cut the leaves crosswise into roughly 2-inch lengths. Wash well and spin dry.

In a large skillet or sauté pan, warm the oil over low heat. Add the garlic, shallots, and rosemary and sweat gently until softened but not browned, 4 to 6 minutes. Add the paprika, ½ teaspoon salt, and a small pinch of cayenne (or to taste). Stir for 30 seconds, then stir in the escarole and cover the pan.

Reduce the heat to low and cook for 10 minutes, turning over with tongs every 2 to 3 minutes, until tender but still bright green.

Serve within 5 minutes or let stand uncovered for up to 20 minutes and reheat slightly before serving.

PARMESAN·ROASTED ONIONS

*M*ake these bright, succulent onions once, and you'll be tempted to replace that holiday menu fixture, creamed onions. Not only is there a lot less peeling involved, but you can prepare the onions in advance: Precook the onions, scoop them out, and make the filling. Then, cover the onions and filling separately and refrigerate until about forty minutes before serving time. Bring them to room temperature and fill and roast as below. • SERVES 6; MAY BE DOUBLED

---

6 small yellow onions

2 tablespoons extra-virgin olive oil

¾ cup dry white wine

¾ cup chicken stock or broth
(canned low-sodium is fine)

Salt and freshly ground black pepper

3 sprigs of thyme

½ cup dry bread crumbs

½ cup finely grated Parmigiano-Reggiano or
other *grana padana* cheese

Scant ¼ cup brine-cured black olives, such
as kalamata, pitted and coarsely chopped
(optional)

2 tablespoons heavy cream

½ teaspoon dried thyme

1½ tablespoons coarsely chopped flat-leaf
parsley

Preheat the oven to 425°F.

Slice off the top quarter of the onions, then peel them and very slightly trim the bases, so they will sit upright.

Place a large, ovenproof sauté pan over medium-high heat and add the oil. Place the onions in the pan, cut sides down, and cook just until nicely browned, about 5 minutes. Remove the pan from the heat, turn the onions root side down, and drizzle the wine and chicken stock over the tops. Season evenly with about ¼ teaspoon salt and a little pepper. Add the thyme sprigs to the pan and bake for about 1 hour, until the bases of the onions are just tender when pierced with a small, sharp knife.

Transfer the onions to a work surface, reserving the pan with the liquid in it (leave the oven on if you are finishing the onions right away). Cool slightly, and with a small spoon, scoop out the insides of each onion, leaving a layer ¼ to ½ inch thick all around (this is about 2 layers of the onion). Chop enough of the scooped-out onion to make ½ cup (reserve the remaining onion for another use).

In a medium bowl, combine the chopped onion with the bread crumbs, Parmigiano, olives (if using), cream, thyme, parsley, ¼ teaspoon salt, and some generous grindings of pepper. Return the onions to the original pan and divide the filling among them. Return the pan to the oven and bake until the onions are very tender, the filling is hot, and the tops are crispy, about 20 minutes.

Spoon some of the remaining pan juices over each onion and serve at once.

CREAMY CARROT SPOON BREAD

*T*his colorful side dish adds a sweet note to the fall, winter, or holiday table. Rather than being dense like a pudding, it is light and almost soufflé-like in texture. Look for young carrots with their green tops on whenever possible; larger, older carrots develop a woody texture as they age. Avoid bagged mini carrots, too, since they are made by machine from these same inferior carrots. • SERVES 8

1½ pounds young firm carrots, peeled and
    cut into 2-inch lengths

1 tablespoon unsalted butter, plus additional,
    softened, for greasing

¼ cup finely grated Parmigiano-Reggiano or
    other *grana padana* cheese

¼ cup heavy cream

4 large eggs, separated

1 tablespoon superfine flour
    (such as Wondra)

Salt and freshly ground black pepper

Ground nutmeg

1 tablespoon finely chopped dill or fennel tops

In a large pot of lightly salted boiling water, cook the carrots for about 30 minutes, until completely tender.

Preheat the oven to 400°F. Grease a 1½-quart soufflé dish with softened butter.

Drain the carrots well and, in a food processor, puree until smooth. Transfer the carrot puree to a large bowl and whisk in the Parmigiano, the 1 tablespoon butter, cream, egg yolks, flour, ½ teaspoon salt, ¼ teaspoon pepper, and a pinch of nutmeg.

In a very clean metal bowl, use an electric mixer to beat the egg whites to soft peaks. With a rubber spatula, stir about one third of the egg whites into the carrot mixture; gently fold in the remaining whites and spoon the mixture into the prepared soufflé dish. Set the dish in a roasting pan. Fill the pan about halfway up the sides of the dish with very hot water.

Bake for about 30 minutes, until the center of the pudding no longer jiggles. Scatter with the dill and serve at once or place on the buffet.

Those Fabulous Murals

Of Tavern's many eye-popping hallmarks, its murals stand out for their quieter characteristics, lending a rather bucolic note to the otherwise glitzy interior. The four murals are as stylistically different from one another as the rooms they decorate. Stepping into Maximillian's Pavilion is about as close to standing in the middle of modern-day Central Park without doing just that, while the Park Room is graced by a turn-of-the-twentieth-century rendering of its namesake. In the Crystal Room, winged horses and whimsical flowers dance among floating fairy-tale castles on a narrow panel just beneath the rococo ceiling. Artist Ron Genereux refreshed this mural several years ago; he also replaced the mural below it, on the pocket doors. It portrays an Italianate fantasy garden punctuated by captivating architectural follies; Warner lives on in that mural, depicted as one of the topiaries doing his beloved dancing-bear imitation.

In fact, that's why Warner loved murals so much: they can bring to life whatever one can imagine. Murals were another expression of his talent for setting the scene.

As awe-inspiring as the murals are, their origins are perhaps even more so. After dozens of years of the same look of the Pavilion Room, when it was decided to rename it Maximilian's Pavilion, Kay commissioned a new mural from Ron Genereux, one that would truly bring Central Park inside Tavern. Ronnie spent hundreds of hours in the park taking photographs—more than 10,000 in all—from dozens of angles and heights. Using that cache of photos as his guide, he reduced the park's 834 acres to 167 linear feet (that's the length of an Olympic-size swimming pool), taking artistic license here and there. He adjusted the positioning of trees and plants to what he considered their better advantage, depicted all blossoming foliage in full bloom (although they do not in actual fact bloom simultaneously), and repositioned the iconic Ladies Pavilion and the Bow Bridge. Ronnie manipulated the skyline, too, deleting most of the Park's urban features, with the exception of the Dakota, our family home for so long. As a nod to Kay's desire to include the park's antique carousel in the mural, which had been nixed due to other artistic considerations, Ronnie placed a miniature version of it on a footpath leading into Tavern on the Green, the only other edifice represented, with a gift tag announcing "For Kay."

This monumental work, a magnificent addition to Tavern's fine arts collection, took eighteen months to complete, with as many as ten artists helping Ronnie in oils on the giant canvasses. Typically, such large murals are done in acrylics, but they don't yield the same richness and depth of color as oil paints. In this case, we know it was worth the added expense!

II

DESSERTS

NEW YORK CHEESECAKE

*S*ome desserts come and go on Tavern's menu, but cheesecake has remained a fixture since 1976, not least because Warner loved it. It remains the most requested dessert today—in fact, there would probably be a riot if it were ever replaced. Some guests request this cheesecake for birthday celebrations; the snow-white surface makes it easy to "write" a message on with a piping tip and bag.

Bring a bit of the Tavern home with this phenomenal cheesecake. Topped with a tart layer of sour cream, it is the only recipe you'll ever need for this classic confection! It's best when made the day before. • SERVES 10 • *photograph on page 260*

CRUST

1½ cups graham cracker crumbs
  (about 12 double graham crackers)

2 tablespoons sugar

Scant teaspoon cinnamon

6 tablespoons (¾ stick) unsalted butter,
  melted

FILLING

1 pound cream cheese, softened

¾ cup (6 ounces) whole-milk ricotta

2 tablespoons heavy cream

⅓ cup sugar

1 teaspoon fresh lemon juice

2 teaspoons best-quality vanilla extract

3 large eggs, lightly beaten

SOUR CREAM TOPPING

1 cup sour cream

1½ tablespoons sugar

½ teaspoon best-quality vanilla extract

Line the base and partway up the sides of a 10-inch springform pan with a sheet of heavy-duty aluminum foil, molding it closely to the pan and smoothing the wrinkles. Cut a circle of parchment paper that is about ¾ inch larger than the diameter of the pan. Spray the inside of the pan with nonstick spray, then press the circle of parchment onto the base, centering it exactly, and smoothing the wrinkles onto the metal (the paper will extend up the sides by about ½ inch, making it easy to remove the cheesecake from the base).

In a medium mixing bowl, combine the crumbs, sugar, cinnamon, and enough of the butter to just bind the mixture. Use the remaining butter to thoroughly grease the paper-covered bottom and all the way up the sides of the pan. Turn the pan on its side and add one third of the crumb mixture. With your fingertips, press the crumbs around the sides of the pan, turning it as you go to make an even crust that reaches about two thirds of the way to the rim. Set the pan base down, add the remaining two thirds of the crumb mixture, and press it with your fingertips into the corners and evenly across the base of the pan.

Preheat the oven to 300°F.

In a medium mixing bowl, combine the cream cheese, ricotta, heavy cream, sugar, lemon juice, and vanilla and beat with a handheld electric mixer until fluffy. Add the eggs and continue beating until smooth. Spoon the filling into the prepared crust.

Bake for 40 minutes, or until the center is almost firm. While the cheesecake is cooking, whisk together the sour cream, sugar, and vanilla extract.

Cool the pan on a rack for 30 minutes, leaving the oven on. Slowly pour the topping over the top of the cake in an even layer, pouring around the edges first and letting the topping find its level in the center. Bake for 20 minutes more (the topping will firm up as it cools). Cool to room temperature, then cover and refrigerate overnight.

Run a thin, round-bladed knife around the inside rim all the way down to the base to release the cheesecake above and below the crust. Release the sides of the springform pan and, using the parchment paper, slide the cheesecake from the base to a flat, round serving platter, for slicing.

CAN YOU WRAP THAT UP, PLEASE?

Tavern has seen its share of sticky fingers, especially around the holidays when some guests assume the Christmas ornaments are favors to which they may help themselves (they're hot-glued to their caps and double-wired to the tree's branches!). Nothing prepared the staff, however, for the gutsy attempt of one would-be thief. He tried to steal *Satisfaction*, an original nineteenth-century painting that was then bolted to the brick wall on which it hung. The thief had managed to loosen some of the bolts that secured the painting to the wall when a hostess chanced upon the scene and the man fled. The painting, which has long been reproduced on the cover of our dessert menus, is now double-bolted.

KAY'S FAMOUS
CHRISTMAS PUDDING

*I*n the United States, a pudding is a soft and spoonable dessert. But in all the countries of the old British Empire, the word "pudding" signifies *any* kind of dessert. Thus, the often-heard phrases "What's for pudding?" and "Where's me pud?" This Chrismas "pudding" has graced British tables for generations and is not in danger of going out of style in this century or even the next few, perhaps because it is so rich, chewy, and delicious (note that a little goes a long way!). There are two traditions associated with this dish: Just before the pudding goes into the oven, the cook adds a silver charm or coin (be sure to wrap it in parchment paper!) and makes a Christmas wish.

You will need a six-cup rimmed pudding bowl (that's two and a half Imperial pints) to make this classic dessert. (If you get a U.K.-made product—the best choice—"size 24" will be printed on the base; the rim is necessary for securing the muslin taut over the top before steaming.) Anytime after at least four weeks of maturing at room temperature, the pudding may be wrapped and frozen for up to one year. • SERVES 10 TO 12

½ cup flour

Salt

½ teaspoon mixed spices (say, a pinch each of coriander, ginger, cloves)

¼ teaspoon ground cinnamon

¼ teaspoon grated nutmeg

Finely grated zest of 1 small scrubbed lemon (see Note, page 41)

1 ounce slivered almonds, coarsely chopped

8 ounces (1¼ cups) dark raisins, chopped

4 ounces (⅔ cup) currants, chopped

4 ounces (⅔ cup) golden raisins, chopped

2 ounces (⅓ cup) mixed candied citrus peel, chopped

¼ pound beef suet, shredded

4 ounces (about 1½ cups) fresh white bread crumbs

½ cup firmly packed dark brown sugar

2 tablespoons molasses

2 tablespoons brandy or dark rum, plus additional, for serving

1 tablespoon fresh lemon juice

3 large eggs

⅓ cup Guinness stout or milk, plus additional as needed

Softened butter, for preparing the pudding bowl

Brandy Butter (recipe follows), for serving (optional)

In a large bowl, combine the flour, a pinch of salt, and all the spices. Add the lemon zest, almonds, raisins, currants, golden raisins, and candied citrus peel. With a fork, blend together until evenly mixed, then work in the suet, bread crumbs, and sugar (use your hands if the fork is not achieving an even blend). Make a well in the center.

In a small saucepan over low heat, warm the molasses until runny. Remove the pan from the heat and add the brandy and lemon juice. In a bowl, beat the eggs well, then stir them into the molasses mixture.

Pour the liquid from the saucepan into the well in the center of the dry ingredients and immediately add the Guinness. With a large spoon, stir all the ingredients together until they are evenly moistened and well mixed.

Cover the bowl with a clean towel, and leave overnight at room temperature. Cut a circle of baking parchment that will fit perfectly inside the rim of the pudding bowl.

Stir the mixture to judge its consistency and, if desired, add a well-wrapped coin or charm and make a wish. The mixture should have a soft dropping consistency; if it seems at all dry, add a touch more Guinness. Generously grease a 6-cup rimmed pudding bowl with the softened butter.

Spoon the pudding mixture into the bowl, filling it to within 1 inch of the top. Cover with the parchment circle and then top with a piece of muslin or a clean towel. Tie a length of kitchen twine quite snugly underneath the rim of the bowl, to secure the muslin taut over the pudding.

Place the pudding in a large, deep saucepan, and add enough boiling water to come one third of the way up the bowl. Cover the saucepan and steam gently for 6 hours, adding more boiling water when necessary.

Carefully remove the pudding bowl from the water and place on a wire rack to cool to room temperature. When the pudding is cool, discard the muslin and the baking parchment. Replace with a fresh layer of baking parchment, then cover with a clean piece of muslin or towel and tie as before. Store in a cool but light place, such as a pantry, until the day you plan to serve. (Do not make the cover airtight or mold may develop. After the pudding has matured at room temperature for 1 month, it can be frozen in its bowl—or turned out and frozen well wrapped in a freezer bag or aluminum foil. The pudding will keep more than 1 year in the freezer.)

On the day the pudding is to be served, re-cover with a new round of lightly buttered parchment paper and large pieces of aluminum foil, and steam briskly, as before, for 2 hours.

Turn the pudding out onto a warmed platter. At serving time, when all the guests are assembled, drizzle the top with a little brandy or rum and ignite with a long match. Serve with Brandy Butter on the side, if desired.

BRANDY BUTTER

8 tablespoons (1 stick) butter, softened

¼ cup Baker's, or superfine, sugar

⅓ cup confectioners' sugar

2 tablespoons brandy or rum

1 ounce ground almonds

Pinch of ground cinnamon

Combine the butter and both sugars in a bowl; with a wooden spoon or a handheld electric mixer, beat until fluffy and very pale. Gradually beat in the brandy or rum, then fold in the almonds. Transfer to a small serving dish and, if desired, refrigerate overnight to develop the flavor. Return almost to room temperature, sprinkle with cinnamon, and serve. • MAKES ABOUT 1 CUP

POACHED PEARS
WITH LEMON-RICOTTA STUFFING
AND TOASTED ALMONDS

*P*resentation is every bit as important as taste at Tavern. Before any dish leaves the kitchen, the expeditor—the last person who inspects the plate before it goes through the swinging doors and out to the dining room—makes sure it's garnished properly and not a drop of sauce is out of place. For this lovely fall or winter dessert, sizzled almonds are the flavorful garnish; scatter them with a light hand, allowing some to fall around the edges of the plate.

Don't substitute canned pears in this recipe; they're too sweet. If the pears are a little less ripe than you would like, simmer them in the syrup for 5 minutes before removing from the heat and covering with a towel.

This is an ideal make-ahead dessert; the pears may be poached up to forty-eight hours before serving, the lemon-ricotta mixture assembled and the almonds toasted up to two hours ahead. • SERVES 6

---

5 cups water

2 tablespoons fresh lemon juice

1 cup granulated sugar

2 vanilla beans, split lengthwise, or ¾ teaspoon best-quality vanilla extract

3 almost-ripe Bartlett pears, peeled, halved, and cored

3 tablespoons butter

½ cup sliced raw almonds

LEMON-RICOTTA STUFFING

8 ounces whole-milk ricotta

2 tablespoons Baker's, or superfine, sugar

Finely grated zest of 2 scrubbed lemons (see Note, page 41)

1 teaspoon ground cardamom

In a small saucepan, combine the water, lemon juice, granulated sugar, and vanilla beans. Bring to a boil over high heat, stirring constantly, until all the sugar has dissolved. Add the pear halves and return to a boil, then adjust the heat so the water barely simmers and cook for 2 to 3 minutes, depending on the size of the pears.

Remove the pan from the heat and immediately spread a clean, folded kitchen towel directly into the water, on top of the pears. Let stand until the pears and the liquid have cooled to room temperature (the heat of the liquid will gently cook the pears through). If you wish, transfer the pears to a covered container and refrigerate in their poaching liquid for up to 48 hours.

Place a small skillet over medium-high heat and add the butter. When the foam has subsided and the butter is beginning to brown, add the almonds and sizzle for 2 to 3 minutes, until the butter is foamy and pale golden brown and the nuts are aromatic. Don't let the butter burn—reduce the heat as necessary. Drain on paper towels.

In a bowl, combine the ricotta, superfine sugar, lemon zest, and cardamom. Mix together with a fork. Taste for seasoning and adjust with sugar and cardamom, if necessary. Cover and refrigerate for up to 2 hours before serving, if desired.

If the pears or the ricotta mixture have been refrigerated, let stand at room temperature for 30 minutes. In a small saucepan, simmer the poaching syrup briskly until reduced by about three quarters, and syrupy. Place a halved pear on each of 6 plates and top with a generous scoop of the lemon-ricotta mixture. Scatter the sizzled almonds, and serve. Pass the reduced poaching liquid on the side, so guests can drizzle a little over the top.

TIRAMISÙ

*F*or several years, the Valentine's Day menu at Tavern included this classic Italian dessert. Its name, literally translated, means "pick me up," a reference to its layers of ladyfingers soaked in espresso. It was certainly a love match with our guests, who relished every bite. We even like to think it moved some to pop the question!

Note that this dish must be refrigerated for at least twenty-four hours, or it won't slice nicely into portions. (Of course, this makes it an ideal—and impressive—make-ahead dessert!) • SERVES 8

---

3 large egg yolks (see Note, page 231)

1 tablespoon Kahlúa

2 teaspoons chocolate syrup, such as Hershey's

¼ cup Baker's, or superfine, sugar

1¼ cups mascarpone cheese, at room temperature

¾ cup heavy whipping cream

Four 3½-ounce packages ladyfinger cookies

2½ cups espresso or very strong coffee

Cocoa powder, for dusting

Chill a large bowl in the refrigerator for 10 minutes.

In the bowl of an electric stand mixer, combine the egg yolks, Kahlúa, chocolate syrup, and superfine sugar. Beat the mixture at high speed for 2 minutes; it should be quite thick and leave a trail when the beater is lifted away.

Place the softened mascarpone in a large mixing bowl, and gently fold in the beaten egg-and-chocolate mixture. Put the cream in the chilled bowl and whip to stiff peaks; fold into the mascarpone mixture.

Dip each ladyfinger briefly into the espresso, and arrange in rows on the bottom of a 9 x 9-inch ceramic, earthenware, or glass baking dish. Gently spread an even layer of one third of the mascarpone mixture over the ladyfingers, and top with a second layer of coffee-dipped ladyfingers. Spread this layer with another third of the mascarpone mixture, make a third layer of ladyfingers, and end with the remaining mascarpone. Cover the pan tightly with plastic wrap, and refrigerate for at least 24 hours and up to 36 hours.

To serve, cut into squares, dusting each portion generously with cocoa powder.

APPLE BROWN BETTY

*F*ragrant, buttery croissants are perhaps second only to warm bagels as New Yorkers' preferred accompaniment to their morning cup of coffee. The flaky crescents are essential to this brown betty, though day-old versions are preferred for best results. If you don't happen to have slightly stale croissants on hand, place fresh ones in a large roasting dish and dry in a 200°F oven for twenty minutes. • SERVES 8 TO 10

Butter and flour, for preparing the baking dish

6 day-old croissants, torn into 2-inch chunks

3 pounds (about 6 large) cooking apples, peeled, quartered, and cored, and cut into ¾-inch chunks

1½ cups best-quality bottled applesauce

¾ cup fresh orange juice

¾ cup plus 1 tablespoon sugar

1 teaspoon ground cinnamon

¾ cup golden raisins or dried cranberries

16 tablespoons (8 ounces; 2 sticks) unsalted butter, melted

½ teaspoon ground ginger

Preheat the oven to 350°F.

Butter and flour a 12 x 9-inch or similar-size earthenware, ceramic, or glass baking dish.

In a very large bowl, combine the croissants, apple chunks, applesauce, orange juice, ¾ cup of the sugar, the cinnamon, raisins, and all but about 2 tablespoons of the melted butter. Toss the mixture well (use your hands for the best mix), making sure all the ingredients are evenly coated with the butter. Press the mixture into the pan, compacting it a little, and brush the top with the remaining melted butter.

Sprinkle with the remaining 1 tablespoon sugar and the ginger, and bake for about 1 hour 15 minutes, until the top is golden brown and the butter and juices are bubbling around the edges. Cool in the pan for at least 1 hour and up to 3 hours.

Before serving, if desired, warm in a very low oven for 20 to 25 minutes.

CHOCOLATE·ESPRESSO MOUSSE

*A*t first glance, guests may think these adorable mousse-filled demitasse cups are simply espresso. But on first "sip" they'll realize they need a little spoon to scoop out the ethereal stuff. The mousse can also be served in Chinese teacups, or even in tiny sake cups if it is part of a dessert buffet.

At Tavern, only the best chocolate is used for all chocolate desserts; Valrhona is our brand of choice. You need to start the dessert well in advance. Work quickly when folding the egg whites and yolks into the chocolate mixture for the lightest results.

• SERVES 8

---

9 ounces best-quality dark, bittersweet chocolate (preferably 60% cocoa), coarsely chopped

7 tablespoons sugar

1 teaspoon powdered espresso

12 large egg whites

Salt

2 large egg yolks, brought to room temperature for at least 30 minutes (see Note)

1 cup heavy whipping cream, very cold

Ground cinnamon, for serving

Place a large metal bowl over a saucepan of barely simmering water. Be sure the base of the bowl does not touch the water. Add the chocolate, 3 tablespoons of the sugar, and the espresso powder. Let warm until the edges of the chocolate begin to melt, then stir occasionally until the chocolate is completely melted and the mixture is smooth, about 15 minutes. Remove the bowl from the pan and let cool for 5 minutes.

In a large, perfectly clean bowl, using a handheld electric mixer on medium speed, beat the egg whites with a pinch of salt for 1 minute. Increase the speed to high and continue beating until soft peaks form. Scatter 3 tablespoons of the sugar over the top and beat for 1 minute more, until glossy but not too stiff.

To lighten the chocolate mixture, quickly but thoroughly whisk in the egg yolks and ¼ cup of the beaten egg whites. Switch to a rubber spatula and gently but quickly fold in the remaining egg whites.

Spoon out and divide the mixture among 8 demitasse cups or small teacups. Cover the cups with squares of plastic wrap and refrigerate for at least 8 hours and up to 24 hours.

To serve, beat the whipping cream with the remaining tablespoon of sugar until almost stiff, then use a pastry bag fitted with a star tip to pipe a rosette in the center of each mousse (or, just dollop on with a spoon). Dust the cream with a little cinnamon and serve.

NOTE · This dish contains raw egg yolks. The elderly, pregnant, the very young, and those with compromised immune systems may wish to avoid consuming raw egg yolks if salmonella is a problem in your area.

KAY LEROY'S TARTE TATIN

*T*he late food writer Craig Claiborne once wrote in *The New York Times:* "Mrs. LeRoy said this week that she had researched all the cookbooks at her disposal and had made five hundred tarts before she developed the one, *perfect* tarte Tatin. This is her formula."

You can substitute any firm, local baking apple for the Golden Delicious (such as Gala). Red Delicious apples, however, will not hold their shape during the baking process. If using Granny Smith apples, increase the sugar by about two tablespoons.

If possible, make this dish in a French *tarte Tatin* pan: ten inches in diameter, copper on the outside and tin or stainless steel on the inside, about two inches deep. If you don't have—or want to invest in—this classic pan (which ensures even browning of the caramel), a deep nine- or ten-inch cast-iron skillet will do the job nicely. • SERVES 6 TO 8

FOR THE PASTRY

1½ cups flour

½ teaspoon salt

8 tablespoons (1 stick) very cold unsalted butter, cut into 8 pieces

3 to 4 tablespoons ice water

FOR THE TARTE

14 tablespoons (7 ounces; 1¾ sticks) unsalted butter, softened

⅔ cup plus 1 tablespoon granulated sugar

7 tablespoons firmly packed dark brown sugar

6 large Golden Delicious apples

1 tablespoon water

⅔ cup heavy whipping cream (optional)

In a food processor, combine the flour and salt and pulse to blend. Add the cold butter and pulse on and off 3 or 4 times for a few seconds each, until the mixture resembles coarse meal. Remove the cover and sprinkle 3 tablespoons of the ice water over the top. Pulse again several times. If the mixture does not begin to form a shaggy mass on the center stem within 5 to 10 seconds, remove the cover and sprinkle the remaining tablespoon of ice water over the top, then pulse again.

Transfer the rough mass to a lightly floured work surface and, working quickly to avoid toughening the pastry, bring together into a round, flattened disk. Wrap the dough disk in plastic wrap and chill for at least 1 hour before rolling out. (The dough may be made up to 1 week ahead and kept chilled. If refrigerated for longer than 3 hours, let stand at room temperature for 20 to 30 minutes before rolling out.)

Preheat the oven to 450°F.

In the Tatin dish or skillet, combine 12 tablespoons (1½ sticks) of the softened butter, ⅓ cup of the granulated sugar, and 3½ tablespoons of the brown sugar. Blend thoroughly with a fork and pat the mixture around the sides and base of the dish with a small rubber spatula.

continued

Peel, quarter, and core the apples and slice them about ¼ inch thick. Arrange the slices over the butter and sugar base in an overlapping, circular, and symmetrical petal-like design. When finished, the apples should come just to the rim of the pan and no higher.

Melt the remaining 2 tablespoons butter. Stir in the remaining 3½ tablespoons brown sugar and scatter this mixture over the tops of the apples.

Roll out the pastry into a circle ⅛ inch thick and cut it to fit as precisely as possible over the apples, without overlapping the edge of the pan. Fit the pastry over the apples and cut a small slit in the center of the pastry to allow the steam to escape.

Bake the tart for 30 minutes, or until the pastry is lightly browned.

Remove the dish from the oven and increase the oven heat to 550°F. Make a round of foil to fit over the dish to prevent the pastry from burning. Cover the pastry with the foil and bake for about 1 hour, until the liquid that forms around the apples has changed from a runny yellow to a dark, oozing, sticky amber. (This can be checked by carefully tilting the pan and looking under the crust.) Note that oven thermostats in home ovens vary, and it may be necessary to adjust the heat if the tart starts to burn. On the other hand, the oven must be hot to enough to caramelize the filling.

When the tarte is done, let it stand for 15 minutes to 1 hour before unmolding.

Remove the foil and place a serving plate over the top of the pan, then quickly invert the tarte. The tops of the apples should be dark brown with caramelized butter and sugar.

Combine ⅓ cup of the granulated sugar and the water in a heavy, thick-bottomed saucepan. Place over medium-high heat and bring to a simmer. Simmer the sugar syrup gently, without stirring, until it is almost—but not quite—dark amber brown. Remove the pan from the heat. With a silicone pastry brush and working as quickly as you can, before the caramel hardens as it cools, paint a thin layer of caramel over the surface of the apples. Let the tarte cool.

While the tarte is cooling, combine the cream and the remaining 1 tablespoon sugar in a bowl and whip to soft peaks.

Slice the tarte and serve with a dollop of the sweetened whipped cream, if desired.

BANANA BREAD PUDDING
WITH BOURBON-CHOCOLATE SAUCE

"It must be fabulous": This line was one of Warner LeRoy's top three refrains. He would undoubtedly apply it to this dressed-up version of one of his favorite comfort foods. It's a triple threat of raisin-studded banana bread, silky custard, and rich chocolate—decadence with a distinctive Southern drawl.

When the occasion calls for a truly indulgent, rich dessert, this is your ticket. The banana bread is truly wonderful on its own and would make a lovely hostess gift. Don't even consider making the bread with unripe bananas! • SERVES 10 TO 12

---

5 cups whole milk

1 teaspoon best-quality vanilla extract

1 cup granulated sugar

1 loaf Banana-Bourbon-Raisin Bread
(recipe follows)

About 4 tablespoons (½ stick) unsalted
butter, softened

1 teaspoon best-quality vanilla extract

5 large eggs

5 large egg yolks

Confectioners' sugar, for serving

Bourbon-Chocolate Sauce
(recipe follows; optional)

Wrap the outside of a 10-inch springform pan tightly with foil, smoothing the wrinkles. (This will prevent the custard from leaking into the hot-water bath, or bain-marie.)

In a heavy saucepan, bring the milk to a bare simmer with the vanilla and sugar, stirring until the sugar dissolves. Remove the pan from the heat and let stand for 10 minutes.

Preheat the broiler.

Cut the banana bread into ⅓-inch-thick slices. Lightly butter one side of each slice and halve the slices diagonally to form triangles. Arrange the triangles, buttered side up, in one layer on 2 large baking sheets and broil about 4 inches from the heat until golden, about 2 minutes. Arrange the triangles in the springform pan, toasted sides up and overlapping slightly, layering until all the triangles have been used. (The pudding may be prepared up to this point and kept covered for up to 6 hours.)

Preheat the oven to 400°F. Place a rack in the center position.

Rewarm the milk mixture slightly over low heat. In a large heat-proof bowl, whisk together the whole eggs and yolks. Add the warm milk to the bowl in a thin stream, whisking all the time.

Ladle the custard evenly over the toasts (the custard will not completely cover them). Set the springform pan inside a slightly larger roasting pan and add enough very hot tap water to the roasting pan to reach about halfway up the side of the springform.

continued

Bake the pudding for 40 minutes, or until puffed. Reduce the heat to 375°F, cover the pan with foil, and bake for about 10 minutes more, until the custard is set. (Poke the center with a spoon to be sure there is no raw custard still inside.)

Remove the pan from the water bath and cool the pudding to warm room temperature. (At this point, you can cover the pan and refrigerate it overnight. If so, before serving, warm in a low oven to crisp the top and then cool slightly to warm room temperature.)

Just before serving, run a knife around the inside rim to release the pudding from the ring, release the springform clip, and remove the ring. Place the base on a platter, and dust the pudding with confectioners' sugar. Cut into wedges to serve, with the bourbon-chocolate sauce on the side, if desired.

BANANA·BOURBON·RAISIN BREAD

1¼ cups golden raisins, currants, or standard raisins

3 tablespoons good, richly-flavored, aged bourbon

Softened butter and flour, for preparing the loaf pan

2 cups flour

¾ cup sugar

1¼ teaspoons baking soda

½ teaspoon salt

3 *very ripe* bananas, peeled and mashed with a heavy fork (about 1½ cups)

¼ cup buttermilk

2 large eggs, lightly beaten

⅓ cup canola oil

In a small bowl, cover the raisins with the bourbon and let stand for 25 minutes. Drain, reserving any bourbon remaining.

Place a rack in the lower third of the oven. Preheat to 350°F. Butter and flour a 9-inch loaf pan, preferably nonstick.

In a large mixing bowl, combine the 2 cups flour, the sugar, baking soda, salt, and raisins and toss. In another bowl, combine the bananas, buttermilk, eggs, oil, and the reserved bourbon and, using a wooden spoon, mash together. With a rubber spatula, gently fold the banana mixture into the dry ingredients until all the ingredients are evenly moistened. Spoon the batter into the prepared pan and bake for about 1 hour, until the loaf is firm and golden brown and a toothpick inserted in the center comes out clean.

Cool in the pan for 5 minutes, then turn out onto a rack. The bread will keep, tightly wrapped and refrigerated, for up to 1 week. • MAKES ONE 9-INCH LOAF

BOURBON·CHOCOLATE SAUCE

½ cup whole milk

½ cup heavy cream

8 ounces dark, bittersweet chocolate, finely chopped

1 tablespoon good, richly flavored, aged bourbon

In the top of a double boiler or in a bowl set over a sauce-pan of barely simmering water (be sure the base of the bowl does not touch the water), combine the milk, cream, and chocolate. Cook, stirring frequently, for 3 to 4 min-utes, until the chocolate has melted and the mixture is smooth. If serving right away, stir in the bourbon. At this point the sauce may be cooled to room temperature and refrigerated overnight. If you do this, reheat gently in the double boiler and stir in the bourbon just before serving.

◆ MAKES ABOUT 2 CUPS

OSCAR GLORY

Tavern is a favorite spot during Oscar season. Julia Roberts spent an evening with us early in 2001, when she was up for an Oscar for *Erin Brockovich*. She came for a party for the National Board of Review, awed the staff with her beauty and charisma, and a few weeks later won the Oscar. Another Oscar winner, Marty Richards, the producer of *Chicago*, also had a memorable night at Tavern—but with a twist: Somehow during the evening he lost a $40,000 watch! Luckily, one of the waiters found the timepiece and returned it to the famed producer the next day.

PUMPKIN·PECAN CAKE
WITH MAPLE–CREAM CHEESE FROSTING

*A*very festive alternative to the standard pie, this cake has all your favorite Thanksgiving spices and flavors, plus a luscious maple-perfumed frosting. As always, buy your pecans from a purveyor with a high turnover so that you have the freshest available. If you can find candied pecans, by all means use them; they'll put this already indulgent cake over the top. • SERVES 12

CAKE

3 cups flour

2¼ cups sugar

½ tablespoon baking soda

1 tablespoon baking powder

2½ teaspoons ground cinnamon

¾ teaspoon ground nutmeg

¾ teaspoon ground allspice

Salt

1½ cups canola oil

5 large eggs, at room temperature

1½ teaspoons best-quality vanilla extract

24 ounces canned, solid-pack pumpkin puree

¾ cup golden raisins

¾ cup pecan pieces

Softened butter and flour, for the cake pan

FROSTING

1½ pounds cream cheese, softened

8 tablespoons (1 stick) unsalted butter, softened

⅔ cup pure maple syrup, plus additional as needed

BAKE THE CAKE

Preheat the oven to 350°F.

In a large bowl, combine the flour, sugar, baking soda, baking powder, cinnamon, nutmeg, allspice, and ½ teaspoon salt. Whisk to blend. In a large measuring cup, whisk together the oil, eggs, and vanilla. Pour the egg mixture into the dry ingredients, and add the pumpkin. With a handheld electric mixer, beat just until evenly blended; the batter will be very thick. Fold in the raisins and pecans.

Use the softened butter to generously grease a 10-inch round cake pan with 3-inch sides (such as a springform). Add 2 tablespoons flour and shake the pan back and forth and around, coating the butter with a fine layer of flour; discard any flour that does not stick to the butter. Spoon the batter into the prepared pan, and smooth the top until it's level.

Bake for 65 to 70 minutes, or until the sides begin to shrink away from the pan and a toothpick inserted into the center of the cake comes out clean. Cool on a rack to room temperature. (If desired, cover and refrigerate up to overnight before frosting. In any case, make sure that the cake is completely cool before you frost it, or the warmth of the cake will melt the frosting on contact.)

MAKE THE FROSTING AND FINISH

In a large bowl, beat the cream cheese, butter, and maple syrup vigorously with a wooden spoon until fluffy. Taste; add a little more maple syrup if desired.

Run a small knife around the edge of the cake pan to release the upper edge, and turn out upside down onto a work surface (the cake is very resilient). Using a long, serrated bread knife, slice the cake horizontally into 3 even layers, placing your hand on top to help guide the knife evenly (turn the cake several times to be sure you are cutting even layers). Transfer the bottom layer to a large cake plate (use the original bottom of the cake as the top layer—it will be nice and flat).

Spread the bottom cake layer with about a quarter of the frosting; then place the second layer over it, matching up the edges, and spread it with another quarter of the frosting. Top with the third layer. Frost the top and sides of the cake evenly with the remaining frosting. Space the whole pecans equidistant around the top edge of the cake.

Refrigerate for 1 to 12 hours to firm the frosting. For the best flavor, return to room temperature before serving in wedges.

THE ART OF FRUIT SALAD

You will never find honeydew melon in the fruit salad at Tavern because Warner LeRoy simply did not like it. It was too pedestrian; every deli in New York City includes it in their bland to-go mix of fruits. But a massive silver bowl of seasonal combinations was and remains a fixture on the banquet table, always splashed with a spirit or liqueur and served with a creamy yogurt sauce.

In recent years we have come, once again, to appreciate the superior flavor of ingredients in their season. As you assemble your own fruit salad, buy what's in season and forgo such temptations as using blueberries in November or apples in July. The tangy yogurt dressing is good in any season, of course, but it may be omitted for a simple, sparkling presentation. • SERVES 8 (BUT ENDLESSLY ADJUSTABLE)

SUMMER

2 ripe nectarines, pitted and cut into 1-inch chunks

3 ripe peaches, pitted and cut into 1-inch chunks

2 pints blueberries

2 pounds watermelon, seeded and cut into ¾-inch chunks

2 cups green or red seedless grapes (frozen, if desired)

1 cup quartered or halved strawberries

1 to 2 tablespoons Baker's, or superfine, sugar, to taste

3 tablespoons Grand Marnier or Frangelico liqueur

2 tablespoons finely chopped mint leaves (see Note)

WINTER

2 Fuji or Gala apples, peeled if desired, cored, and cut into ¾-inch chunks

1½ cups pineapple chunks, fresh or from a jar

1 small ripe cantaloupe, seeded and cut into ¾-inch chunks

2 cups seedless red or green grapes (frozen, if desired)

2 grapefruits (white or pink), all pith removed and segments peeled and cut into ¾-inch chunks

2 blood oranges or navel oranges, all pith removed and segments peeled and cut into ¾-inch chunks

1 cup blackberries

½ cup sweetened, shredded coconut (see Note)

2 tablespoons orange flower water

1 to 2 tablespoons Baker's, or superfine, sugar, to taste

YOGURT DRESSING

1 cup plain, full-fat yogurt

1 teaspoon zest from a scrubbed lemon (see Note, page 41)

2 tablespoons fresh lemon juice

1 to 2 tablespoons sugar (granulated or superfine)

Use the ingredient lists above as a guideline, and pick and choose among the suggestions depending on your taste and the season. In reality, you will be led by the contents of your farmers' market or supermarket. The Grand Marnier in the summer salad and the orange flower water in the winter salad may be replaced with the spirit or liqueur of your choice (Cassis, Pernod, dark rum, etc.), always keeping in mind the season and the resulting "personality" of the salad. For elegant occasions, choose only a few different fruits with complementary colors and flavors.

For added texture and temperature contrast, freeze the grapes in a single layer on a baking sheet for at least 12 hours (and up to a week), and serve frozen.

The chosen fruit may be assembled in a large, beautiful bowl up to 1½ hours before serving and held, covered, in the refrigerator. Whisk together all the ingredients for the yogurt dressing 30 minutes to 1½ hours ahead, and hold, covered, in the refrigerator.

Just a few minutes before serving, to keep the flavors fresh and clean, toss the fruit with the sugar, liqueur, and fresh mint or coconut, or top with the yogurt dressing (if using).

NOTE · **If you wish, you can replace the mint or coconut with crumbled gingersnaps or almond macaroons; chopped almonds, hazelnuts, or walnuts; or slivered basil.**

WHEN HEF CAME TO TAVERN

Another grand party at Tavern—and perhaps the only one at which many of the guests were nearly naked—was the twenty-fifth anniversary of *Playboy* magazine. Legendary publisher Hugh Hefner was there, flanked by dozens of the women who had appeared in the magazine's pages. The media world turned out in force to honor the occasion. Among the luminaries was Clay Felker, another famed publisher. Hefner had once worked for him at *Esquire*, but quit when he was denied a five-dollar-a-week raise. That night, Felker presented Hefner with a replica five-dollar bill and told him, "All is forgiven. Please come home." Of course, the hugely successful Hefner had already built his own empire, but it was a nice sentiment from a respected colleague and lent a humorous note to a fabulous evening.

THE ART OF
THE CHEESE PLATE

*C*hoosing from the cheese cart has always been a favorite part of dining out in Europe, and now the cheese cart has come to America. To make your own small sampler at home, select unique and culturally diverse cheeses and pair them with care.

Avoid passing around an unwieldly cheese platter—the cheese soon begins to look hacked up, and there is a lot of awkward reaching after the first pass. Instead, individually plate two or perhaps three carefully chosen cheeses and accompany them with appropriate bread and drink, and a complementary nibble.

As a general rule, allow 1 ounce of each cheese per person, plus 1 tablespoon or so of nuts, dried fruit, a vegetable, or other accompaniment, and anywhere from 2 to 6 ounces of the complementary wine or liqueur.

Here are some examples to start off the creative process:

MAYTAG BLUE AND AGED VERMONT WHITE CHEDDAR WITH RADISHES AND APPLEJACK

Two of America's most respected cheese are complemented by cool, crisp, and peppery radishes and a thimbleful of fiery spirits from America's orchards.

BREAD: Quartered slices of seeded rye.

ÉPOISSES AND ROQUEFORT WITH WALNUTS AND MARC DE BOURGOGNE

ÉPOISSES: One of the greatest cheeses from Burgundy, arguably the finest gastronomic region in France, Époisses is a washed-rind cheese. Happily, the liquid used for washing it is Marc de Bourgogne, the grappa-style eau de vie made from the dregs of the wine grapes after Burgundy's great wines are made. If Époisses is unavailable, substitute Pont-l'Évêque or Livarot.

ROQUEFORT: France's King of Cheese needs no introduction—but make sure to locate a ripe, soft specimen.

BREAD: Sliced fresh baguette.

SCAMORZA AND PECORINO ROMANO
WITH FIG CAKE AND VIN SANTO

SCAMORZA: Similar to mozzarella but with a denser, dryer texture, it is available either plain or smoked.

PECORINO ROMANO: A tangy, salty sheep's-milk cousin of Parmigiano-Reggiano, with a granular texture and an inedible rind.

BREAD: Long, slim slices of fresh focaccia or grissini (breadsticks). Or both.

CABRALES AND MANCHEGO
WITH CELERY HEARTS AND PEDRO XIMÉNEZ

CABRALES: A rich and intense aged, blue-veined goat's cheese from the Asturias region of Spain. A country cousin of the more refined Roquefort, Cabrales is considered by some cheese connoisseurs to be one of the greatest unsung cheeses of the world.

MANCHEGO: Unarguably the pride of Spain and now widely available, this cheese has a distinctive crosshatch pattern on the rind, which is not edible. If sheep's-milk Manchego is hard to find, substitute a cow's-milk version.

BREAD: Choose quartered slices of a rustic boule, or thin slices of baguette.

KEFALOTYRI AND MILD FETA
WITH DRIED FIGS AND RETSINA

KEFALOTYRI: A good Greek melting cheese that is reminiscent of Romano, though softer and less salty.

FETA: The classic, much-used soft sheep's cheese that has been embraced worldwide.

BREAD: Quartered pita bread.

NOTE · Cold cheese is tasteless! If you buy your cheese from a reputable purveyor and plan to serve it within 24 hours, please do not refrigerate it. The flavor will be sadly diminished, like looking at a beautiful landscape through a piece of mesh fabric. If you do refrigerate the cheese, allow it to come to room temperature for at least 3 and up to 24 hours before serving. (The only exception is a soft and exceedingly fresh perishable cheese such as burrata, which is best served with a slight chill.)

LEMON·FRANGELICO SOUFFLÉ
WITH FRESH RASPBERRY SAUCE

For many couples visiting New York City for the first time, Tavern on the Green is on the list of requisite stops. There's hardly a more romantic place to eat in all of Manhattan. In the warmer months, the staff makes an effort to seat couples at a lovely table in the garden, while in the winter, the cozy Chestnut Room is ideal for an intimate meal. This dessert *à deux* is the kind of seductive sweet that makes an evening at Tavern so memorable.

Softened butter and granulated sugar, for the soufflé dish

2 tablespoons flour

3 tablespoons whole milk

4 tablespoons granulated sugar

2 large egg yolks

1 tablespoon unsalted butter, softened

1 tablespoon plus 2 teaspoons Frangelico liqueur or Grand Marnier

1 teaspoon best-quality vanilla extract

Finely grated zest of 1 scrubbed lemon (see Note, page 41)

3 large egg whites

Salt

Confectioners' sugar

Fresh Raspberry Sauce (recipe follows; optional)

Use the softened butter to thoroughly grease a 3-cup soufflé dish or small baking/gratin dish, then dust the base and sides with sugar, shaking out the excess.

If you will be cooking the soufflé right away, preheat the oven to 400°F. Place a rack in the lower third of the oven.

In a small saucepan, whisk together the flour and 1 tablespoon of the milk; whisk in the remaining milk and 3 tablespoons of the granulated sugar. Place over medium-high heat and whisk frequently until the liquid thickens to a paste. Whisk for 30 seconds, then remove from the heat. Let cool for 1 or 2 minutes, then whisk in the egg yolks one at a time, whisking well between each addition; the sauce will be very thick. Whisk in the unsalted butter, Frangelico, vanilla, and lemon zest.

In a perfectly clean bowl with clean beaters, use a handheld electric mixer to beat the egg whites with a pinch of salt to soft peaks. Sprinkle the remaining 1 tablespoon sugar over the top and continue beating until the peaks are stiff and glossy.

Stir a quarter of the beaten egg whites into the Frangelico mixture to lighten it, then fold in the remaining egg whites gently but quickly. Spoon the mixture into the prepared soufflé dish and, if desired, cover loosely with aluminum foil and hold in the refrigerator for a maximum of 30 minutes before baking (be sure to preheat the oven to 400°F about 20 minutes before you plan to start cooking the soufflé).

Place the soufflé in the oven and immediately turn the temperature down to

375°F. Bake until it is puffy, golden, and no longer jiggly in the center, about 20 minutes.

As soon as the soufflé is done, dust the top with a little confectioners' sugar and serve at once, before it has a chance to deflate. If desired, offer a small sauceboat of raspberry sauce for drizzling.

FRESH RASPBERRY SAUCE

1 small basket raspberries (about ¾ cup), picked over

1 to 3 teaspoons Baker's, or superfine, sugar

1 to 3 teaspoons water

In a mini-prep or standard food processor, pulse the raspberries until smooth. Add the sugar to taste and a little water to achieve your preferred drizzling consistency. Refrigerate, covered, for up to 2 hours before serving.

♦ MAKES ABOUT 1 CUP

A Thousand Points of Light

$\mathcal{C}$andlelight is synonymous with nighttime banquets and private parties, with towering candelabra on tables and—perhaps most remarkable—votive candles studding the glass "walls" of the Crystal, Park, and Terrace rooms. Longtime interior designer Paul Brummer developed a way to suspend the tiny candles in the double-paned windows to astonishing effect. When lit, a single votive gives an illusion of having three flames.

To achieve this, Paul wraps clear exterior mounting tape around spotlessly clean votives, then fastens the tape to the window. Depending on the occasion, Paul will use variously colored votives—say, pastel for Easter and red for Valentine's Day.

Here are some of the clever decorator's tips for bringing Tavern's light home:

- Avoid pre-filled votives; they don't have the key reservoir space between the candle and the glass, which allows the wax to settle so that the flame is exposed.

- Suspend votives on your dining room and bathroom mirrors for a festive touch when expecting guests.

- Wrap glass votives in fabric, ribbon (sheer looks best), parchment paper, or scrapbooking paper to customize them; secure the material with two-sided tape, making sure to leave a quarter to a half inch of the glass exposed around the top.

12

The

HEIGHT

of

BEAUTY

HOW TO BUILD A
BEAUTIFUL SPREAD

From the moment Warner reopened the doors of Tavern on the Green in 1976, New Yorkers put it on their shortlist of preferred party spots. Not only did he create a one-of-a-kind venue with jaw-dropping décor, but Warner knew how to stage a world-class buffet, the entertaining style of choice for most clients whose guest list numbers more than fifty.

More than 25,000 events have taken place in the former sheepfold since its grand makeover. The list is as diverse and illustrious as the citizens of the city itself. Hollywood luminaries and boldface names have shown up in droves for the many movie premiere bashes held here (see page 300). And Tavern has hosted the opening-night parties for some of the most memorable plays and musicals of the last generation (see page 301). Our neighbor, Lincoln Center, brings the taste and talent of the day into Tavern, for after-theater celebrations and the annual party after the opening screening of the New York Film Festival.

In addition, there are MTV's post-award receptions, Carnegie Hall celebrations, and benefits for such national charities as the Nature Conservancy and the Leukemia Society, all of which draw tons of marquee names. With more locally oriented non-profits (such as Goddard Riverside Community Center) and scores of corporations (American Express, Coca-Cola, Cartier, Merrill Lynch, and Time Warner among them) and trade groups holding functions at Tavern, it all adds up to more than a thousand banquets annually, and 120,000 guests to feed!

To accommodate multiple simultaneous fetes, our banquet staff sometimes expands beyond the 14,000 square feet of space in its six dining rooms. With Dr. Seuss–like whimsy, we've been known to erect tents in the parking lot and gardens, outfitting them it with wooden floors, fabric walls, and, of course, chandeliers hanging from the floating ceilings. In all, the restaurant can play host to three thousand people at once!

When the party calls for buffet-style service, Tavern's banquet professionals have adopted Warner's bent for bringing over-the-top touches into the dining room. A profusion of flowers arranged by the in-house florist, festive tablecloths, and color-coordinated napkins are a given. But the showpiece is the buffet table itself, where particular attention is paid to how everything is arranged. Gleaming silver chafing dishes, copper fondue pots, cloth-lined wicker baskets, thick wooden carving boards, stacks of china, and vessels of silverware all come together at varying heights—the key to bringing movement and life to the table. Pedestals, platters, compotes—even mini "stages" made from wood blocks and draped with napkins—bring a sculptural element to the spread. The buffet tables, in effect, always look as if they're inspired by still-life paintings. But a Tavern buffet-style banquet often includes a bit of live theater, too. À la minute preparations are a hallmark, whether a toqued chef is preparing blini, sushi, bananas Foster, or crepes suzette.

Some of the most memorable buffets at Tavern have centered around a theme. Consider the menu for the opening-night party for the 2002 revival of the musical *Oklahoma!* Tavern offered barbecued baby back ribs and buttermilk fried chicken along with Oklahoma filet of beef and country ham. There were warm biscuits with butter and fried okra. A spread of desserts offered up crispy, crunchy, creamy, and smooth options: fresh fruit, deep-dish pies, bread pudding with bourbon sauce, cheesecake, peanut brittle, mini pecan pies, and cookie platters.

. . .

Putting together a Tavernesque buffet at home doesn't require tens of thousands of square feet, a set of ornate chandeliers, or closets full of special tableware. In fact, you don't even need a formal dining room to make a buffet the celebratory focal point of a gathering. The key lies not only in putting delicious food on the table, but in presenting it appealingly (our belief in the beauty and practicality of varying heights is something to bear in mind).

Always consider the ease with which guests can help themselves to the offerings. When you want to invite more guests than can fit around your dining table, place a long, wide serving table in the center of the largest space in your house, leaving room around it so that guests can access it from either side.

Pull out your nicest linens, silver, lanterns, candlesticks, and stemware. And look beyond the linen closet for your table covering. A length of fabulous fabric will do the trick, especially if it suits the season or occasion.

Resist the urge to crowd the table with decorative objects; for the most part, every piece should do double duty to make the best use of space. Use handsome bowls, platters, and terrines for serving.

Choose pieces of varying shapes, heights, and widths. Set the highest dishes down the center of the table, and arrange the remaining in graduated order out to the edges of the table (you don't want to force guests to reach over the standing rib roast to help themselves to the roasted potatoes). Overturned bowls, footed compotes, stacks of books, and large cans—anything, in fact, that provides a sturdy surface and affords height that can be cleverly disguised with fabric or table linens—are all perfect candidates for propping up food.

Consider the order in which items should be placed on the buffet when deciding what serving pieces to use. Place sauces, chutneys, and dips in bowls or gravy boats in front of the dishes they are meant for; a baffled guest is an awkward and even unhappy one! Guests shouldn't have to backtrack as they move along; arrange a stack of plates at one end of the table, followed by the salad course, cold side dishes, hot dish, bread, hot sides, and silverware. Bundle the silverware in a napkin and tie it with a decorative ribbon or string; this makes it effortless for guests to pick up their cutlery while holding on to their plate.

Unless you own or want to rent several chafing dishes, limit the number of hot dishes to those that can be served quickly and straight from their cooking vessels. Light chafing dishes at least twenty minutes before guests arrive; arrange other dishes on the table about ten minutes before the party starts.

Garnishes can make the blandest-looking dish come alive; fresh herb branches, leaves from fruit trees, and edible flowers are just a few of the simple decorative elements you can use to give each dish a finishing flourish.

As we do at Tavern, make a show of desserts by giving them a table of their own; use the same principles for arranging them as you would the meal.

EIGHT BUFFET PARTY MENUS

*T*he menus that follow are intended only as guidelines or suggestions. Most are ambitious parties, intended to serve many guests, that will require help—from family, friends, or someone hired for the event. Especially for a smaller party, feel free to cut one or two dishes from the menu; you'll still be entertaining in Tavern on the Green style!

Summer Garden Party

SANGRIA D'ESPAÑA (*PAGE 20*)

TUNA TARTARE ON RUFFLED CHIPS (*PAGE 44*)

BRUSCHETTA OF HEIRLOOM TOMATOES
WITH BURRATA CHEESE (*PAGE 56*)

CUCUMBER-AVOCADO PUREE
(*PAGE 75; SERVE IN SMALL GLASS TUMBLERS*)

SUMMER SEAFOOD AND PESTO LASAGNA (*PAGE 101*)

BLACK PEPPER ORZO WITH LAMB SAUSAGE, FETA,
AND MINT (*PAGE 122*)

HALIBUT AND TOMATO GRATIN, FOR A CROWD (*PAGE 133*)

GRILLED AND HERB-MARINATED GIANT SHRIMP ON COLD
SESAME-PEANUT NOODLES (*PAGE 144*)

SIRLOIN BURGERS WITH CHIMICHURRI SAUCE (*PAGE 184*)

SPINACH, BACON, AND MUSHROOM SALAD (*PAGE 199*)

TIRAMISÚ (*PAGE 268*)

THE ART OF FRUIT SALAD (*PAGE 280*)

Spring Bridal Shower Lunch

MIMOSA (PAGE 27)

CARROT AND GINGER SOUP WITH DILL CRÈME
(PAGE 89; SERVE IN SMALL GLASS TUMBLERS)

GOAT CHEESE—RADICCHIO QUESADILLAS (PAGE 62)

OLIVE OIL—POACHED TUNA NIÇOISE
WITH CONFIT TOMATOES (PAGE 138)

SMOKED CHICKEN, WILD RICE, AND APRICOT SALAD (PAGE 198)

WARM FINGERLING POTATOES
WITH WHITE WINE—CHIVE SAUCE (PAGE 246)

BRAISED BABY PEAS IN VERMOUTH BUTTER (PAGE 252)

CHOCOLATE-ESPRESSO MOUSSE (PAGE 270)

Sweet Sixteen Birthday

GOAT CHEESE—RADICCHIO QUESADILLAS (PAGE 62)

PEACHES WRAPPED WITH BASIL AND PROSCIUTTO (PAGE 69)

SHRIMP AND FETA BAKED SHELLS (PAGE 104)

BUFFALO CHICKEN SALAD WITH MAYTAG BLUE DRESSING (PAGE 200)

SMOKED TURKEY CLUB SANDWICHES WITH CLASSIC SLAW (PAGE 208)

CRISPY ROASTED POTATOES, FOR A CROWD (PAGE 244)

ROASTED GREEN BEANS WITH SIZZLED HAZELNUTS (PAGE 249)

PUMPKIN-PECAN CAKE
WITH MAPLE—CREAM CHEESE FROSTING (PAGE 278)

Silver Anniversary

THE MIDTOWN MANHATTAN (PAGE 23)

GRATINÉED OYSTERS WITH LEEK CREAM (PAGE 54)

CROUSTADES WITH THREE FILLINGS (PAGE 57)

ASPARAGUS AND PARMESAN RISOTTO (PAGE 119)

ROASTED PROSCIUTTO-WRAPPED SCALLOPS (PAGE 143)

BEEF STROGANOFF (PAGE 179)

ROASTED GREEN BEANS WITH SIZZLED HAZELNUTS (PAGE 249)

Bar Mitzvah Brunch

CLASSIC BLOODY MARY *(PAGE 29)*

HOMEMADE MUESLI WITH WARM FRUIT SALAD *(PAGE 223)*

HOME-CURED SALMON "PASTRAMI" HAND ROLLS *(PAGE 47)*

CHICKEN HASH WITH SAUSAGE, MUSHROOMS, AND BASIL *(PAGE 232)*

GOAT CHEESE AND SOUR CHERRY BLINTZES *(PAGE 226)*

POTATO LATKES WITH CHIVE CRÈME FRAÎCHE *(PAGE 224)*

BREAKFAST BERRY STRATA *(PAGE 222)*

NEW YORK CHEESECAKE *(PAGE 262)*

Fall Fireside Supper

OH! WHAT A PEAR! *(PAGE 27)*

MUSHROOMS STUFFED WITH BACON AND BLUE CHEESE *(PAGE 64)*

CURRIED APPLE SOUP
(PAGE 90; SERVE IN SMALL GLASS TUMBLERS OR DEMITASSE CUPS)

SWEET CORN CHOWDER WITH SMOKED PAPRIKA MAYO
(PAGE 86; SERVE IN SMALL GLASS TUMBLERS OR DEMITASSE CUPS)

POLENTA "NAPOLEON" WITH PORCINI-SAUSAGE RAGÙ *(PAGE 117)*

BELGIAN ENDIVE AND ROASTED BEET SALAD
WITH CITRUS VINAIGRETTE *(PAGE 203)*

WARM POTATO SALAD WITH DOUBLE-SMOKED BACON
AND FRESH ROSEMARY *(PAGE 207)*

SQUASH CRISP *(PAGE 242)*

BRAISED ESCAROLE *(PAGE 254)*

APPLE BROWN BETTY *(PAGE 269)*

Holiday Extravaganza

FLIRTINI (PAGE 26)

BLINI WITH DOMESTIC CAVIAR (PAGE 43)

LAMB CHOPS WITH ITALIAN SALSA VERDE FOR DIPPING (PAGE 66)

LOBSTER AND FENNEL BISQUE WITH TARRAGON
CRÈME FRAÎCHE (PAGE 76; SERVE IN DEMITASSE CUPS)

ARTICHOKE, PECORINO, AND PASTA TIMBALE (PAGE 94)

STANDING RIB ROAST OF BEEF
WITH HORSERADISH-ONION RELISH (PAGE 180)

POTATO—BLUE CHEESE GRATIN (PAGE 247)

CREAMY CARROT SPOON BREAD (PAGE 257)

LEEK AND BROCCOLI BREAD PUDDING (PAGE 250)

THE ART OF THE CHEESE PLATE (PAGE 282)

KAY'S FAMOUS CHRISTMAS PUDDING (PAGE 264)

New Year's Brunch

MIMOSA (PAGE 27)

CLASSIC BLOODY MARY (PAGE 29)

CHRISTMAS DEVILED EGGS WITH CAPER MAYONNAISE AND
RED AND GREEN CAVIAR (PAGE 65)

CREATING A LOX PLATTER (PAGE 236)

ALMOND-CRUSTED FRENCH TOAST (PAGE 235)

CHICKEN HASH WITH SAUSAGE, MUSHROOMS,
AND BASIL (PAGE 232)

NEW YORK HERBED NOODLE PUDDING (PAGE 97)

ROASTED PORK SANDWICH WITH BLUE CHEESE AND
CRANBERRY-PEAR CHUTNEY (PAGE 210)

POACHED PEARS WITH LEMON-RICOTTA STUFFING
AND TOASTED ALMONDS (PAGE 266)

TIRAMISÙ (PAGE 268)

PORTABLE POTABLES

A festive party always features refreshing drinks, both alcoholic and non-alcoholic.

Set up your bar away from the buffet table. This eases the flow of traffic and also promotes mingling among the guests. You can fashion a bar out of a simple card table or your living room console table, or clear some books from a shelf in the bookcase and use that as a makeshift drinks station.

A separate bar is another opportunity to make the room sparkle: Gleaming stemware and highballs, shimmering silver ice buckets, and jewel-toned fruits piled into clear glasses for garnishes are decoration in and of themselves.

If you opt to have a full bar, hire a bartender to mix drinks or a signature cocktail (see Chapter 2). Alternatively, you can make it less formal—and easier on yourself—by setting up a self-service bar with wine, beer, one or two liquors, and mixers.

A MECCA FOR MOVIE PREMIERES

Amadeus

Annie

Black Rain

Bobby Deerfield

Brighton Beach Memoirs

Fatal Attraction

Gorky Park

Howard's End

A League of Their Own

Let's Spend the Night Together

The Mirror Has Two Faces

The Prince of Tides

Return of the Jedi

Robin Hood: Prince of Thieves

Sabrina (1995)

Santa Claus: The Movie

Saturday Night Fever

Sea of Love

Six Degrees of Separation

Star '80

A Star Is Born (1976)

Stardust Memories

Stir Crazy

Sweet Liberty

Twister

Wings of Courage

THEATER OPENING NIGHTS

Abe Lincoln in Illinois (1993 Lincoln Center Theater revival)

The Act

Ah, Wilderness (1998 Lincoln Center Theater revival)

An American Daughter

Anything Goes (1987 Lincoln Center Theater revival)

Arcadia

Big Deal

Big River

Burn This

Carousel (1994 Lincoln Center Theater revival)

The Chairs (1998 revival)

Damn Yankees (1994 revival)

A Delicate Balance (1996 revival)

A Doll's House (1997 revival)

Dream

Dreamgirls

Fiddler on the Roof

Gypsy

I Remember Mama (1979 musical version)

In the Summer House (1993 Lincoln Center Theater revival)

Juan Darien

King of Hearts

The Last Night of Ballyhoo

The Little Foxes

Macbeth

Measure for Measure

Medea

Moon over Buffalo

My Fair Lady (1993 revival)

My One and Only

Private Lives

The Real Thing

Same Time Next Year

Sex and Longing

Side Show

The Sisters Rosensweig

Six Degrees of Separation

Sophisticated Ladies

The Sound of Music (1998 revival)

Speed-the-Plow

State Fair

Steel Pier

Sweet Charity

Sweet Sue

The Tap Dance Kid

The Tenth Man (1989 Lincoln Center Theater revival)

Triumph of Love

Victor/Victoria

Waiting for Godot (1988 Lincoln Center Theater revival)

Zorba (1983 revival)

An Elegant Setting

A table setting at Tavern epitomizes our approach to creating an experience. Every setting receives the care and consideration that is our hallmark. Warner insisted on round fifty-four-inch tables set for ten guests, all the better to cozy up in conversation. He also preferred raised centerpieces such as candelabra; the stems had to stand tall enough for guests to be able to see past them. For banquets, guests always have the option to choose them, along with thirty different tablecloth designs. Warner didn't stop at setting a four-armed piece of sterling in the center of the table, though. Flowers always figured into the mix, intertwined in the candelabras' arms and forming collars around the pillar candles set into them. He was known to have stated he would sooner close the restaurant than not have flowers on the table.

Some find Tavern most breathtaking just before the crowds come through the doors, when the tables are perfectly set and undisturbed, the glasses glistening, the flatware shining, and the china reflecting the shimmering crystals of the chandeliers overhead. Such beautifully set tables make an indelible impression on guests, and they're actually fairly simple to prepare once you know what elements you need and where each one goes on the table. Tavern's tablecloths are as much a part of the décor of the room as they are an element of the table setting. A proper table is covered with a tablecloth—the most formal going to the floor. For some events, two table coverings are used: a floor-length tablecloth and a complementary overlay, positioned on the diagonal to reveal the corners of the under piece.

Next, place a flat dinner plate in front of each chair and flank it with a knife and tablespoon on the right (the knife is closest to the plate and the blade faces it) and two forks on the left—the smaller salad fork on the far left and the larger dinner fork between it and the plate. To the left of the forks, place a small bread and butter plate with a butter knife set across the top; the blade should face the bottom. Tavern's tables are always set with a dessert spoon and fork; place a teaspoon with the handle on the right above a dessert or cake fork with the handle on the left, horizontally above the dinner plate. As for glassware, two glasses—a larger stemmed water glass and a smaller, longer-stemmed wineglass (you can use any style glass as long as one is smaller than the other)—are placed above the knife with the wineglass to the right of the water goblet. Cloth napkins (never use paper for a special meal!) can be folded in myriad ways and placed on the center of the plate—never tucked into the water glass (a pet peeve of Warner's, you'll never see this on a Tavern table!).

It's easy to follow the same principles at home and set an elegant table for your guests. A floral centerpiece is key. You may not need a candelabra, but anything elegant that doesn't obstruct the view across the table—a bud vase or a small bouquet—will add a touch of sophistication.

ACKNOWLEDGMENTS

It has taken the collaboration of many people to put together this book. To sift through thirty years of memories, photographs, parties, and history, deciding what goes and what stays, is no easy task. Actually, it was a labor of love for my mother and me, as well as for my sisters, Bridget and Carolyn, both of whom have made some of their own history at Tavern. (In fact, Bridget's Tavern experiences have contributed to the success of her own hospitality venture, the New London Inn, in New London, New Hampshire.)

Their memories and insights were invaluable, as were those of many others, including Edmundo Baquerizo, Jasmine Bojic, Jim Burgess, Maggie Burkhart, Paul Brummer, Shelley Clark, Julian Calderon, Guillermo Colorado, John D'Antonio, Michael Desiderio, Ron Genereux, David Hart, Bryan Kalman, Don McHenry, Erica Meyerson, Sonia Mirabeaux, Nicolle Paqua, Bob Policastro, Rodney Shepherd, Brian Young, William Zambrotto, and Zina Zimmerman.

My mother and I are also grateful to Brigit Binns and Kathleen Hackett for their indispensable assistance in assembling the text. The team at Artisan Books, led by publisher Ann Bramson and our patient, painstaking editor, Trent Duffy, has been supportive throughout; we appreciate the efforts of Stephanie Huntwork, Jan Derevjanik, Nancy Murray, Sigi Nacson, and Erin Sainz.

Finally, much gratitude to our fabulous photographer, Ben Fink, and to our agents, Michael Psaltis and Joe Regal of the Culinary Cooperative.

—JENNIFER OZ LEROY